Basic Parenting 101:

THE MANUAL YOUR CHILD
SHOULD HAVE BEEN BORN WITH

Philip Copitch, Ph.D.
Family Therapist

HERE TO SERVE YOU:

Hutzpah Press titles are available in quantity discounts for promotions, premiums and fund raisers.

Our titles can be custom imprinted with your name and information.

FOR FURTHER INFORMATION PLEASE CONTACT:

HUTZPAH PRESS
PO BOX 400
Igo, CA 96047

EMAIL: DrPhil@CopitchInc.com
www.CopitchInc.com

DEDICATION:

I once had a very compulsive patient who for six months taped each session then transcribed the tape. We would start the next session with her questioning me on the "minutes" from our last meeting. At the end of therapy, I asked her jokingly what she was planning to do with the hundreds of pages of notes she had compiled.

She looked me straight in the eye and said, "After you are dead, I am going to publish them and make a fortune."

I have been blessed with the honor of helping families grow to be more creative and caring. Over the years, many have told me at the end of a family therapy session, "This is a lot to remember, you should write it down for me to take home."

So, I dedicate this series to the parents who asked, no demanded, that I write it down.

And, to Geri, the only one I know who can put up with me.

Thank you for encouraging my behavior.

Philip Copitch, Ph.D.
2000

Tell me, I forget.
Show me, I remember.
Involve me, I understand.

Table of Contents

INTRODUCTION 7
1. HOW CHILDREN LEARN 11
I'M PETRIFIED OF 12
AMY AND THE CHOW CHOW 15
HOW DID AMY LEARN TO BE FEARFUL OF DOGS? 15
GENERALIZATION 18
DESENSITIZATION 19
BILLY THE BOMBER 22
EXTINCTION 26
PUNISHMENT 28
TIMING IS VERY IMPORTANT 30
SHAPING 35
MODELING 37
BRIBERY DOES NOT WORK 38
THE POWER OF A TOKEN ECONOMY 39
2. HOW TO BUILD YOUR CHILD'S SELF ESTEEM 43
WHAT DO YOU REALLY WANT FOR YOUR CHILD? 43
WHAT IS THE SINGLE BIGGEST "GIFT" WE CAN GIVE OUR CHILDREN? 44
HOW IS SELF ESTEEM BUILT? 45
THREE BASIC LEVELS OF SELF ESTEEM 47
SELF ESTEEM IS NOT CAST IN STONE 49
WORDS COUNT 50
SELF ESTEEM AND BEHAVIOR COMPLIMENT EACH OTHER 52
THE PARENTAL ROLE OF NURTURING 55
GIVING THE GIFT OF HIGH SELF ESTEEM 56
SHOWING ONE'S LOVE 57
THE ROLE OF TIME 58
BUILDING TRUST 58
TEACHING HONESTY 60
A HEALTHY FOCUS ON YOUR CHILD AS A MEMBER OF YOUR FAMILY 62
ADVOCATING VERSES JUDGING YOUR CHILD 62
THE POWER OF PRAISE 68
TEACHING RESPECT 73
YOUR CHILD'S TEMPERAMENT 77
CARETAKER VERSUS CAREGIVER 79
3. TIME OUT IS NOT PUNISHMENT 83
IT IS A STOP GAP MEASURE 83
PUNISHMENT VERSUS DISCIPLINE 84
THE GOAL OF TIME OUT 87
DEFINING "TIME" 87
ROUTINE COUNTS IN TIME OUT PROCEDURE 88
HOW TO START A TIME OUT 88
DOING A TIME OUT 90
ENDING A TIME OUT 90
ADVOCATING FOR GOOD CHOICES 91

HOW CHILDREN TEST THE TIME OUT PROCESS 93
OOPS! WHAT TO DO IF YOU MAKE A MISTAKE 96
WHO'S RESPONSIBLE? 97
BUT WE ARE NOT ALWAYS AT HOME! 97
"I WANT TO TALK CODE" 98

4. FAMILY RULES— THE DIFFERENCE BETWEEN A HOUSE AND A HOME ... 101
THE ART OF DISCIPLINE 102
MUST, MAYBE AND MINOR RULES 108
WHERE ARE WE TODAY: HOMEWORK ASSIGNMENT #1 110
DR. PHIL'S THREE M'S OF RULE TYPES 111
MINOR 111
MAYBE 111
MUST 111
A TYPICAL 3M LIST 112
MAYBE RULES CAUSE CONSTANT CONFLICT 113
ONLY PARENTS CAN BREAK A MUST RULE 117
MUST RULES BUILD A FAMILY 123
POSITIVE CONSEQUENCES OF BEING A MEMBER OF YOUR FAMILY: HOMEWORK
ASSIGNMENT #2 125
MUST RULES SHOULD BE WRITTEN DOWN 127
WHO WRITES THE MUST RULES? 128
HOW DO YOU WRITE A MUST RULE? 128
WHAT REALLY COUNTS FOR YOU: HOMEWORK ASSIGNMENT #3 134
CHILDREN LEARN BY CONSEQUENCES 137
PUTTING IT ALL TOGETHER 138

5. CONTROLLING CHAOS: BASIC PARENTING 101 IN ACTION: 149
ANGER, YOUNG CHILD 151
BED-WETTING 156
LYING 164
SIBLING RIVALRY 170
SOILING 174
STEALING 178
TEACHING RESPONSIBILITY 182
UNCOOPERATIVE BEHAVIOR IN SCHOOL (8 YEAR OLD) 190
UNCOOPERATIVE BEHAVIOR: SCHOOL MORNINGS, (TEENAGER) 202
UNCOOPERATIVE BEHAVIOR IN SCHOOL (TEENAGER) 205
WHAT DO I NEED TO KNOW ABOUT STREET DRUGS? 208
WHINING 222

IN CLOSING 225
INDEX 227

UNIVERSITY OF LIFE / COLLEGE OF HARD KNOCKS

INTRODUCTION

Most Colleges and Universities in the United States start their students' education in core classes. These classes are the *core* of knowledge that students will need as a base to balance and understand the rest of their academic training. In my education these classes were called 100 and 200 level courses. So, if you were planning to major in the massive field of psychology or chemistry you would start your college career with Basic Psychology 101 or Basic Chemistry 101.

Usually on the first day of a 101 class you would encounter some weathered instructor explaining that this class will be the *foundation* of all things to come. That you should learn your lessons well because if the foundation is weak all knowledge built upon it will be unstable. As cliche as it sounded I, as a young student, learned that it was true. I found that the more advanced courses were not actually harder, just built on the foundation of the lower level courses. I watched fellow students just squeeze by Psych 101 only to find themselves totally lost and discouraged in Psych 201. The foundation course must be truly understood to be useful.

It seems that everything comes with directions. My car manual explains even the most basic of things such as where the key fits into the ignition. On airplanes they show you how to attach your seat belt. The paper cover on the chop sticks at my corner Chinese restaurant shows you (kind of) how to hold chop sticks. I own com-

In this area, the side bar, you will find funny and/or uplifting stories or examples associated with the main text. Most people find the side bar to be the part of the series that gels their understanding. These stories are placed here for more than comic relief. Learning can be hard work and a little humor can go a long way. These stories are also here to stimulate your thoughts and memories. I challenge you to look for the deeper meaning, to read between the lines and to ask yourself this

puter manuals, home fix-it manuals, and even a manual about how to take care of a boa constrictor. All so I can do something that I want to do or wish to do better.

As a family therapist I am often told, "My kid didn't come with directions," or "Isn't there a kid instruction book?" This was the impetus for the writing of *Basic Parenting 101*. My goal is to give a *core* of knowledge to every parent.

There are a lot of parenting books on the market. Most do a good job of explaining techniques on how to deal with your child. I recently saw a commercial for a book that asked questions such as, "Should you give coffee to a child who is having an asthma attack?" And, "Will the dryer quiet a colicky baby?" Most books on families and parenting explain "how." "How to stop your child from wetting the bed." Or, "116 ways to discipline without spanking." This is all well and good, but, all children are individuals. All families are unique. In fact aren't your children the best, the brightest kids you have ever met? If any child can figure out how to destroy *parenting technique #17*, wouldn't it be your child? I'm positive that my children can find a way up, over, around or through any technique. They are professional children. They take pride in their work. If it is their goal to teach me that, technique #17 is useless, I'm positive that they can.

Cookbook type parenting books can be very valuable. If you read about a new way of accomplishing a goal, great. You have added to your bag of tricks. This is important because parenting tends to be time sensitive. For example, you have 1.2 seconds to pick a parenting technique that can fix this moment's crisis. It takes a lot of skill to pick and implement the correct "trick" for the correct situation. The more options you as a parent possess, the better.

In this book the intent is to focus on the *whys* and *how-to's* of parenting. Why does Tommy suck his thumb? Is it normal for Mary to be interested in boys? How come I have to say everything eleven times to get Bobby to do anything? Why do the kids constantly bicker? How come whatever you suggest your daughter should wear is the dumbest idea since the last time you suggested anything? Why does riding with you make your fourteen year old, "just want to die!"

If you have an understanding about *why* then you have a excellent opportunity to pick the correct technique (*the how*) to deal with the situation. By understanding how your child's mind works, how your child learns, and how your child communicates, you can help them to cope with their job of growing up.

Don't get worried, this book is not an overview of the stages of human development. We will discuss developmental issues, but you will not find any charts or graphs on when Sissy should poop by herself or when Sammy should do his homework with self motivation.

Developmental charts have their place, but not here. What we will look at is why does Billy need to argue every step of the way? We will learn why arguing over dumb stuff will be important in your child's relationships as an adult. By knowing the *why*, you will find your child easier to deal with. If you have an understanding of the developmental need for the parent-child conflict, you will find the conflict to be only a minor inconvenience. One mother of six told me at the end of a parenting class, "I love children, but boy is that different than living with them! Knowing that my kids are acting like normal, healthy kids makes my life so much easier." We will investigate what is "normal" when it comes to children.

We will also look at the *hows* of parenting. How do you get a three year old off the supermarket floor? How do you teach responsibility to an eleven year old? What really works to change a bad attitude into a cooperative attitude?

By blending the *why's* with the *how-to's* you will find the *art* of parenting.

I suppose I am now that weathered psychology instructor. So, as we begin, I ask you to open your thoughts, relax and let's tour the minds of our children. With knowledge you will find power. The power to love and support the most important people in your world, your children.

I was once drafted by my sister to assemble a swing set. It was a beautiful spring day and I allotted an hour to put the swing set together before I had to be off doing serious teenage activities such as, hanging out with my friends and doing nothing. After fifteen minutes of setting up, propping up, forcing in and swearing at, I got frustrated and threw down a long metal pole in disgust. My sister, who was supervising me by sipping ice tea, smarted off, "That doesn't look right, did you read the directions?" After I growled something in her direction "I" decided that I should read the directions.

I found the thin direction booklet and read the introductory paragraph. "Now that you have tried to put your swing set together without reading these directions, please disassemble and align all parts as illustrated in Figure 1." Wow! I guess I am not the only one who doesn't read directions until I have to.

The universe is made of stories, not atoms.
Muriel Rukeyser

Chapter 1

How Children Learn

1. HOW CHILDREN LEARN

How do children learn? This is a relatively new question. Until about 100 years ago, people assumed that children were just smaller versions of adults. But, since the industrial age, our view of children, as well as our expectations of ourselves has multiplied immensely.

My five year old, Joshua, was explaining to his grandmother that the remote control was a beam of light and that the beam of light went from the remote control to the VCR. His grandmother understood all that but just wanted CNN. Joshua gave up explaining the concept and just removed the pile of papers from in front of the VCR's sensor. Of course, Josh's grandmother thought he was a genius. I hope so— well, I am his father, and I also think he is a genius. One thing for sure, Josh is able to learn. You see, a few weeks prior, Ethan, age eight, had a similar but not as polite a conversation with his little brother about the infrared wonders of the remote control.

Ethan: Give me it. Give me it now.

Josh: No! I want to turn it up!

Ethan: Josh, Josh, Hurry up then ... you're so slow!

Josh: I'm not slow, it's broken. The thing don't work!

Ethan: Give it to me, I'll do it!

At this point the channel changer was dropped purposefully at Ethan's feet just as he tried to snatch it.

Ethan: What's wrong with this dumb thing. Josh, Josh ... move the papers from in front of the VCR ... Get out of the way ... Mom, Josh won't let me watch TV!

Josh learned that the channel changer will not work if the VCR sensor is covered with papers. He stored this knowledge and was able to retrieve it from the depths of his memory when his grandmother had a similar problem.

This is a remarkable ability. Without trying we humans gather and store information in our minds, then retrieve it later when we need it. This is the most basic definition of learning. Our children are predisposed to learn. They are wired to be curious and to store information.

In this chapter we will look at the basic ways in which a child learns. By understanding this process we as parents can become

WHAT'S THAT NOISE?

The uterus isn't exactly the quietest place to hang out. Not only can a baby hear the sounds of his mom's body—her stomach growling, her heart beating, the occasional hiccup or burp—but he can also hear noises from beyond. If mom sits in a movie theater with state-of-the-art sound or walks by a noisy construction site, odds are the fetus will react to all the ruckus by kicking or shifting around.

Of course, not all sounds are the same. Perhaps the most significant one a baby hears in utero is his mother's voice. Around the seventh and eighth month, a fetus's heart rate slows down slightly whenever his mother is speaking, indicating that mom's voice has a calming effect.

By the time they're born, babies can actually recognize their mother's voice. In one study, doctors gave day-

Continued on page 12

better teachers of life's lessons.

Continued from page 11

old infants pacifiers that were connected to tape recorders. Depending on the babies' sucking patterns, the pacifiers either turned on a tape of their mother's voice or that of an unfamiliar woman's voice. The amazing result: "Within ten to twenty minutes, the babies learned to adjust their sucking rate on the pacifier to turn on their own mother's voice," says the study's coauthor William Fifer, Ph.D., an associate professor of psychiatry and pediatrics at Columbia University's College of Physicians and Surgeons. "This not only points out a newborn's innate love for his mother's voice but also a baby's unique ability to learn quickly."

Laura Flynn McCarthy
Parenting

I'M PETRIFIED OF ...

Mrs. Rizzo was very embarrassed. She entered my office and sat in a chair taking up as little space as she could possibly shrink into. She made no eye contact. She spoke softly, fighting off tears. The weight of the world was resting on her shoulders.

"I'm depriving my daughter of what she deserves." She testified, "I'm acting so selfish. But, I just can't help myself. I feel stupid coming to you with my problem. I'm sure you have <u>real</u> problems to deal with." Mrs. Rizzo was embarrassed to tell me that she was petrified of balloons. She had been fearful of them for many years. In fact, she can vividly recall the first time a balloon frightened her. She was six or seven years old.

I was at my aunt's home helping to set up for my cousin's birthday party. I was blowing up a balloon and I pushed my air into it as hard as I could. I wanted to see how big it could get. Just then, Boom! It exploded. I was so shocked, I froze. I couldn't take the next breath. My aunt grabbed me and shook me. She thought I had swallowed part of the balloon. I finally took a deep breath and started to cry. My mother came running into the kitchen and yelled at my aunt for letting me blow up the balloon. My mother was positive that I could damage my eye with a piece of exploding balloon.

The Rizzo family was planning a huge birthday party for Mary who was turning eleven. Mary had asked for a clown theme party. Mrs. Rizzo had okayed the plan and found a clown to entertain. The clown was a happy go lucky senior citizen who had a local reputation for fussing over each child during a party. When Mrs. Rizzo went to meet the jolly Jumpin' Judy she was treated to a small show of clown antics. One part of Jumpin' Judy's show included joke telling and balloon animal antics. Jumpin' Judy would tell rapid fire jokes and blow up and tie balloon animals to illustrate the pun. In over forty years the jokes had barely changed. The kids loved them. Mrs. Rizzo explained:

She took a little green balloon off the table. She snapped it onto a hand held pump. In seconds it grew to a long thin curving tube. Pop! I couldn't catch my breath. I felt lightheaded. The room started to spin.

I felt a heavy weight on my chest and I started to perspire. Judy, said something like, "Oops, I made a balloon angel." Then she noticed me. She asked if I was okay. I told her I had to go and practically ran to my car. That afternoon I went to work, I'm a waitress. There was a small kiddie party. The balloons scared me so much I told the manager that I had the flu and needed to go home. I must have looked like I had the flu. He wouldn't let me drive home until I was feeling better. I've ruined Mary's party! I told Jumpin' Judy no balloons!

What Mrs. Rizzo was suffering from was an anxiety attack brought on by her unrealistic fear of balloons. In a few sessions Mrs. Rizzo's fear was alleviated. Mary's party was a complete success, balloons and all.

So, what happened? How did Mrs. Rizzo become fearful of balloons? It happened through a process called **classical conditioning.**

Classical conditioning was first defined by Russian physiologist Ivan Pavlov (1849-1936). You have probably heard of the Pavlovian Response which is usually thought of as a dog salivating to the sound of a tuning fork or bell. Pavlov found, during an experiment to understand the way salivary glands work, that the dogs salivated well before the food was placed in front of them. He noticed that the dogs salivated when they heard footsteps coming down the hallway. At first this made no sense, until it was observed that the food dishes were also carried down the same hallway. The dogs had learned that sometimes the sound of footsteps coming down the hall resulted in food being placed in front of them. Pavlov's observation and subsequent research was so revolutionary to the understanding of learning that he was honored with the Nobel Prize for his work.

People can be conditioned to positive or negative things. Mrs. Rizzo became conditioned to fear balloons. Let's look at how this occurred.

Mrs. Rizzo was born with the ability to feel fear. She has a naturally occurring response to fearful situations. This feeling of anxiety is a normal part of a person's neurological makeup. This fear is an **unconditioned response**. In short hand this is written "**UCR**." By definition a UCR is a naturally occurring response (behavior or feeling) to an **unconditioned stimulus (UCS)**. A stimulus is something in the world that causes a behavior. If Mrs. Rizzo was walking in the woods and heard a loud growl she would naturally feel fear. The loud growl would be the unconditioned stimulus and the fear would be the unconditioned response. Mrs. Rizzo did not have to learn to be fearful, that has been part of her since birth. The growl elicited, caused, her fearful behavior.

Quick Reference Guide

CLASSICAL CONDITIONING-

Unconditioned Stimuli: A stimulus that causes an involuntary response of the autonomic nervous system.

Unconditioned Response: A naturally occurring behavior of the autonomic nervous system. (Involuntary)

Conditioned Stimuli: A stimulus that acquired its power to cause a behavior. It initially lacked such power.

Conditioned Response: A learned response of the autonomic nervous system caused by a conditioned stimulus.

As a diagram this looks like:

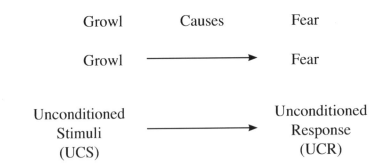

Prior to age seven, let's say, Mrs. Rizzo was not fearful of balloons. But, when the balloon and the fear provoking loud pop (unconditioned stimulus) were connected in her mind, Mrs. Rizzo became fearful of balloons. The balloon is now said to be a **conditioned stimuli (CS)**. By definition a conditioned stimuli is a stimulus that acquired its power to cause a behavior. It initially lacked such power. The learned response is called a **conditioned response (CR)**. By definition a conditioned response is a learned response of the autonomic nervous system caused by a conditioned stimulus. This connection is the process of classical conditioning, one of the ways we all learn. With repeated exposure, Mrs. Rizzo became so fearful of balloons she didn't want to be in the same room with them.

By unintentionally connecting the balloon popping with her fear, Mrs. Rizzo's brain connected the two as being about the same stimuli. She learned to be fearful of balloons.

As a diagram this looks like:

At fist-

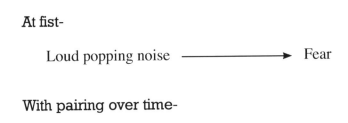

With pairing over time-

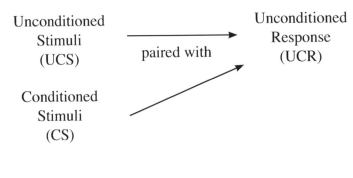

-or

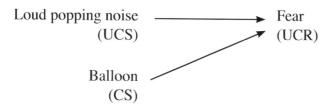

Over time this changes to look like:

$$\text{Balloon (CS)} \longrightarrow \text{Fear (CR)}$$

Repeated pairings of the balloon (CS) with the loud noise (UCS) taught Mrs. Rizzo to experience fear when she was in close proximity to a balloon. Please note, this was not a choice that Mrs. Rizzo had. She would have loved not to feel the fear. In fact, she believed the fear to be unrealistic. But her fears were very real, even overpowering. She was unable to override her conditioned response by thought. Mrs. Rizzo needed to be unconditioned. In eight hours, over a two week period, she unlearned her fear of balloons. (We will discuss how we "unlearn" later in this chapter.)

AMY AND THE CHOW CHOW

Amy was a tall thin girl of nine when I first met her. She was social, outgoing, and quick witted. Her mother was very concerned that, as she put it, "Amy has screaming fits whenever she sees a dog." As it turned out, Amy was well known for her uncontrollable screaming whenever she saw a dog, even a puppy. Dogs were so fear provoking for Amy, that when she was in the school library a poster of a chow chow and a kitten set her off into a siren of tortured fear. Amy's mother explained, "The principal suggested I bring her to a therapist before it got out of hand. Out of hand! She would have to <u>explode</u> to get more out of hand."

Amy's mother had no idea why her daughter was so fearful of dogs. Amy was well adjusted, she had never been attacked by a dog, and she seemed to love all other animals.

HOW DID AMY LEARN TO BE FEARFUL OF DOGS?

Below you will find a diagram for classical conditioning. Fill in the blanks and see if you can explain how Amy learned to be petrified of pooches.

Make up your own scenario as a starting off point. Try to imagine the process it would take to become fearful of a dog. I advise you to only take a few minutes on each question. This is just for fun. I will go over my theory on the next page. Enjoy figuring out the puzzle.

A few questions to ponder:

What caused Amy's <u>initial</u> fear?

_____

_____

_____

_____

_____

_____

How did Amy learn to be afraid of dogs? (Your best guess)

_____

_____

_____

_____

_____

_____

What got paired in Amy's mind?

_____

_____

_____

_____

_____

How would you diagram the classical conditioning?

```
_____              _____
 (UCS)    paired with   (UCR)

_____
 (CS)

_____              _____
 (CS)                   (CR)
```

WHAT CAUSED AMY'S <u>INITIAL</u> FEAR?

Amy's initial fear was an unconditioned response. Amy was born with a full package of feelings. One of these feelings is her ability to be fearful. For the most part this ability is very helpful. It helps her to react to danger, to protect herself. This fear is a response of the autonomic nervous system, a reaction. If we had to think about pulling our fingers away from a hot stove, versus having that response controlled by the autonomic nervous system, we would all possess burn scarred fingers. The autonomic nervous system (not under our direct thought control) is substantially faster than cognition (controlled by thought). We will never know exactly what happened. However, we can come up with a likely scenario.

One weekend at the lake, I observed a young couple and their toddler playing in the sand. At one point, the curious toddler wandered twenty feet astray and went to visit a lonely puppy staked out next to a blanket and a large ice chest. The toddler showed no fear of the puppy. The puppy showed no fear of the toddler. In a few minutes the two of them became close friends. So close that the puppy wound his leash around the toddler's feet, pulling him to the ground. At this moment, mom observed the new friendship. She ran over and picked up her small child. He began to cry. Mom became upset and yelled at the bouncing puppy for scratching her leg. As she carried her child back to her blanket she told him in a stern voice, "You stay with mommy, that doggy could bite you."

The toddler, who was not interested in sunbathing, escaped from his mother and ran towards the puppy. At this point mom screamed, frightening her child and all others in ear shot. The baby plopped down on his bottom and cried heavily.

I would think that this kind of pairing would cause the average child to learn to fear dogs.

WHAT GOT PAIRED IN AMY'S MIND?

Somehow Amy experienced the pairing of a fear provoking stimulus, such as mom's screaming (UCS), with the presence of a dog (CS), causing fear to be a conditioned response (CR).

Quick Reference Guide

CLASSICAL CONDITIONING-

Unconditioned Stimuli: A stimulus that causes an involuntary response of the autonomic nervous system.

Unconditioned Response: A naturally occurring behavior of the autonomic nervous system. (Involuntary)

Conditioned Stimuli: A stimulus that acquired its power to cause a behavior. It initially lacked such power.

Conditioned Response: A learned response of the autonomic nervous system caused by a conditioned stimulus.

Generalization (stimulus): The tendency of a stimulus, similar to the conditioned stimulus (CS), to cause the conditioned response (CR).

Desensitization: A process of unlearning unwanted responses learned through classical conditioning. (Sometimes called classical extinction)

HOW WOULD YOU DIAGRAM THE CLASSICAL CONDITIOING?

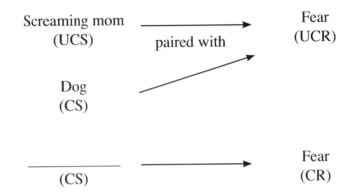

GENERALIZATION

Amy became fearful of all sorts of dogs. She was uncomfortable around collies and perplexed with poodles. In fact, even a poster of a chow chow scared her. This is due to a phenomenon called stimulus **generalization**. Amy, as with all of us, generalized her fear to similar stimuli. The shape of the dog, the size of the dog, or the disposition of the dog did not matter. Anything in her "fear category" was defined as a *dog*, and to Amy all *dogs* provoked fear. By definition, generalization is the tendency of a stimulus, similar to the conditioned stimulus (CS), to cause the conditioned response (CR).

We often see stimulus generalization when young children begin to learn language. Most parents have at least one embarrassing incident associated with when baby finally calls her father "Dada." Over the next few days or weeks she calls every man she sees, "Dada." This generalization is the natural progression of learning. It tends to decrease as a person gets older. However, it is still a powerful reality even for adults. I have seen many adults in the corporate world experience stimulus generalization to their own detriment.

Mr. Carlson was having angry thoughts about his new supervisor. He openly stated that he barely knew the new boss. He had no history of trouble with other supervisors. When I asked him who his new supervisor reminded him of, he shed light on his internal conflict. "Now that you mention it," he pondered, "He looks a lot like my brother. He is such a dishonest bastard I can't stand him!" Even in his explanation I wasn't sure if he was talking about his brother or the new supervisor. Mr. Carlson was experiencing stimulus generalization.

DESENSITIZATION

Earlier we met Mrs. Rizzo, a woman who was overwhelmed in the presence of balloons. Her fear brought much discomfort to her work and home life. Mrs. Rizzo and I used a learning process called **desensitization** to decrease Mrs. Rizzo's fear of balloons.

Desensitization simply involved <u>re</u>teaching Mrs. Rizzo that balloons are not fear provoking. This reteaching took shape by having Mrs. Rizzo spend time with balloons when she did not feel anxious. This sounds so simple, but it tends to be very tricky. In Mrs. Rizzo's case, the fact that she was coming to my office to deal with her fear of balloons caused her to feel nervous.

While sitting privately in the waiting room, I explained to her that we were going to solve her problem with balloons. And, that we would solve this problem at her speed. This was very important to her. She was trying to trust me but, in the back of her mind she was concerned about having to confront her fear. If you think about it, she had spent most of her life avoiding her fear. By avoiding balloons she did not have to deal with her discomfort.

Mrs. Rizzo and I continued our session sitting at a round table. I asked her to teach me what it was about balloons that scared her. I softly asked questions about her discomfort.

Dr. Phil:	How close to a balloon can you come before feeling discomfort?
Mrs. Rizzo:	I can't touch them.
Dr. Phil:	I understand, touching them would make you feel uncomfortable. Could you watch a balloon on TV?
Mrs. Rizzo:	Sure. It can't hurt me.
Dr. Phil:	Could you hold a photograph of a balloon?
Mrs. Rizzo:	I could, it isn't real.
Dr. Phil:	Would you be okay with a balloon on a chair across a large room?
Mrs. Rizzo:	Yes, but I couldn't go over to it. You're not going to make me do that are you?
Dr. Phil:	As I told you in the waiting room. I work <u>for</u> you. I will not make you do anything. Is that okay with you?

Quick Reference Guide

CLASSICAL CONDITIONING-

Unconditioned Stimuli: A stimulus that causes an involuntary response of the autonomic nervous system.

Unconditioned Response: A naturally occurring behavior of the autonomic nervous system. (Involuntary)

Conditioned Stimuli: A stimulus that acquired its power to cause a behavior. It initially lacked such power.

Conditioned Response: A learned response of the autonomic nervous system caused by a conditioned stimulus.

Generalization (stimulus): The tendency of a stimulus, similar to the conditioned stimulus (CS), to cause the conditioned response (CR).

Desensitization: A process of unlearning unwanted responses learned through classical conditioning. (Sometimes called classical extinction)

Mrs. Rizzo:	It sure is. I don't want to touch a balloon! (She said with a sour face.)
Dr. Phil:	Would you feel relaxed if a balloon was sitting over there on the couch? (I pointed to the couch 15 feet away.)
Mrs. Rizzo:	Would I have to touch it?
Dr. Phil:	No.
Mrs. Rizzo:	I could do that.
Dr. Phil:	How about if the balloon was half way between us and the couch?
Mrs. Rizzo:	No, No way ... That is just too close.

Just the thought of the balloon 7 feet away on the floor was causing her agitation.

Dr. Phil:	Could you hold a balloon?
Mrs. Rizzo:	I don't think so.
Dr. Phil:	Could you blow up a balloon?
Mrs. Rizzo:	Are you nuts! (She looked astonished.)

What this gentle line of questioning accomplished was a hierarchy of fear. A way of measuring and categorizing Mrs. Rizzo's level of fear. At the top of the hierarchy, the most fear provoking activity was blowing up a balloon, at the other end was watching a balloon on TV. The bottom of the hierarchy was the starting point of Mrs. Rizzo's relearning and the top of the hierarchy was Mrs. Rizzo's goal. (At this point we didn't even talk about the specifics of "our goal." That could send Mrs. Rizzo running into the street yelling, "Dr. Phil is crazy, Dr. Phil is crazy ... He wants me to blow up a balloon!" That would really get the eye doctor's staff next door talking. I simply told Mrs. Rizzo that our goal was for her to become comfortable around balloons.)

Mrs. Rizzo's balloon fear hierarchy looked like this:

HIGHEST LEVEL OF FEAR

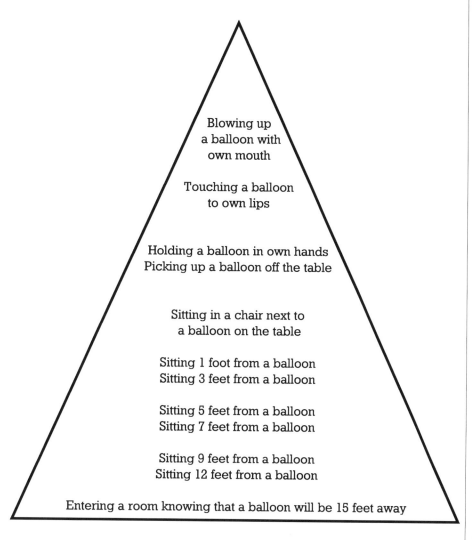

Blowing up
a balloon with
own mouth

Touching a balloon
to own lips

Holding a balloon in own hands
Picking up a balloon off the table

Sitting in a chair next to
a balloon on the table

Sitting 1 foot from a balloon
Sitting 3 feet from a balloon

Sitting 5 feet from a balloon
Sitting 7 feet from a balloon

Sitting 9 feet from a balloon
Sitting 12 feet from a balloon

Entering a room knowing that a balloon will be 15 feet away

LOWEST LEVEL OF FEAR

The hierarchy is pyramid shaped. At the top we have the most fear provoking activity while at the bottom the lowest fear provoking activity. If we extend the pyramid, we would have all things that cause no fear whatsoever. Sometimes we need to start dealing with a problem very far from the top of the pyramid. We start where we can start, without passing judgment.

I met with Mrs. Rizzo, every few days over a two week period. Each time we started at the highest place on the hierarchical pyramid that she was comfortable. Then we slowly moved up the pyramid. This movement was simply a question of choice, "May I bring the balloon one foot, a half foot or an inch closer?" If she said no, we talked about controlling our discomfort by breathing. If she said yes, I slowly moved the balloon closer. At no point was pressure used. The goal was for Mrs. Rizzo to get used to the presence of the balloon, for her to relearn the pairing of the balloon as a neutral stimulus. Mrs. Rizzo was being reconditioned to the true nature of

The process of desensitization is critical in dealing with children who have failed repeatedly in school and are "turned off" to learning in school. In much the same way as the individual runs from the snake, these children "run" from learning through belligerence, apathy, or any other technique that gets them away from the stimuli they have learned to fear.

Donald MacMillion

Anything learned can be unlearned.

the balloon.

The conditioned stimulus (presence of balloons) was weakened when it appeared alone so often that Mrs. Rizzo no longer exhibited the conditioned response (fear of balloon). At this point Mrs. Rizzo's fear of balloons is said to be *desensitized*.

By our fourth session, Mrs. Rizzo was comfortable sitting holding an inflated balloon. During the fifth session she was comfortable blowing air into a deflated balloon. At the end of only two weeks, Mrs. Rizzo was happily talking about the upcoming birthday party. Through the process of extinction we unpaired the initial conditioning by reconditioning a new response to balloons. Mrs. Rizzo felt triumphant.

The same process was implemented to recondition Amy with her fear of dogs. We developed a hierarchy of contact with dogs that caused Amy's fear. We methodically relearned a more comfortable relationship for Amy with dogs. Within a month, Amy and I went to the county pound to befriend dogs and cats.

Due to the powerful effect of classical conditioning, we parents need to keep our eyes open to what we may be accidentally teaching our children by pairing conditioned and unconditioned stimuli. Children are sponges needing to soak in information. I was in a local supermarket and heard one mom say, "I told you not to touch that. If you touch that, the policeman (pointing to a uniformed guard) will take you off to jail! Do you want to go to jail?" The guard playing along with the mom, put his hand on his gun and leered at the toddler. It will not take many pairings such as this for a toddler to learn that "police" take you to jail and that police are scary. I point this out, because this innocent looking interaction is well learned by our children.

In classical conditioning the process of learning is thought to be "passive." The child elicits a response. This response is reflexive in nature. The loud noise makes the child jump. The puff of air makes the child's eye blink. The child is passively being influenced by the stimuli. Next we will learn about an interactive teaching method called operant conditioning.

BILLY THE BOMBER

Billy was referred to my office by his probation officer. That within itself was a cause for alarm. You see, Billy was a scrawny, blond haired, mouse of a child. He was nine years old on the day I met him. He was frail looking and at first glance he looked all of six. Billy had been expelled from three schools in a nine week period. Other students' parents had formed impromptu groups in two of the schools to demand that Billy be stopped. Things got so out of hand, the principal of the third school called the police and requested

I would rather make my name than inherit it.
W.M. Thackeray

assistance from the county probation department.

Earlier in the week, when I talked to the probation officer by phone, he asked if I was willing to see this lad. "Sure, he sounds like my kind of kid," I exclaimed. "Really?" He queried, "What did I say that makes you think this is a nice kid?" I explained:

> I didn't say he was a nice kid. I said he was my kind of kid. It seems to me that this kid must be brilliant. He has three principals perplexed and is able to get parents to come to school. Parents don't even show up for teacher conferences any more. I'm looking forward to meeting him.

Through no fault of his own, Billy lived in a foster home. His mother had severe mental problems and his father was not known. Billy had not had contact with any family members since he was three.

Billy was brought to my office by his foster mother. He had lived with her for about three months. (He was asked to leave his last foster home due to his negative behaviors.) When I first met Billy he bopped into my office and plopped into a stuffed rocking chair. He looked me straight in the eye and announced, "So, you're my new shrink. Why you so !@#$% fat?"

"Because I eat too much." I answered. "How come you're here?" (At this point I knew I was in for a great therapeutic ride, Billy was most definitely my kind of kid.)

Billy:	I had to come here because the !@#$% told me to.
Dr. Phil:	You do what you're told?
Billy:	Most of the time, I only *@%! up some times. How about you, are you a !@#$%& up?
Dr. Phil:	Sometimes, mainly when I try hard.
Billy:	You don't mind if I !@#$% swear?
Dr. Phil:	Swear? What do you mean?
Billy:	You know fat man!
Dr. Phil:	I don't care about words very much. You can swear in here if you need to. So, how come you had to come here?
Billy:	Mr. Dickhead (probation officer) told my new

How to teach your children not to listen ...

Most parents tend to talk to their children from the negative. "Didn't you finish your homework yet?" "Stop yelling at your brother!" or "Didn't I tell you yesterday ..." This parental negativity tends to teach our children to stop listening.

Responses may be altered by their effects on the environment
                    E.L. Thorndike

Law of Effect: Behaviors (responses) that lead to positive outcomes (as defined by the child) are increased and behaviors that lead to negative outcomes are decreased.

mom that I had to.

Dr. Phil: How come?

Billy: Because the kids all call me 'Billy the Bomber.'

Dr. Phil: How come?

Billy: 'Cause I can spit so good.

Dr. Phil: Spit good?

Billy: Yeah, don't you @##@$, oh- I'm sorry. Don't you listen?

Dr. Phil: Sure I do, but I just don't understand.

Billy: Man! When the kids get in my face I spit at them.

Dr. Phil: Does it work?

Billy: Sure enough. They all fall down, or run. No one likes to get spit on. Don't you know nothin'?

Dr. Phil: Give me a break, I'm fat. I just don't get it. You like to spit on your friends?

Billy: No man! I don't have no friends. I spit on the other kids.

Dr. Phil: Oh, I get it. You don't have any friends.

© 2000 CopitchInc.com

"Check this out Charley, I've taught that scientist to give me food every time I hit this lever."

"Wow, they aren't as dumb as they look."

Billy: I didn't come here to talk about friends, I came here to talk about spittin'!

As it turned out, Billy had learned to keep people away by spitting at them. He had quite a record. He wasn't allowed on any school bus. He wasn't allowed out at recess. He wasn't allowed in a classroom desk row. His spitting worked very well for him. He had pushed his world away. Parents in the school secretly talked about Billy the Bomber. It got back to the principal of school number two that Billy must be crazed because of the AIDS virus and that he was endangering the other children by spitting on them. The facts didn't seem to matter. Billy didn't have AIDS. But the rumors persisted.

Billy was in need of crisis counseling. Before Billy could attend another school, his spitting behavior had to stop. As we discussed earlier, any behavior that can be learned can be unlearned. Seeing Billy was in control of his behavior (spitting), desensitization through classical conditioning would not work. As you recall, in classical conditioning, the child is passively taught. In this case, Billy was involved with his learning.

When the response of the child influences their surroundings, it is known as **operant conditioning**. In the model of learning called operant conditioning, the responses of the child "operate" on the environment to produce rewarding consequences.

In 1911, E.L. Thorndike explained the **Law of Effect**. Thorndike showed that when learning, *responses may be altered by their effects on the environment*. What this means in plain speak is that behaviors (responses) that lead to positive outcomes (as defined by the child) are increased and behaviors that lead to negative outcomes are decreased. Simply, Thorndike noted what we all know, if something works for us, we do it again, if it doesn't work for us, we stop doing it.

Let's go back to Billy. Somehow he had learned to spit when he was upset. When I asked Billy how he started spitting, he told me, "I always have." I'm pretty sure Billy didn't pop out of the womb and spit at the hospital staff, at least not intentionally. Spitting, for Billy was an adaptive behavior. One he learned to use to get a need met, "...get kids out of my face."

I would imagine it all started something like this. Little Billy was feeling picked on by some other child. He felt frustrated. He felt angry. He wanted the other child to leave him alone, then it happened. Splat! Billy spat at the other child. The other child was not overcome with joy and he ran off to some adult to tell on Billy. Did you see the reinforcement? Billy was reinforced when the other kid got out of his face right after Billy spat at him. Billy got his needs met. Billy was rewarded (kid left) for his behavior (spitting). A behavior that is reinforced will increase.

The reward in Billy's case was the removal of an adverse

Quick Reference Guide

Operant Conditioning-

Negative Reinforcer: The removal of an adverse stimulus that increases the likelihood of a response. A reward.

Positive Reinforcer: A stimulus that increases the likelihood of a response. A reward.

Punishment: The presentation of an aversive stimulus following an undesired response that decreases the likelihood of the undesired response.

Extinction: The process in which a learned response is no longer reinforced, reverting to its preconditioned level.

Successive Approximation (Shaping): The process of rewarding for a behavior each time it gets closer and closer to the desired behavior.

Modeling: A hands on form of shaping behavior. It is learning by imitation.

Operant Conditioning-

Negative Reinforcer: The removal of an adverse stimulus that increases the likelihood of a response. A reward.

Positive Reinforcer: A stimulus that increases the likelihood of a response. A reward.

Punishment: The presentation of an aversive stimulus following an undesired response that decreases the likelihood of the undesired response.

Extinction: The process in which a learned response is no longer reinforced, reverting to its preconditioned level.

Successive Approximation (Shaping): The process of rewarding for a behavior each time it gets closer and closer to the desired behavior.

Modeling: A hands on form of shaping behavior. It is learning by imitation.

stimulus (the other kid). This is an example of **negative reinforcement**. By definition, negative reinforcement is the removal of an adverse (negative) stimulus that increases a response. We know it increased Billy's response (spitting), he was raining down like El Nino.

Negative reinforcement tends to be tricky to understand. Many confuse it with punishment. But you can keep it clear in your thoughts if you remember that it is a reinforcement; it increases the likelihood of a behavior. It is a reward. The reward in negative reinforcement is the removal of the negative stimulus.

One day, for the fun of it, when I was setting the dinner table, I placed a small piece of candy under each of my children's plates. By the end of the meal I had forgotten about their little surprise. When one of the boys started to clear his plate he found the candy. What fun! Both boys thought that this treat should be repeated at every meal. The next morning, my youngest, then four, came to the breakfast table and tilted his bowl, spilling milk and cereal. "What are you doing?" I questioned. "Where is my candy?" he asked sadly. I had accidently taught my four year old to spill his cereal. Which, incidentally, he did regularly without my help. For days my kids looked under stuff at every meal. The boys were positively reinforced to look under their plates. This is an example of **positive reinforcement**. By definition, a positive reinforcer is a stimulus that increases the likelihood of a response. Finding the candy under the plate increased the likelihood of the children looking under the plates.

EXTINCTION

Mrs. Messick was concerned about her four year old daughter. She explained:

> Wendy is a very bright little girl. She is so sweet, but... she refuses to pick up after herself. It has become a huge battle. I'm getting to the point that I'm afraid to ask her to pick up her own toys. When I do she throws a fit. She yells and screams as if she is being beaten. I'm concerned that my neighbors may think that I'm beating her. But she has to learn how to pick up after herself.

My advice to Mrs. Messick was to ignore the screaming and be honest to her reasonable request. This turned out to be a real chore for Mrs. Messick. The following week she told me what had happened.

I did just what you told me. At first I thought that

this would never work. I even told my husband that you were silly. I just didn't think that something this major could be solved so simply.

I visited all my neighbors and told them a little about my problem. I told them that we never beat Wendy and that the increased screaming over the next week was your fault. I'm sorry Dr. Phil, I just didn't think it was going to work.

That same afternoon I told Wendy that she was a big girl and would have to pick up after herself. She seemed to accept this with no problem. Just before dinner I asked her to pick up her toys in the living room. She went nuts. In minutes she was screaming at the top of her lungs. I ignored her. After three or four minutes she was the loudest I had ever heard her. After about five minutes of this screaming she came into the kitchen and calmly asked why she had to pick up her toys. I told her again about being a big girl and her responsibility. She went nuts, again! I did what you told me and calmly walked away. She followed me— screaming! I went into the bathroom and she sat at the door crying and yelling about how picking up her toys was too hard to do all by herself. She even kicked at the bathroom door a few times. This went on for another five minutes. Then she stopped. The house was too quiet so I went looking for her. She was in her room playing with the toys that had been in the living room. She seemed just fine ... as if she had never cried at all. Over the next few days we played the same game, but only for a few minutes each time. It seems like a miracle. The last few days she just picked up her toys as if she had never had a problem. She just complains a little, just like a kid should.

With a big smile on her face she asked, "How do I get my husband to pick up his dirty clothing?"

What seemed like a miracle to Mrs. Messick is actually called **extinction**. Mrs. Messick extinguished Wendy's learned behavior (the tantrum) by not reinforcing Wendy's crying and screaming behaviors. Remember, behaviors have to be reinforced or they weaken (occur less). When mom backed down and picked up Wendy's toys she was teaching Wendy to tantrum. The positive reinforcer of picking up Wendy's toys was working quite well for Wendy. But Mrs. Messick did not want to teach this so, she had to extinguish that learned behavior. By not reinforcing Wendy's crying tantrum the tantrum stopped working for Wendy. By definition, extinction is the process in which a learned response, which is no longer reinforced, reverts to its preconditioned level.

It is also interesting to note that Wendy's crying was a negative reinforcement on her mom's behavior of picking up Wendy's toys. When mom backed down and picked up the toys she was able to turn off the aversive stimulus of Wendy's crying. This removal of an adverse stimulus reinforced mom to continue picking up the toys. (This circular reinforcement can keep us parents up at night if we think too hard about all the layers of reinforcement in our life.)

PUNISHMENT

For most parents, punishment is the most often used behavior controlling mechanism. While shopping in a local supermarket I observed a little boy who looked to be about four years old. His mother's patience was wearing thin. Over the next four or five minutes her statements went from, "Not now Tommy!" to "Tommy, damn it! Do you want a spanking?"

When I got to the checkout, by chance, there was Tommy, sitting in the child seat looking angry. Mom was conducting business with the cashier when she spied Tommy reaching for the candy shelf just inches from his grasp. Slap! Like a King Cobra, mom slapped Tommy's hand without missing a beat of her checkout conversation.

Tommy recoiled his hand. Held it to his chest and seemed only a little bothered by the slap. This is what most parents understand punishment to be. Tommy got his hand slapped so he should now know not to reach for candy. Specifically, Tommy's reaching is the response that his mother found to be undesirable. The slap is an aversive stimulus designed to decrease the likelihood of the undesired response. The slap caused Tommy to replace the undesirable behavior (reaching for candy) with a different behavior, not reaching for candy (desired response).

This looks like:

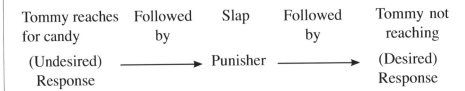

Tommy reaches for candy — Followed by — Slap — Followed by — Tommy not reaching

(Undesired) Response ⟶ Punisher ⟶ (Desired) Response

By definition, punishment is the presentation of an aversive stimulus, following an undesired response, that decreases the likelihood of that undesired response.

The actual use of punishment is quite complicated. A few seconds following mom slapping Tommy's hand Tommy reached his left foot out towards the candy shelf. Mom slapped the foot and exclaimed, "Tommy, stop being a pain, just sit still!" Tommy then reached with his right foot and was able to kick the candy box off the shelf. M & M packets covered the floor. Mom got angry. Tommy got angry. The cashier seemed unfazed. As mom pushed the cart with screaming Tommy out of the store, the cashier said to me, "People should leave their damn kids at home, they give me a headache."

Punishment is a powerful teaching tool. However, it has two major draw backs to its effectiveness. First, for punishment to be effective it must be severe. If not, its effectiveness is only temporary. Second, punishment brings to the relationship powerful feelings such as anger and revenge which can destroy a positive learning situation. Let's look at each of these drawbacks individually.

For punishment to be effective it must be severe, if not the lesson is only learned for the short term. Tommy did not truly learn not to reach for the candy. If the punishment was severe enough to teach that we would call it child abuse. My friend Stephan is a locksmith and he is very good at his job. I bring this up because once he suffered an accident to his hand. He was preparing to take out the garbage. When he was pushing the refuse down into the can a glass jar, under the top papers, broke. A large piece of glass protruded up and severely cut his hand between his thumb and palm. The damage was massive, limiting the movement of his thumb. Years later I watched him while he was closing up his shop. As he was taking out the garbage I asked him what he was looking for. "I'm looking for something to push the garbage down with," he said as he held up his damaged hand, "You won't catch me using my hand to do it." Stephan had learned, through the learning process of punishment, not to push garbage into a garbage can with his hand. The lesson had been well learned over fifteen years earlier.

For Stephan, the act of pushing garbage down (response) was followed by the severe pain of the glass cutting deep into his hand (punisher) causing a different behavior. He now uses something to push the garbage down (desired response). Please note, this just happened. Stephan was punished by chance, severely. Due to the severity, the lesson was well learned.

In the real world of parenting, for punishment to work, the severity of the punisher would be much too severe for a parent to implement. Tommy's mom could probably teach Tommy not to reach for candy by criminally (child abuse) hurting Tommy's little hand. Obviously, this would be outrageous. Most parents learn that punishment produces only short term learning.

The second major undesirable effect of punishment is the emotional turmoil that can develop.

On a regular basis I have parents tell me:

I can't believe I can't get through to my kids.

Will my children ever learn?

Quick Reference Guide

Operant Conditioning-

Negative Reinforcer: The removal of an adverse stimulus that increases the likelihood of a response. A reward.

Positive Reinforcer: A stimulus that increases the likelihood of a response. A reward.

Punishment: The presentation of an aversive stimulus following an undesired response that decreases the likelihood of the undesired response.

Extinction: The process in which a learned response is no longer reinforced, reverting to its preconditioned level.

Successive Approximation (Shaping): The process of rewarding for a behavior each time it gets closer and closer to the desired behavior.

Modeling: A hands on form of shaping behavior. It is learning by imitation.

What do I have to do to get through to them? I grounded them last week for the exact same problem!

And I hear children say:

My parents don't understand ... all they do is yell at me.

My folks don't even know who I am!

What do I have to do to get my parents to understand. They grounded me last week for the same thing. I just don't care!

Mr. Knapp came to my office out of frustration. He said his fourteen year old daughter, Ellen was out of control. "I can't get her to do anything. Even when I spank her she just yells, 'You don't own me!' I've grounded her, taken away her stuff and told her that she can't have her driver's license next year. Nothing seems to get through to her!"

Ellen was a bright and stubborn young lady. During our first family counseling session, she stated the situation quite clearly. "I don't care what my mom and dad do! They can't hurt me. I haven't cried from a spanking since I was seven!"

What Mr. Knapp was experiencing was the disruptiveness of emotions that destroy the limited effect of punishment. The act of punishing a child brings up in the child many disruptive thoughts and feelings. These feelings tend to get in the way of our goal as parents, to teach our children appropriate social behaviors. It is common for a child to receive punishment for a misbehavior, only to stomp off to their room and spend the next few hours focusing on their parents' behavior, the act of punishment, rather than their own inappropriate behavior.

We will discuss this more in the section, THE ART OF DISCI-PLINE, in Chapter 4.

TIMING IS VERY IMPORTANT

Mrs. Babcock read in a children's magazine about a parenting technique that helped toddlers pick up after themselves with little fuss. So she tried it. She made a chart on a piece of paper showing the days of the week followed by three circles. She told her daughter, Mandy (age 3), that after breakfast, lunch, and dinner it was clean up time. She explained to Mandy that if she helped clean up her toys with mommy, mommy would put a sticker on the correct circle. Mandy was very excited by the colorful stickers. Over the next two weeks Mandy was reasonably helpful in picking up her belongings.

On the two week anniversary of the sticker chart mom couldn't locate the stickers. She looked high and low but had to tell Mandy that she had no stickers to give. Mandy went ballistic and threw her toys at her mom. From what I was told, Mandy was an accurate little pitcher, future Baseball Hall of Fame material.

To this point we have discussed continuous schedules of reinforcement, which simply means, every time the correct behavior is shown, the child receives a reward. Every time Mandy helped with the clean up, she received a sticker for her chart. One act of helping earned one reward sticker. This is written as 1:1 (1 to 1).

In the real world, reinforcement is seldom 1:1. In the real world reinforcement is usually *partial* (not 1:1). Psychologists have investigated this fact and have grouped reinforcement into schedules. There are four major groups of reinforcement parents need to understand. Each type of reinforcement has its place in teaching our children.

FIXED-RATIO SCHEDULE OF REINFORCEMENT

In a fixed-ratio schedule, reinforcement is given after a fixed number of correct behaviors. So, in the example above, Mandy was reinforced on a schedule of 1:1. Every time. However, if she had been given a sticker after three helpful cleanup experiences, the ratio would be 3:1 (3 behaviors to 1 reward).

Learning with a fixed-ratio schedule tends to be the quickest of all schedules. This makes sense. Mandy was able to connect the reward with the desired behavior easily. However, unlearning behavior (extinction) is also quick with a fixed-ratio schedule of reinforcement. Mandy knew right away that she wasn't receiving any reinforcement so she stopped picking up.

Workers who get paid by the piece or by commission tend to be highly productive as long as the reinforcement is received. I once knew a commissioned car salesman who almost got into a fist fight with the sales manager when asked to vacuum the showroom. In the salesman's eyes he was there to sell cars. He didn't get paid to pick up around the showroom. Without the direct reinforcement both the car salesman and Mandy refused to help out around the place.

FIXED-INTERVAL SCHEDULE OF REINFORCEMENT

In a fixed-interval schedule, reinforcement is given to the first desired behavior following a specific period of time. For example, Mr. Randel was a strict parent. He believed that his military training was pivotal in his success as an adult. In the Randel family bedroom inspections were Sunday at 5 PM. At 5 PM sharp, Mr. Randel walked through his children's rooms. If they were shipshape he would leave their allowance on their pillows. He was proud to say, "At 5:01 my children's rooms are perfect." He was sheepish to say,

Quick Reference Guide

Schedules of Reinforcement-

1. Fixed-ratio schedule of reinforcement: Reinforcement is given after a fixed number of correct behaviors.

2. Fixed-interval schedule of reinforcement: Reinforcement is given for the first desired behavior following a specific period of time.

3. Variable-ratio schedule of reinforcement: Reinforcement is given after a varying number of desired responses.

4. Variable-interval schedule of reinforcement: Reinforcement is given for the desired behavior based on a varying interval of time.

"By Monday morning the rooms look like a war zone. I can't believe how undisciplined my children are."

A fixed-interval schedule of reinforcement tends to show rapid learning, but the results are sporadic. The Randel children, all nine of them, cleaned their rooms Sunday afternoon. The Randel children learned to anticipate the reinforcement and were ready to receive it at 5 PM Sunday.

A fixed-interval schedule of reinforcement is used in most school testing situations. The student knows when the test is and studies (crams) just before. Right after the test the desired behavior, studying, rapidly decreases.

VARIABLE-RATIO SCHEDULE OF REINFORCEMENT

My beloved wife, Mrs. Copitch, is an elementary school teacher. She has this classroom currency called *Copitch Cash*. If you are caught being kind, helpful or just down right wonderful you receive $1 *Copitch Cash*. At the end of the week the *Copitch Cash* can be used in the class store or saved for bigger and better goodies. Don't tell the students, but Mrs. Copitch wants every child to earn lots of *Copitch Cash* throughout the week. She knows, hopefully from all her proof reading of my work over the years, that a variable-ratio schedule of reinforcement is a powerful and long term learning mechanism. Let's say, for example, that Mrs. Copitch wants every child to earn at least three dollars in *Copitch Cash* per day. The students know that there is potential cash to be had. They just don't know when they are going to be "caught being nice." Sometimes they do nice things 36 times before getting caught. Other times they get caught on their third nice behavior. This schedule of reinforcement takes a little longer to teach but the durability of the behavior is greater.

In a variable-ratio schedule, the reinforcement is given after a varying number of desired responses. In the adult world, a variable-ratio schedule of reinforcement is the key to how a casino gets gamblers to play slot machines. The slot machine is programmed to let the gambler win, get reinforcement, at a varying ratio, over a set number of plays. This reinforces the gambler to put money into the machine. The gambler *knows*, "This machine is just about to pay off." A variable-ratio schedule of reinforcement is very powerful. I have had patients, after putting their rent money into a slot machine, tell me, "If I only had a few more dollars. I just know the machine was ready to pay." What the person doesn't see is that the machine is programmed to *let you feel* that the reward is just one pull away.

God could not be everywhere, therefore he made mothers.

The Talmud

VARIABLE-INTERVAL SCHEDULE OF REINFORCEMENT

Jason was 16 when I met him. He had been expelled from school for smoking in the bathroom on three separate occasions. He asked his parents to help him stop smoking and, after months of failed attempts, Jason and his family were convinced that Jason had, what his father described as, an "Addictive Personality."

Jason told me how he got started smoking. When he was 13 he thought that he had to try cigarettes. He stole a smoke from his father's jacket. Jason whispered as he told his story.

> I snuck out into the back yard and lit it up. It was so exciting. Getting over on my parents was great. I hated the cigarette. It was nasty and made me choke. But every night for a month I stole another.
>
> Then my father became suspicious. He started taking his pack of cigarettes up to his room at night. Some nights he forgot. I would steal one and smoke it. This went on for months. I guess I was smoking 2 or 3 cigarettes a week. I was hooked. I now smoke a pack and a half a day. I can't stop.

Without knowing it Jason was defining a learning schedule. Every night for a month (fixed-ratio schedule of reinforcement) Jason was reinforced for stealing and smoking a cigarette. The reinforcement was his excitement of "getting over" on his parents. Then, when his father became suspicious and began taking his cigarette pack to his room, Jason was only reinforced at a variable interval, every few nights. Jason never knew if tonight was the night. Jason didn't know the reinforcement schedule, but the reinforcement was powerful. Even with a nicotine patch Jason could not stop smoking.

A variable-interval schedule of reinforcement taught Jason that the reinforcement was some time interval away. Maybe one day maybe six days. This is why Jason was having such a hard time staying away from cigarettes even after weeks with no reinforcement.

SCHEDULES OF REINFORCEMENT AND EXTINCTION

A fixed-ratio schedule of reinforcement is usually referred to as constant reinforcement. Due to the constant nature of this reinforcement, extinction of the new behavior tends to be rapid. The other three schedules of reinforcement are usually referred to as partial schedules of reinforcement. Partial reinforcement is extremely effective in maintaining a behavior. The learner is not expecting a reward every time so, the behavior is not weakened as quickly when the reward is not received. Sometimes this works wonderfully, such as when your child is motivated to clean their room without

Quick Reference Guide

Operant Conditioning-

Negative Reinforcer: The removal of an adverse stimulus that increases the likelihood of a response. A reward.

Positive Reinforcer: A stimulus that increases the likelihood of a response. A reward.

Punishment: The presentation of an aversive stimulus following an undesired response that decreases the likelihood of the undesired response.

Extinction: The process in which a learned response is no longer reinforced, reverting to its preconditioned level.

Successive Approximation (Shaping): The process of rewarding for a behavior each time it gets closer and closer to the desired behavior.

Modeling: A hands on form of shaping behavior. It is learning by imitation.

you asking. Sometimes it is a disaster, as Jason found when he tried to stop smoking.

As parents, we need to be attuned to the schedules of reinforcement so that we can teach our children effectively. We must also understand schedules of reinforcement so we can use extinction effectively. As humans we are prone to frustration when what we expect does not occur. Earlier, we found Mandy throwing things at her mother when she did not get the sticker she expected. By understanding the powerful influence schedules of reinforcement have, we can be more patient and understanding when our children experience frustrating situations.

DR. PHIL'S RULE OF 10:1, 100:1, OR 1000:1

Schedules of reinforcement, and children over the years, have taught me that changing an undesirable behavior is very, very difficult. I have a simple but relatively unscientific Dr. Phil Rule. I say it is unscientific because I have no empirical data for the number part of the rule. But, I have not yet found a parent who didn't experience the wrath of this rule.

DR. PHIL'S RULE OF 10:1, 100:1, OR 1000:1 USUALLY SHORTENED TO: DR. PHIL'S 10:1 RULE:

HOWEVER MANY TIMES YOUR CHILD HAS BEEN REINFORCED FOR AN UNDESIRED BEHAVIOR, IT WILL TAKE AT LEAST 10 TIMES THAT NUMBER TO CHANGE THAT BEHAVIOR.

For example. If your child learns that if he whines you will sometimes back down, you are teaching your child to whine using a variable schedule of reinforcement.

An example of this would be when you say "no" to your darling seven year old and he says, "But, mom!" or "Please, please, please..." and then, after a while, you get worn down and change your mind (usually just before you lose it). Take the quantity of whines you taught him to have (variable reinforcement), and multiply it by at least ten to find the number of times he will whine before he believes whining doesn't work any longer (extinction). Use the multiplier of ten if your child is not too bright. The brighter your child the greater the multiplier. For the average kid multiply by 100. For a smart kid, one who will someday run the world, multiply it by 1000.

What this means is, if you teach your child to whine seven times before you back down, you will have to un-teach him 70, 700 or 7000 times. It is important that parents are careful about what they inadvertently teach their children. (See WHINING in Chapter 5 if you need encouragement to continue.)

SHAPING

I once did a weekend seminar for one of those big companies that can afford to advertise during the Olympics or the Super Bowl. The seminar was devoted to helping middle managers learn how to motivate their sales force. On Saturday morning I was surprised to find a room full of bright eyed, white-starched-shirt-wearing, power-tie-toting, middle aged men. I had just crawled out of bed, showered under a tiny water saver shower-head, and had not yet had any coffee. It was 8:30 AM and my day was only thirty minutes old. The men in the audience were awake. Happily awake. I was disgusted. To me, the only way I could be happy at 8 AM was if I was up to deliver my wife's baby. Saturday mornings are for sleeping, everyone knows that. (Except during youth soccer season.)

I talked to the group about my plan for the day and pointed out a few goals and objectives. I asked if there were any questions and waited for some. I have talked to hundreds of parent groups, teacher groups and therapist groups. Someone always has a question. This group looked fearful. It dawned on me that this group wasn't expecting to participate. They thought they were there to listen and absorb information. Boy, were they in for a big surprise.

I called on people. "What is your biggest problem with your work force?" "How do you motivate people to work?" "Tell me your biggest thorns-in-your-side and who put them there?" Finally, after some fifteen minutes, one older gentleman stood up and growled, "Well DOCTOR, I have to spend my weekend here, are you going to tell me how to find employees that will follow directions... I need winners! Where do I find them!?" Then he crossed his arms and plopped himself into his chair. The room became alive with murmuring. It seemed that this man had shared a problem that was common for the attendees. I was so excited. Anger. Pure and simple anger. An emotion I could work with. What a wonderful opportunity. So, I told a story. (I'm a cognitive, behavioral therapist - I always tell stories.)

A couple of months ago I was at Sea World. I saw the dolphin show. This gray sleek mammal leaped out of the pool, did a forward flip over a bright red nylon rope, and dove back into the water. What a sight!

A small boy in front of me asked his grandfather, "How did they teach the dolphin to do that?" The grandfather said, "They go out into the ocean and scare the dolphins out of the water with their big boat engines. The ones that jump the highest they capture and bring here for the show."

This was an intriguing theory but not an accurate one. I postulated the boy's question to my hostile audience: "How do you teach a dolphin to jump over a rope?" I ask you the same question, "How would you teach a dolphin to jump over a rope?"

The most common answer to the question was, "I'd hang a fish from a rope above the water." The problem with this is how to get the dolphin to look up at the fish. Dolphins don't go around in their natural environment, looking up out of the water expecting mackerel. Most fish don't jump out of the ocean. And even the motivated ones that do would not be enough to fill the bellies of many a dolphin.

The way you teach a dolphin to jump is by using a process called **shaping**. Shaping is the process of rewarding a behavior each time it gets closer and closer to the desired behavior. You can't go out into the ocean, with a loud speaker attached to your boat yelling, "Jump! Jump! Come on Flipper, JUMP!" You won't get a dolphin to jump out of the water, do a back flip, smile at the camera and come to the boat to be captured. If you did, you would have what corporate middle managers call a "WINNER!" It just doesn't happen. At first, dolphins don't know anything about show biz.

Dolphins are not fools. They are readily willing to investigate their world and find food. That is their job. At first you have to get the dolphin to recognize the importance of the rope. If you place the rope in the pool so the dolphin can swim above it and below it they will do just that. When the dolphin "accidently" swims above the rope you drop a fish in the pool. After a few chance encounters the dolphin says to itself, "Hmm... I think there is an interesting relationship here. Something is going on between that lifeless piece of seaweed and a fish falling from the heavens. I'll call that new kind of plant, Hmm... rope. Now let's see, if I swim under the rope nothing happens. But, if I swim over the rope, lunch. This I can live with. In fact, I feel encouraged to keep swimming above the rope."

Then the trainer raises the rope. Just a little each time. Not to be mean, but making it harder for our friend Flipper. It's just not much of a show if the rope is in the water. Spectators would say, "Big deal, the dolphin can swim at the top of the pool." You're not going to get $14.50 a head for a dolphin fin poking out of the water playing shark! The trainer keeps raising the rope slowly, over time, until it is well above the water.

We do the same thing with our children. If you want to teach your 18 month old to politely say, "Excuse me mother, could I please have a piece of toast?" You don't wait until the kid is completely verbalizing his needs. If you wait that long, you'll end up with a skinny dead kid. That's not good!

What we want to do is shape the child's behavior. Mom says, "Do you want toast? Toast, toast, toast?" Then one day your little buddy says, " Ta Ta Ta" for toast and you get all excited. You get out the video camera. You call the grandparents. You declare your

The trouble with this world is that too many people go through life with a catcher's mitt on both hands.

child to be a genius. But, at 16, if your son starts saying, "Ta Ta Ta" for toast you'd have his urine checked for street drugs.

You reward as you catch your child making progress. "Ta Ta Ta," works for a while. But in no time "Ta Ta peas" is needed. Then "toes peas" is changed to "toast please" and you don't even think about the fact that your little baby isn't as cute anymore.

This is shaping. Some psychologists call it *successive approximation*. Shaping behavior accounts for the vast majority of complex learned behaviors.

MODELING

Modeling is a hands on form of shaping behavior. It is learning by imitation. When the coach stands next to the little leaguer and shows her how to swing the bat the coach is modeling the desired behavior. When the martial arts instructor repositions a student's hand or foot, showing the correct position, the instructor is modeling the student's behavior.

Many children have acted out a negative behavior they observed another child doing only to be surprised at their parents' response. This is a form of shaping where the child learned from the behavior another child modeled.

Modeling is a powerful learning tool. If the modeled behavior is reinforced it will be maintained. Many parents are correct to be concerned about what their children can learn through inadvertent modeling. For example, children (and adults) will learn behaviors modeled on television or on the big screen.

Excellence I can reach for; perfection is God's business.
Michael J. Fox

Quick Reference Guide

Token economy: A behavior modification system that uses a token as a conditioned reinforcer.

The "Token" currency of Copitch Cash

BRIBERY DOES NOT WORK

Mrs. Conrad was very concerned that Paul, age 14, was not getting his homework done. So, she decided to motivate Paul to do his homework with a deal she heard that had worked for her friend's child. If Paul did his homework every night she would give him $1 per assignment. She and Paul calculated that he could make around $30 dollars a week. Paul was highly motivated to do his homework. Every night for three weeks Paul proudly presented his assignments to his mother. Depending on the night. Mrs. Conrad gave Paul three to five crisp dollar bills she got from the bank for this very purpose. Mrs. Conrad told me:

> I thought I had found homework heaven. Paul was doing his work. We had stopped arguing over his homework. I really thought I was brilliant. I told my friends how easy it was to be a great mother.
>
> Then the report card came home. I was dumbfounded. Paul's grades were worse then ever. He was failing half his classes. I was positive there was a mistake. I was sure that if I showed Paul his failing report card he would feel like a failure. I didn't tell him it came. I had seen Paul's work and he understood his assignments. I was sure the school had messed up. I marched right down to that school. I was furious that they couldn't get their act together.
>
> I found Paul's math teacher in the hallway. Do you know what? My damn kid hadn't turned in any of his assignments. Not one! Every teacher told me the same story. "Paul is a great kid, but not very motivated, he never does his homework." Almost $200 dollars, and for nothing!

This is an example of bribery. Bribery is when we put the proverbial cart before the horse. That is, when we give the reward before the behavior. At first it makes so much sense. If I give you your reward why wouldn't you do what I asked you to do? The simple answer is that we humans, and every other animal we have ever tested in the lab, need to work for our rewards. By giving the reward we are reinforcing the behavior that comes before the reward. In bribery, the behavior just before the reward is doing nothing and that is what we tend to get. Nothing. In the above story, Paul received the reward when he showed his mother the completed homework assignment. There was no incentive to turn the assignment in. If most adults were paid prior to the work period, what incentive would there be for going to work?

An old man sat outside of the walls of a great city. Whenever travelers stopped and asked him, "What kind of people live in this city?" The old man would reply with the question, "What kind of people live in the city you come from?"

If the traveler said, "Only bad people live in the city I come from." The old man would tell them, "You should not stop here. You will only find bad people living here." If the traveler said, "Only good people live in the city I come from." The old man would reply, "You should stop here. You will find good people living in this city."

Yiddish Folk Tale

In my office, Mr. and Mrs. Conrad confronted Paul with the homework fiasco. Paul was calm. He simply said, "Mom, you only paid me to do my homework. You didn't pay me to be a delivery man."

Using a reward as a promise is useless. It does not teach children to complete a task. The child feels manipulated into doing something they do not wish to do. They are behaving for the reward, not because it is the "correct" way to behave. A child who follows the rules because of the bribe is bound to be a spoiled, manipulative individual. Such a child is going to go through life looking for what he can take. What is in it for him.

I will state it very clearly: BRIBERY DOES NOT WORK!

THE POWER OF A TOKEN ECONOMY

I recently read a news story about an enterprising college student who had organized his friends to help him win a war plane. As I understand it, one of the big cola companies had a promotion running that encouraged people to collect cola points. With these cola points one could purchase fun products. So, for example, if you collected 100 cola points you could earn a free cola, for 1000 points you could obtain a hat with a cola insignia. In the commercial one was led to believe that, with some astronomical amount of points, you could win a Harrier Jet. Some enterprising young person pooled his resources and gathered this astronomical amount of cola points. The newspaper article pointed out that the cola company and the advertising company were making the offer of a war plane as a joke. The point collecting self starter was demanding his plane. I wonder how it ever worked out.

I would imagine that the advertising company executives sat around a large oak conference table and pitched their idea to the cola executives. The ad folks said something like, "Well, we believe you will sell a heck of a lot of your soda if kids could save cola points to win a prize. We think that kids would be encouraged to buy maybe a thousand cans just to get a hat. Hats don't cost much, so you'll make a lot of profit. You could also put your company logo on each hat and have every sixteen year old forehead act as your walking bulletin board."

Psychologically speaking, collectable coupons are very rewarding. Many companies have used them to build customer loyalty. I recall my mother saving S&H Green Stamps for years. She loved the little things. My brother and I would beg for the new bike which was only 64 gazillion points. We were dumb struck when mom traded her boxes of stamp books in for an electric can opener. (It made no sense to ten year old me. You can't ride a can opener. Only 63 gazilion more stamps and I would have been the happiest kid on Elm street. Moms. Go figure!)

Stamps, coupons and cola points are real life examples of a **token economy**. A token economy, by definition, is a behavior modification system that uses a token as a conditioned reinforcer. In a token economy behavior is shaped towards being more socially acceptable. For example, a preschool teacher may give out stickers to his students when they pick up their toys appropriately. A very bright elementary school teacher may give *Copitch Cash* when a student uses her words to help another. A high school teacher may give painted checkers to students who return their homework in a timely fashion. In all these classroom situations, the student can accumulate the tokens (stickers, *cash*, or checkers) and use them to buy something at the class store or treasure box.

The delayed reward in the token economy often adds to the "fun" of the recipient's experience. The anticipation is part of the reward. Later we will discuss how we can individualize the reward system for a particular child. But, for now we can look at two examples.

Randy is a rambunctious five year old. His energy level is difficult to contain in the kindergarten class. The teacher was experienced and knew that a token economy could help Randy focus on his work. She explained the procedure to Randy's mother and asked for her to be the giver of the reinforcer. The teacher proposed that throughout the day, Randy could earn points on a chart. If he earned 5 points, Randy would be able to pick a five minute special time with his mother. The special time would occur when mom picked up Randy at the end of the school day. Randy could pick playing with mom on the swings, playing kick ball with mom, or having a story read to him, by mom, in the over-stuffed chair at the back of the room. If Randy did not earn five or more points then his mom was to "play" sad and say, "Oh, what a shame, I was looking forward to our special time. Maybe tomorrow?"

By the end of the first week, Randy had earned his special time with his mother on all but the first day. At the end of the second week mom, the teacher, and Randy decided to change the rules just a little. Instead of it being five or more points to earn five minutes, Randy could earn one minute of special time for every point over five points. By the end of the third week, Randy was consistently earning fifteen minutes of special time with his mom. Mom was happy with the change and spoke openly about how she looked forward to her "special time." Only the teacher and I knew how much of a change had really happened.

At first, Randy was able to earn points for just not being obnoxious in class. By the middle of the second week, Randy could only earn points for being on task with the class. By the third week Randy could only earn points for being in a good mood while being on task. In as little as a month, Randy's behavior went from bouncing around the room to relaxed and creative. Randy was enjoying school and his mother was enjoying her part as the special reward.

Within the token economy the child's behavior is shaped. If we expected Randy to sit and happily do his work from the beginning, he probably never would have earned his first five points.

In Mrs. Copitch's class a student earns *Copitch Cash* for being nice and working hard. This is personalized for each student. Each student is treated as special and as an individual. This class management system allows for more time for teaching and more warm fuzzies along the line of "caught you being nice." Everyone is a winner.

Most token economies are what I call "positive token economies." This means that the child only earns tokens. Personally, I prefer a Positive/Negative Token Economy. In this more sophisticated system, the child can earn (reward) as well as lose tokens (punishment). (Please note that this is much more work for the adult.) For example, in Mrs. Copitch's class if you lose your homework you need to purchase another copy of the homework assignment. A pencil costs a dollar, a bad word costs five dollars. This behavior modification system is a lot of work for the teacher because the child's academic and personal needs must always be factored into the equation. A positive/negative token economy tends to be a warm learning environment that encourages personal responsibility.

CLOSING NOTE

In this chapter we have discussed the mechanisms of teaching that govern the learning process. In the following chapters we will investigate how personality influences the process of an individual's personal development.

Chapter 2

How to Build Your Child's Self Esteem

"Oh yes, Suzanne is doing quite well. She has done her first apartment in early attic."

2. HOW TO BUILD YOUR CHILD'S SELF ESTEEM

WHAT DO YOU REALLY WANT FOR YOUR CHILD?

We start off with a question fundamentally impossible to answer with one answer. At one moment the answer is, "I want my Sally to be happy." Five minutes later... "I want Sally to have a college education." Minutes later, "I want Sally to..." We have hopes and aspirations for our children. We wish them to be well educated, physically healthy, emotionally stable, and to care about us in our old age. The list is almost endless.

I asked parents over the course of a week, "What do you want for your child?" Their answers follow:

-to be happy
-to be safe
-to be smart
-to go to college
-to grow up and have a great life
-to be whatever he wants to be
-to have a better life than my parents
   could give to me
-to do well in school
-to be self confident
-to be thoughtful and kind
-to give to people less fortunate than herself
-to know and love God
-not to get into major trouble
-to have integrity
-to be honest

A mom once told me, "I used to pray that my son would have a great mind. Now, I wonder if God is laughing at me. Sam can remember everything I tell him and he uses my own words against me."

When I look down this list I have to agree. I would think that most parents have a list that is a mile long of what they want for their children. But, let's look at this from the view point of our children. What pressure! What overwhelming, engulfing pressure. Our children are constantly being compared to our goals for them, our expectations.

Now, don't get me wrong. Without parental expectations most children and teens would have difficulty finding food. We need to have hopes and dreams for our children. But, we cannot deny that the goals and aspirations are dropped on our children's shoulders without warning. The weight of our hopes can be overwhelming to many young people.

What goal would you deny your child? We are in agreement

that the list of our hopes is overwhelming, so what would you cross off your list? Would you put a line through, - to do well in school or -to have integrity? I wouldn't think so. We all want the very best for our children.

WHAT IS THE SINGLE BIGGEST "GIFT" WE CAN GIVE OUR CHILDREN?

Hold on. Take a minute to think about this question. If you could give one and only one gift to your child, what would it be? Would you give your child financial riches? Would you give her beauty? Would you give him intelligence? If you could give only one thing that would give your child a leg up in life, what would it be?

I frequently read in the newspaper about the movie star who finds fame and fortune, only to end up in a drug treatment hospital. Or, the business money mogul who has three ex-wives and a few estranged children. We have heard of generals indicted for being stupid, presidents shamed into retirement, or the religious leaders who lead two different life-styles.

So, what is the best thing we can give our children? What "gift" can help a child in good and bad times? What one "gift" will help our children to avoid the horrors of drugs, stay level headed when good times roll in and keep perspective during life's pitfalls?

I propose that the best gift a parent can give a child is the home environment that allows their child to build a high self esteem. Research has shown us that children who possess a healthy self esteem deal with life in the safest ways.

If we as parents help our children to build a strong self esteem we give them the best internal tool to deal with their world. With the internal awareness of their own self worth, our children interact with the world with inner contentment and self assuredness. The side effect of our children having high self esteem is that they view the world through this high self esteem. As I will discuss later, high self esteem is an emotional force field protecting our children in the chaos we call life.

DON'T GET LOST IN THE MEDIA HYPE

I recently heard a conservative radio talk show host rant and rave about liberals wasting money on building self esteem. He was very concerned that a school district had sanctioned a baseball coach for yelling at his loosing team. He proclaimed that "the liberals are so worried about hurting some kid's self esteem that they are taking all the fun out of competitive sports."

The callers to the radio program spoke for the rest of the hour about how the schools, the churches, and our society as a whole were babying children, and making them feel good about doing

Children are poor men's riches.
English Proverb

Children in a family are like flowers in a bouquet: there's always one determined to face in an opposite direction from the way the arranger desires.
Marcelene Cox

mediocre and substandard work. One caller explained that the youth of today were "all stupid and useless." He was sure that if parents whipped their kids when they acted up they would know right from wrong and we just wouldn't have to worry about stuff like self esteem and feelings.

As the radio talk show continued it became obvious that the callers were really angry with the youth of America. Words like "whiny" and "cry baby" were used to define today's teens. "Spoiled" and "selfish" were pinned on the younger children. Callers blamed the teachers, the parents, and the government. The words "self esteem" seemed to be used as a negative. As if "self" or "esteem" were bad words. The radio talk show host stated that, "We have a dumbing down of our schools. Teachers give grades to build self esteem, not based on what kids learn."

Bashing children, schools and parents may make a stimulating topic for a talk show, but it is not helpful. It misses the truth. It misses the essence of society.

One caller blamed forces outside of our solar system for the behavior of today's youth. Even the host thought that was far fetched.

The vast majority of people work very hard to get along with others. Most parents truly care about their children and wish to parent well. Most children love and respect their parents. Unfortunately, we tend to hear only about the negative. Would a talk show or a newspaper keep its audience involved with the following topics:

Mrs. Smith reads to her three
children almost every night.
Or,
Mr. Jones' child has never
been in a fist fight at
Smallville Elementary School

The reality is that most people are caring, hard working people. In fact, most of us are still striving for the things our parents hoped for us. And yes, even as adults, our own parents' goals for us, along with our own aspirations, can feel overwhelming.

HOW IS SELF ESTEEM BUILT?

Let's start off by defining what we are talking about. Self esteem goes by many names. Some call it self worth, others self-confidence. The high brow academic set use words like, "the sense of self " or "ego identity." Shakespeare said it best, "A rose, is a rose, is a rose," or something like that. The reality is that we all know what high self esteem or low self esteem look like, but it is hard to put it into words.

In a nut shell, self esteem is the internal belief we hold about ourselves. What makes it hard to understand and put into words is that it is ever changing. We hold different internal beliefs about our abilities dependent on the situation.

For example, my five year old son informed me that he couldn't pick up a hat in the side yard because of spiders. He hadn't seen any spiders but he was obviously uncomfortable. When he was reminded that he had touched spiders before, he said, "Yeah, but that spider was not hiding to get me!" Is this a self esteem issue? In a way. If, at five, Joshua felt comfortable enough within himself to handle the fears that he pictured, I would not have had to pick up the hat. But, is it a self esteem problem? Definitely not. Josh was not saying to himself, "I'm not able to pick up the hat." He was saying, "I'm afraid of spiders hiding under the hat and attacking me." Often parents confuse low self esteem with fear.

The internal belief we hold about ourselves is somewhat situational. Your child may feel that she is the best baseball player since Babe Ruth, but be uncomfortable about joining the team because she doesn't know any of the other players. When we talk about self esteem, it is important to listen to the child's words. If we focus too much on the child's behavior we often miss the true picture.

So, when we talk about self esteem we are really talking about the internal <u>balance</u> of our beliefs of self worth.

When we are born we enter the world with a personal makeup. This personal makeup is usually called our temperament. The newborn interacts with his world through his temperament.

Newborns seem to be "pre-wired" to investigate their world. Part of their temperament is to investigate and eventually build relationships with their new world.

Infant research has shown that newborns have the ability to "interact" with their caregivers from the first moments of birth. Their eyes are developed enough to focus on their mother's face during the first breast feedings. Infants are able to smell and remember their caregivers.

The individual's temperament is influential in the formation of the feeling of self worth. We take this sense of self with us throughout our life. For example, a sixty year old can truly say that they are the same, but still a different person than they were when they were six. Our feelings of self worth are with us for a lifetime.

THE BIRD NEST

Recently my family and I watched a Discovery Channel program about birds from around the world. The narrator explained how different birds build their nests. Some birds simply moved around a patch of dirt and called it home. Other birds carried twigs and grasses up into a tree and intertwined them to make a nice basket. One swallow carried beak-fulls of mud, making a substantial "clay" pot to call home. A hyper little fellow swiped spider webs and sewed the sides of leaves together making a sturdy green hammock. The

Over the years I have walked along the hallowed halls of many a university. Inevitably, the professors and students use signs and cartoons to share personal philosophies. A popular sign is the cynical view of scientific research. "Never let the facts interfere with your theories."

Not to have control over the senses is like sailing in a rudderless ship, bound to break to pieces on coming in contact with the very first rock.

Mahatma Gandhi

birds did all this by instinct. Each of the different birds was pre-programed with the innate ability to build their species specific nest. This is impressive.

We all build our self esteem in a similar fashion. We pick and choose from our environment to form our belief of who we are. Our temperament tends to initiate the direction of what we notice. Then, as time goes by, our temperament is intertwined with our experiences to form the "self." Most researchers believe that the self is pretty much built by age two. Then, by age three we start an internal dialog with ourselves and we develop our opinion about who we are. This is the onset of self esteem.

THREE BASIC LEVELS OF SELF ESTEEM

Most people think of self esteem as either high or low. It is important to understand that self esteem is a continuum. No one really has a truly high self esteem, rather they tend to possess mostly high feelings of self worth and an understanding about their limitations. Similarly, individuals with low feelings of self worth believe poorly about themselves in most situations, but are able to get by and outwardly function in their world. They perceive themselves through low esteem glasses, reaching medium esteem in a few limited areas of their life. Figure 1 illustrates the continuum of self esteem.

There are three basic levels of self esteem— high, medium and low.

HIGH SELF ESTEEM

A person with high self esteem feels comfortable in most situations. She tests her beliefs and has had experience trusting her belief system. She is self confident. She is aware that she thinks well on her feet. She knows that even well developed plans often need minor corrections. She is internally assured that she can deal with life's ups and downs. She is aware that she does not have all the answers while, at the same time, she knows deep in her soul that she can figure out most of the answers she will need.

An example of high self esteem:

Ellen is twelve years old. She is a hard working student who is somewhat bored in school. She is happy most of the time. Her parents are sure that she is a "good kid" who tends to be argumentative with them. "She is always testing my limits," her mother told me. "But then again, she plans to rule the world." Ellen feels good about herself and safe within her relationship with her parents. She has goals and dreams. She practices her growing skills on her parents. She chooses to back down when her parents give her firm limits.

During the first week of school, eight year old Thomas came home stating that "school was boring." Five year old Eric seemed to love his first days in kindergarten. He ran up excitedly and said, "We did numbers. We had recess. We did story." However, his mother was concerned when Eric then parroted, "It was boring". When mom asked, "What does boring mean?" Eric replied, "Thomas says it, I think it means sweaty."

Instead of saying that man is the creature of circumstance, it would be nearer the mark to say that man is the architect of circumstance. It is character which builds an existence out of circumstance. From the same materials one man builds palaces, another hovels; one warehouses, another villas; bricks and mortar are mortar and bricks until the architect can make them something else.

Thomas Carlyle

MEDIUM SELF ESTEEM

People with medium self esteem are constantly questioning themselves. They know that they have done well but are never really sure if it was their doing or maybe just simple dumb luck. These people tend to have a hollow drivenness. It is not so much a quest for challenge, as in the high self esteemer, it is a never ending test of themselves, to see if they can cut the mustard. This need to prove themselves tends to be very taxing, removing much of the potential enjoyment from even doing well. Individuals with medium self esteem are constantly in self doubt.

An example of medium self esteem:

Milly is an outgoing, happy go lucky, girl of nine. Her parents describe her as "flighty" and "irresponsible." "She is so smart," her mother told me, "that it infuriates me that she screws up all the time." Milly seems to want help constantly. She needs others to direct her. She tends not to follow these directions, preferring to muddle her way through. She puts a lot of energy into almost getting things done, into almost taking control of her world.

LOW SELF ESTEEM

People with low self esteem are positive that they are doomed. They believe that any thought they have will prove to be stupid. Self hate is the reality of people with low self esteem. This self hate leads to the use of societal anesthesia. This anesthesia tends to take the form of one or more of the following: social isolation, alcohol abuse, drug abuse, sexual promiscuity, or severe risk taking. Their mantra is "I don't care." And it is true for them. This internal pain drives them to wish out of a relationship even with themselves. They often mistreat caring individuals in their world. They take the attitude, "If you care for me you deserve whatever I do to you."

People with low self esteem have no respect for themselves and only contempt for anyone who cares about them.

Two examples of low self esteem:

Charles is a chubby boy of twelve. He spends large portions of his day getting noticed by moping around. His mother explains, "He sits around all day, wanting. His teacher tells me he is bright, but he does very little in school." When I first met Charles, he was polite and talkative. He spoke of his dreams and goals. It was quickly apparent that he was positive, at the core of his being, that he would never come close to any of his dreams.

Tyler is a muscular eleven year old referred to my office by juvenile probation. His nickname is "Bull," short for "The Bulldozer." He proudly explained, "Everyone calls me 'Bull' because I push people around. I like to fight. I can beat up everyone in my school, even the eighth graders." Tyler's mother has been asked to find another school. She explains, "Bull is a good boy. He just has a bad temper, like his father. He doesn't mean to hurt anyone, he just doesn't want to be told what to do."

Figure 1: The continuum of self esteem

Now for the good news...

SELF ESTEEM IS NOT CAST IN STONE

One of the most important jobs of a parent is to provide the best building material for the growing self esteem of their child. Just as the bird forages for twigs, grasses, or mud, your child searches his environment for the stuff of self esteem. At first this information gathering process occurs mostly with his caregivers. In time other influences grow in your child's life.

Research has shown us that newborns "pick up" on the feelings in their home. We know that children who are physically cared for, but whose home is in emotional turmoil tend to be prone to stomach unrest, headaches, and sleep disturbances.

Mrs. Rodriguez was going through a messy divorce with her abusive husband. Her six month old daughter was seen by her family doctor three times in one week for diarrhea and concerns of dehydration. Mrs. Rodriguez told me, "The doctor said all the tests came back normal. My baby was just fine. Then he whispered to me, 'Mary, I'm just a country doctor, but how about you send the baby to your mother's. Maybe she is all tied up in knots because of the family problems.' I told him that me and my husband don't argue in front of the baby, but I sent Alexa to my mother's anyway. You know, it was a miracle, she slept on the couch for the first fourteen hours. She got as big as a horse in just a week."

I think there is a lot to be said for country doctoring. Babies and young children are so dependent on their caregivers that it makes sense to me that they are critically attuned to them and their emotional states.

As parents, we can influence our children's self esteem by providing the correct self esteem building blocks. At about the time your child can recognize his own name, he is starting to search his world for information about himself. This information is in the form of verbal and nonverbal messages.

I once asked a young man, who just got an acceptance letter to college, how his mother reacted to the good news. He said, "She is very happy. But, she always told me I was special." "Special?"

When playing on the old tractor, Josh meticulously positioned himself on the seat, fastened the seat belt and called for his big brother to come for a "ride." Big brother happily jumped up on the tractor wheel cover. Josh announced, "I'm Dad." "Where are we going Dad?", Ethan played along. Josh summoned his deepest dad voice, "Son, you know you're not allowed to play on the tractor, what other choice can you make."

Our children are listening. Be careful what you are saying.

One kid told me that his mother's pet line when leaving a store was, "I feel like I'm baby-sitting the world some days."

I questioned. "Yeah, she always told me I was special, you know that I could put my mind to something and figure it out." "When did she tell you that you were special?" I continued. "Boy, knowing my mom, she probably patted herself on her belly and said, 'Whoever you are ... you're special to me.'" He smiled a big proud smile and I knew he was special. Why? Because I believed his mother.

Your child believes you, at least in the beginning. In fact, many child specialists point out that infants and young children perceive their parents to be "godlike." So, what are you saying to your children? What are you feeling towards your children? They are listening, intently.

WORDS COUNT

What you are thunders so that I cannot hear what you say to the contrary.

Ralph Waldo Emerson

Over the years I have asked most new patients, adults and children alike— "What did (do) your parents say to you the most?" The following are the most common answers:

THE POSITIVE SOUNDING LIST

You're so good
You're so beautiful
You're so smart
You can do it if you try hard enough
You're so creative
You could do anything you put your mind to
You can be anything you want to be
I didn't have the breaks you will have
You're an angel
You're a gift from God
You've got such a pretty face
You're so kind to others

THE NEGATIVE SOUNDING LIST

You're stupid
You're clumsy
You're selfish
You act so naughty
You're bad
You're ugly
You're fat
You're evil
You act so silly
Can't you make real friends
You're so disrespectful
You always wake up in a really bad mood

You're just like... (disliked relative)
You're driving me crazy
Are you trying to make me flip out the
    rest of the way?
If your head wasn't attached you'd lose it

Your child absorbs the millions of messages that you give him day after day, year after year. Your child hears the words of your messages and the innuendo, the "between the lines," of your sentences.

Let's do a short four part homework assignment to see what messages you give and/or receive.

HOMEWORK ASSIGNMENT PART 1

Ask yourself what were your parents' pet statements when frustrated with you as a child. It tends to be the statement you tease them about behind their backs now. Please write your answers below.

_____
_____
_____
_____
_____

HOMEWORK ASSIGNMENT PART 2

Ask your children what pet statements you use when frustrated with them. [Parents of very young children find that by observing their child playing they can fill this section out.] Please write your answers below.

_____
_____
_____
_____
_____

HOMEWORK ASSIGNMENT PART 3

Evaluate Part 1 for the hidden meaning. Please write your an-

Without knowing the force of words, it is impossible to know men.
Confucius

The best time for you to hold your tongue is the time you feel you must say something or bust.
Josh Billings

Mrs. Trudeau was very upset when I allowed her daughter to write in her workbook. She explained that she learned in school that books were not made to be written in. She was so upset, that she went as far as to ask if I went to school, then she caught herself and said, "Oh, I'm sorry Dr. Phil, I know you went to school ... but did you have books?"

swers below.

_____

_____

_____

_____

_____

HOMEWORK ASSIGNMENT PART 4

Evaluate Part 2 for the hidden meaning. Please write your answers below.

_____

_____

_____

_____

_____

Most parents are somewhat embarrassed by the hidden messages that they find. You shouldn't be. In fact, you should feel proud that you are looking inward. It shows that you care a lot about your child by the fact that you are evaluating yourself. Only positive can come from your caring enough to look at your own parenting skills.

We will revisit this homework assignment in Chapter 3 when we investigate communication choices.

SELF ESTEEM AND BEHAVIOR COMPLIMENT EACH OTHER

In many cases, self esteem is a self fulfilling prophecy. If your child believes that she can or she cannot accomplish something she tends to be correct. Your child absorbs the millions of messages that are given to her day after day, year after year. If the message is "you are lovable" your child has a wealth of building material. If the message is, "You are inconvenient or bothersome," the building blocks are weak and non-supportive.

Dr. Abraham Maslow (1908-1970) conducted research into human needs. His research showed that humans have a hierarchy of needs. The most powerful "basic need" is survival. This means, when in life threatening circumstances humans will do whatever it takes to prevent hunger and thirst. Once the survival-oriented needs are met, humans focus on secondary needs such as our impulse towards freedom, goodness and justice. Maslow believed that the highest secondary need is self awareness. For a child to comprehend his own abilities his self esteem must be high.

Let's look again at the four children we met earlier. As you recall, Ellen, age 12, possesses a high self esteem. Milly, age 9, has a medium self esteem. Charles, age 12, and Tyler (Bull), age 11, are children with low self esteem. Let's look at how their behaviors and self esteem are intertwined.

TYLER (BULL)

Bull is a very intelligent child who is, what most people would call, an "unwanted child." Not that his mother didn't want him, she surely loves him, it's just that Bull has been parented by absentee parents. His mother has had a long term drinking problem. His father's involvement has been virtually non existent. When I first met Bull, he had just been kicked out of his fourth school and his eleventh foster home. Bull could not recall the names of all of his "moms and dads." He boasts 33 brothers and sisters, all short term relationships from foster home to foster home. When I first asked him what people thought of him, he was very matter of fact, "No one likes me ... They are afraid that I'm going to cut their livers out." The county probation officer (number 6) told me that "...this is one hard kid. He is as tough as a 30 year convict." He said frustratedly, "I can't find a home for this kid, he is so self confident, he walks all over foster parents."

The people in Bull's life, confused bravado with high self esteem. Bull had grown a pretend self. He wore this pretend self like armor. He walked through his world pushing people away, making sure that they never found out how scared and alone he really was. Bull had a favorite line he used when angry. He would make his angry face and screech, "I'll cut your liver out!" This had worked to get him out of many a classroom and foster home. The Juvenile Court judge was very concerned by these outbursts and court ordered therapy. During our second therapy session, Bull and I prepared liver and onions. The process of preparing the calf liver was very emotional for Bull. He was disgusted with the tactile experience. He was brought to tears before we cut a single onion. He wept and told me that he had never thought about what he was really saying.

Thirty days later, at a group meeting at Juvenile Hall, a child care worker spoke of how polite Bull was. When I asked how often he was threatening to cut people's livers out, the worker said, "Bull? He never talks like that." During this same meeting, Bull asked if we would start calling him "Tyler."

CHARLES

Charles is a chubby child who basically refuses to move unless he has to. His favorite thing to do is sit around and be in the way. He has this "in the way activity" down to a science. For a non active

Court ordered therapy is when a judge tells an individual that he needs to see a therapist for a particular psychological problem. In most cases the court ordered patient is not receptive to therapy. He sees the therapist as part of the court and feels contempt for the process. One teen put it very simply, "You can lead a person to the bathroom but you can't make him pee!"

child he works very hard to be noticed. During our third therapy session, I asked Charles what he wanted for his life. He looked down and said I would laugh. With much encouragement Charles told me, "I want to be in a wheelchair." He explained that he wants to be broken from the neck down. "If I'm in a wheelchair, people will have to take care of me ... I can just sit and no one can make me do anything."

People with low self esteem, are positive that they are useless. They are consumed with self hate. The attitude of "I don't care" is easier than having to fail and be disappointed again.

MILLY

Milly is an attractive girl with long, dirty blond hair. She has a big smile that she contorts into silly faces reflecting her moods. Milly is an outgoing follower. She seems to choose her mood depending on the people she is with. She is driven to be accepted by her peers. Milly is a child with many unrecognized talents. Unfortunately, she is filled with self doubt. She does not trust in herself, choosing other's opinions of her over her own. Her need for this constant approval of others tends to get her into trouble with adults. Her parents see her as not trying to accomplish or even as "...just silly Milly."

People with medium self esteem tend to feel uncomfortable most of the time. Even when things are going well for them, they are pushing to obtain the acceptance of others. Due to nagging self doubt, they are dependent on others for emotional stability.

A therapist friend of mine has a poster in her office that reads, "It's easier to build a child than repair an adult."

ELLEN

Ellen is an intelligent child raised in a lower income family. She respects and appreciates her parents. Due to illness, Ellen's family has had more than their fair share of turmoil.

When I asked Ellen about her world, she explained that she was luckier than most. Her attitude was quite simple. "My parents are important to me. I am important to them. So, I must be an important person." This self confidence permeates her life. She knows that she can problem solve quite well but, if she gets into difficulty, she can turn to her parents for support. Please note the word "support." She knows that her parents support her. Ellen does not expect her parents to solve her problems. She knows that is her job. She looks to her parents for advice. And, according to her mother, most of the time she doesn't adhere to it.

People with high self esteem make life choices based on feeling important and cared for.

JUST A THUMB NAIL SKETCH

These four children are just a thumb nail sketch of three basic esteem profiles. As you recall, we discussed earlier that self esteem is a continuum open to change. Unfortunately, low self esteem has a spiral effect to it. Low self esteem tends to be a behavioral black hole sucking the life out of a person. High self esteem tends to lead towards making sound life choices.

THE PARENTAL ROLE OF NURTURING

By definition, the word nurturing means to bring up, to sustain. When we think of parenting we tend not to think of the minimal role but the expansive role of being a wonderful parent.

A teen made it very clear to me once when I asked her about her father. She explained, "I don't have a father. I had a sperm donor." Other teens have taught me that a *father* or *mother* is the person who makes your life possible, but a *dad* or a *mom* loves and cares for you.

Over the years, it has always impressed me that children with limited parental support can develop high self esteem. Marcus, a third year college student, told me about Mr. Harlum, his high school shop teacher. Marcus had no family to speak of. He lived his high school years in a foster home with fair but non loving foster parents. He explained his sense of family. "I never felt like I belonged. Then I met Mr. Harlum. I was just another street kid looking to go nowhere fast. Mr. H. taught me that I was somebody. He liked me for me. So now, I think of what Mr. H. would suggest I do. I find this very helpful so I don't do dumb stuff."

Marcus taught me that in as short a time as a shop class, over the course of a few years, you can learn that you count. That if Mr. H. says you are worth caring about, you surely are.

THE ART OF BEING A CARING PARENT IS FOCUSING ON YOUR CHILD

The art of being a caring parent cannot be underestimated. It is important that your children *feel* that you truly see them for who they are and that you don't just observe their behavior.

Many parents feel as if they are constantly putting out forest fires. They feel that they do not really get to parent, they only get to keep the family from burning down the home. In

There is no such thing as a "self-made" man. We are made up of thousands of others. Everyone who has ever done a kind deed for us, or spoken one word of encouragement to us, has entered into the makeup of our character and of our thoughts, as well as our success.

George Matthew Adams

I have a sign in my office that simply states: Process Counts.

Stop showing me up. Mom says you listen better than I do!

the next section we will look at how to focus on what really counts and how not to be distracted by the hot spots of hopelessness and frustration.

GIVING THE GIFT OF HIGH SELF ESTEEM

In this section we will look at five major parental focal points that help to instil the gift of high self esteem in our children. In general, these focal points form the *attitude* of our parenting.

For example, I was asked to attend an activity on a Friday night. I was interested in going. In fact, I would have enjoyed going. It was easy to decline the invitation due to the fact that my family and I had prior plans. The prior plan stemmed from the decision, many years ago, to have a "family night."

A family night is just what it sounds like, a night for family. No matter how hectic the week is, no matter how chaotic the world is around us, Friday night we think small and peaceful. We, as a family, share each other's time and attention.

Family night was a conscious choice we made to insure that my wife and I do not lose track of what matters. By making this one decision, we actually have made millions of other choices.

By choosing the family we have chosen not to go our separate ways. We have chosen not to take work assignments that take us away from our children. We have chosen not to bring work home on Friday night. We have chosen not to attend an adult activity. The ripple effect of this one choice is infinite.

My wife and I made this choice based on what really counts to us. It is based on the role we wish to play in our children's lives. Our number one goal is to be good and caring parents. With this fact in mind, we are able to focus on what will help us accomplish this goal. We need to assist our children in developing and maintaining high feelings of self worth. By knowing what we really want we are able to meet our goals.

As a therapist, I often see parents who are drawn away from their family by other goals that are very important to them. On one hand, they wish to be good and caring parents, while on the other hand they also wish to achieve in their job or their social group. This type of conflict can destroy a family. Recently, one father was so angry with his 16 year old daughter that he slapped her when he found her lying. He consulted with me initially because he felt like a failure and he was concerned that he was loosing his daughter to the streets. During the first family session it was obvious that the members of this family truly loved each other. When I asked what the number one problem was, the family consensus was, time. Father felt he was being pulled in all directions, mainly work and home. Mother felt that she was a taxi cab driver with no real life. And all three children complained about constantly being nagged at

Even the gods love jokes.

Plato

to hurry up or complete some task. Near the end of this first family session the father and 16 year old daughter started to talk about not feeling wanted. Father was heart felt about just being a cash cow or a decision maker and daughter was in tears about how her father was always at work even when he was at home.

This highly functioning family had lost its reason to be a family. That reason is mutual support and closeness. By week three of family therapy, this family made only one notable change. This one change had a ripple effect of happiness and family security. The one change was to have a scheduled dinner time three times per week.

Let's look at how we can build self esteem through some simple choices.

SHOWING ONE'S LOVE

For your child to experience high self esteem, he must experience your love for him. It is not enough for you to love your child. Your child must "know" that he's loved by you. It is the perception of the child that counts. You need to expose your child to your love in such a manner that he believes, at his core, that he is *lovable*. This sounds so simple, but like many things that are seem simple the doing is very hard.

Most parents start family therapy from the emotional standpoint, "I love my child." In fact I often hear, " I love him so much ... Why does he act this way!"

Your focus needs to be, "Does my child feel and experience my love?" This feeling and experience are the cement between parent and child that holds the self esteem building blocks together. Dorothy Briggs, author of <u>Your Child's Self-Esteem</u>, puts it clearly, "No child can *feel* lovable if he does not *experience* love." It is imperative that we interact with our children in a way that they feel and experience our love.

I was fortunate to take a course in graduate school from Dr. Jeffrey Smith, a celebrated psychologist and long time professor at Stanford University. When I showed up to my first class I had no idea who the instructor was. He arrived a few minutes early and very slowly walked to a chair at the front of the room. He sat slowly. He spoke softly. He explained that he was an old man. He had a terminal disease and he hoped to be alive long enough to teach this 18 week course. He apologized for his frailty. He explained that he would understand if anyone would like to transfer to another instructor. He spoke about looking forward to meeting all of us young people. (Most were in their thirties.)

Dr. Smith captivated the class. It was obvious to us that he wanted to die as he lived, a teacher. He let us know that we were special to him, that his world had greater meaning because we were a part of it.

Dr. Smith allowed us to experience his love. Soon after the course ended, Dr. Smith died. His wife mailed us our final exams. Until the end, Dr. Smith taught. He took the time to write a note on each final exam. My note was hard to read. The hand that penned it was weak. He wrote, "I like to think of you, by contrast, with your strong, positive spirit, working with children, Jeffrey"

The people you love need you to let them *feel* your love. Only when our children feel our love can they experience the fact that they are *lovable*.

THE ROLE OF TIME

America is a nation preoccupied with "doing." Parents often explain how they show their love for their children with their list of "doing." You know what I mean. "Well, I take Suzy to piano, then drop Scotty off at the soccer field. Then I buzz across town to pick up Sally to take her off to Youth Leadership at the church." This is all well and good, but as many a bumper sticker will attest, this is taxiing. We must not let ourselves confuse "doing" with "being." When we *do* we are aiming at the completion. When we are *being* we are experiencing the wholeness of the activity.

Think back to your courtship days. You demanded time together. You enjoyed just *being* with the other person. This is how we humans show our caring for another. We simply say, with our actions, "I wish to be with you rather than doing anything else in the whole wide world." This attention is the "quality" time that builds relationships. One mom put it, "Life is the moments." I must agree wholeheartedly, *life is built on small moments*.

Your child absorbs your love in these small moments. The slight hug, the wink at the dinner table. The approving nod, the supportive "no." Yes, that is right, these small moments are not always "yeses," often they are supportive and definite "no's."

Most contact with our children tends to be in the "do" mode. We really have no choice. If you don't push a kid out of the house at 7:03 the school bus leaves at 7:06 without him. We must remind ourselves to experience the small moments. If we do not remind ourselves, the hustle and bustle of the real world will infect us. We will become taxi cab drivers ferrying lonely little people from soccer practice to swim lessons.

How do we make sure that we do not get caught up in the rush? By planning and adjusting our attitude. If I'm in a rush, I can't enjoy shopping with my three year old. Shopping with a happy hyper helper is at least 25% more time consuming than shopping alone. All my hoping is not going to change this fact of three year old dynamics. So, I have to plan and adjust my attitudes. This attitude shifting skill, keeping in mind the big picture, is the true art of parenting.

BUILDING TRUST

We all need to know that we can trust our loved ones. Without this trust, people feel like they are walking around their own home on egg shells. Basically, what trust means is that we can predict how someone will act in a given situation.

Trust is learned. We learn whether we can or cannot trust another by observing the same-ness of the another's words and actions. Even very young children key into this word and action same-ness. All things being equal, children will believe the behavior over the words of their parents. *Behavior counts.*

One thirteen year old girl, while talking about visitation scheduling, told her father very coldly. "You say that you will pick me up at nine in the morning, but you show up at ten." Without knowing it she was telling her father that she did not trust him. She did not feel special to him. Trust is a very difficult feeling to earn and it is quickly lost. The quickest way to lose your child's trust is through double messages. These double messages are usually subtle. But remember, your child's job is to understand her world so she has almost infinite patience to observe and learn who you really are.

Mrs. Cole sat in my office and was very upset. She explained that her three children did not respect her. She was just a maid. She "hated" to go home. She found herself finding things at work to do after hours so that she didn't have to go home to her bickering children.

When I asked Mrs. Cole how come she thought her home was so uncomfortable she snapped, "Oh, I know, I hear it all the time. My kids are like a broken record, 'Mom you said ... You lied!'"

As it turned out, Mrs. Cole was constantly feeling cornered by her children. She had learned to just say yes to get the kids out of her face, to postpone the situation. Then, when she felt stronger or just had to say "no" her kids pulled out their pet scream ... "Mom you said. You lied!"

We need to make sure that our words and our actions match. When I was in the "Super Store" buying a case of something I don't have room to store— I heard, "If you hit your brother one more time, I'll spank you so hard!" I hear this inconsistent statement all the time. (I even half joke that the stores should have a verbal abuse check out, or a "swat you until you learn" area.) Telling a child that hitting is wrong by threatening to hit is extremely inconsistent. The following are some typical inconsistent statements parents have told me about just this week in sessions:

> I told Bobby that smoking was bad for him. I told him that the next time I caught him smoking I would make him eat a whole cigarette.

There is qualitative difference between being looked at and seen.
Dorothy Briggs

Sara is such a little boss that I told her to shut up, and I really meant it this time!

Michael is over 18. If he thinks he is a man... I told him that I expect him to start paying rent. I was so pissed at his room... I told him he owes me $25 a month or he'd better start looking for a new place to live!

I told him... "How would you like it if I poked you?" Then I poked him right in the chest ... He is so damn dumb, he didn't learn, You know what that kid did? He spit right in my face!

The parents depicted above are all caring concerned individuals who really wish to do the best for their children. Unfortunately, the only one really listening to the messages between the words are their children.

Our children need to experience their parents as real people. We destroy trust by putting on the airs of a role. For example, one common area where parents put on an act is with adult problems. After a disturbing phone conversation, your child may ask what's wrong. Many parents will actually lie to their child and say, "Oh, nothing." This act of trying to protect your child actually erodes the trust you have built. I am not saying that you should share the details of your adult world. What I'm saying is that you need to be honest and caring. "Oh, I'm upset ... I need to be by myself for a few minutes." This respects your child and teaches a real life lesson, that even adults have feelings that they need to figure out. This way your behavior, your sad expression, and your words, "Oh, I'm upset ... I need to be by myself for a few minutes," are consistent. This consistency between your words and your behavior are what allows trust to grow.

Behavior and words need to match. For example, when you say to your child, "It's time to go," you also need to move towards the door. When you say, "It's time to go," but you stand there talking to a friend or watching one last football play, you teach your child that your words do not count. Your actions tend to have more power than your words.

TEACHING HONESTY

Many parents demand 100% honesty from their children. This is a tricky proposition when we do not demand it of ourselves. In fact, I doubt that it is possible to be 100% honest. More often than not, honesty is a gray area. If we say, "In a minute ..." we know that we are generalizing. We do not really mean sixty seconds. For many children, at their discretion, one minute means just that, sixty seconds. "But mom, you said, 'in a minute'... it's been three minutes!" This whiny child's statement is true, but is it really true? What we are talking about here is the spirit of the law of honesty not the letter of the law of honesty.

An important part of building trust is picking your words correctly. I find myself saying, "If all goes well ..." a lot when talking to children (and most adults). "If all goes well, I will be at your school at 3:00." "If all goes well, we can go shoe shopping Saturday afternoon." This teaches people that I am basically an honest person. This keeps me away from the "YOU SAID!" indignation of the mortally wounded child.

However, on a very subtle note, I do listen carefully for the honesty of life. For example, if I am walking by the bathroom and notice that a damp towel is left on the floor I tend to get involved. "Whose towel?" I call down the hall. "Mine dad, I'll take care of it in a minute," an innocent voice responds. I'm not concerned about the "minute" word, I am concerned about my child's intent to be honest. So, an hour later when I see the towel still drying on the floor my focus changes.

"Ethan (the former innocent) you led me to believe that you were going to take care of the towel"

"Yeah!" He mumbles. "I was, I'm going right now."

"After you pick up the towel, come and find me, we have to talk about being honest."

"I was honest, I'm getting the towel right now!"

Calmly I explain, "This isn't about the towel, this is about your word. I'm not worried about the towel, I'm worried about your word."

In a few minutes I will, again, explain that I put a lot of faith in his words. That when I get my hug and kiss good night, I really mean the words, "I love you." When I hear the words, "I love you," I want to believe them. If a person is willing to deceive me about a nothing towel on the bathroom floor, how can I be sure about really important words such as, "I love you?"

Please note, the towel is an inconvenience. Honesty is a necessity to help your child feel loved and protected.

As parents we need to watch our words carefully. We need to be careful not to teach dishonest behavior. For example, recently a family got into a heated discussion about answering the phone. The voices got loud. It was clear that the issue was not the phone, but rather trust and honesty issues around the phone. In this particular situation, mom had a sister that she didn't care for. So, she refused to answer the phone in case her sister called. When the sister did call, the children were instructed to tell her, "Oh, mom is out ..." or "Mom is in the bath." Mom was surprised, when I pointed out, that she was teaching her children to lie.

Relationships are built on small moments, if these moments are dishonest, the relationship cannot be stable.

Children begin by loving their parents. After a time they judge them. Rarely, if ever, do they forgive them.

Oscar Wilde

A HEALTHY FOCUS ON YOUR CHILD AS A MEMBER OF YOUR FAMILY

As a therapist I am usually called when the family is in conflict. I tend to hear similar stories about how Johnny doesn't listen, or that, "Nothing has worked." It is common for a parent to spend fifteen minutes telling me about the negative behaviors that Johnny has shown. When I ask, "Tell me something positive about your son." Mom or dad are usually taken back. "Well, ah ... Johnny is a good boy ... (pause) He is really good at ..." At this point I can see the tension drain from the parents' faces. For some time now, they have been fearful for their son. The circumstances being what they are, all they can see are Johnny's negative behaviors.

To feel loved a child needs to be seen. Too often parents only look at their child's negative behaviors. For whatever reason they stop seeing their child and start looking at just their child's behaviors. This is a major shift in parenting. If you focus on the negative, your child will have to perform more negatively to feed his need for attention. Your child needs, at the core of his being, your attention. So, won't he have to act out just to get your attention?

After explaining the above, one father growled back. "Ahhh, that's just psycho-babble wishi-wash. My kid should just fly right. He knows we love him, he is just choosing to be a royal pain in the @$!" Over the next few weeks this caring father learned that he was correct. His child was "choosing" to act out. He also found that he was teaching his son to act out. With a few minor parenting changes, this family started to enjoy being together again.

In the next section we will look at the attitude of parenting. Things we can do to help our children grow up to be loving, caring, respectful and happy individuals.

ADVOCATING VERSES JUDGING YOUR CHILD

The quickest way to destroy a relationship is
to judge another's behavior as a character flaw.

Mr. Holms was ailing and close to death. He contacted me and asked for an appointment for himself and his younger brother. There was only one catch. Mr. Holms had not talked with his younger brother for over forty years. Mr. Holms, now seventy-two, was fearful that he would die without making things right. Mr. Holms, Sam, wanted to say good-bye to his seventy year old brother, Elliot. They had lived within 100 miles of each other all this time. Except for the occasional wedding or funeral, they avoided each other. The brothers' wives organized the meeting.

I opened the session by thanking the two men for agreeing to meet. Both men were nervous. After a pause, Elliot said, "Well, I hear you wanted to see me before you pass away." Five minutes later the conversation got around to how this long silence got started.

"It was a nothing, I told him he was a bum for losing his job." Sam confessed. "I didn't mean anything by it, but he punched me in the mouth."

"I sure did, I socked him one good. He said I was not going to be able to take care of my family. I showed him. I always had a bigger house. I always had a fancier car."

Sam protested. "I never said that you were not going to take care of your family."

"You did too, you lying * ^ $&% ^ $. You said I was a bum and that you would have to give me money." Elliot turned and looked at me, tears welled in his eyes. "I never took a penny from him, Doctor." He clenched his fist. "I never needed him."

Wow! What a session. The men left together and went with their wives for coffee. (Two years later, as of this writing, they are both going strong. In fact, their wives informed me that they both cheat on their golf scores.) Forty years of silence because one brother felt his character was being attacked by another. Wow!

Our character is the combination of qualities that makes us who we are. It tends to be our moral or ethical strength or lack there of.

Often, without thinking, parents change a problem behavior into a personal character attack. Mrs. Patton was very upset that her daughter, Jenni was caught at school with different clothes on than she left home in. As it turned out, Jenni was keeping a "cool" set of clothes in the woods by her home. On the way to school she was pulling a "super girl" changing act and attending school in rather revealing garb. Mom found out when a teacher called home concerned about a "...less than modest top that was distracting male students in fourth period English." Mrs. Patton had a cow! A week later, in my office, she repeated, "I told her that no daughter of mine was going to be a whore. I was furious ... I screamed at her that she was going to end up no good and whoring herself just to pay for her drugs!"

Let's look at this conflict. Jenni was not accused of prostitution or drug abuse. Mrs. Patton, in a calm moment, was able to say that she didn't think that Jenni was either. But in the heat of conflict, mom's worst fears came out — hard. Mom's character attack was so strong that Jenni ran away from home and hid in the basement of the family's church for three days. (It all worked out well in a few months.)

What was the issue? Remember, Jenni was inappropriately dressed for school according to the school and mom. Jenni, on the other hand, thought that she looked great, like some girl on the TV

It takes great wisdom to realize that all feelings are legitimate: the positive, the negative, and the ambivalent.

Haim Ginott,
Ph.D.

show 90210. It took three weeks to get to the issue of Jenni's school clothing. It took another week to get to Jenni's lying, with her behavior, by changing clothes on the way to school. A character attack kept this family in crisis for a month.

It is usually the little, hard to notice, character attacks that erode a person's self esteem. Your children listen carefully to your words. Even to the hidden meanings between your words. (I know it doesn't feel like it, but it is true. Words like "bedtime", or "homework" are regularly tuned out. But what you think and feel are heard and made part of your child's core makeup.)

Let's revisit the negative sounding list of examples from earlier. This list is full of clear cut character attacks.

THE NEGATIVE SOUNDING LIST: REVISITED

You're stupid
You're clumsy
You're selfish
You act so naughty
You're bad
You're ugly
You're fat
You're evil
You act so silly
Can't you make real friends
You're so disrespectful
You always wake up in a really bad mood
You're just like... (disliked relative)
You're driving me crazy
Are you trying to make me flip out the
    rest of the way?
If your head wasn't attached you'd lose it

Not one of these statements can truly define a child's character. But, with repetition, the child will believe that it does. For example: Kyle was a shy twelve year old. He was referred to my clinic because he was molested by an uncle. When I met him in the waiting room the conversation went like this:

Dr. Phil: Welcome to the neighborhood, you must be Kyle.

Kyle: (Looking at his feet) I guess.

Dr. Phil: How about we get together and talk?

Kyle: (Looking at his feet) Why?

Dr. Phil:	Your mom told me I had to.
Kyle:	(Looking at his feet) Did she tell you that you are stupid?
Dr. Phil:	Not yet.
Kyle:	(Looking at his feet) I don't want to .... (big sigh)
Dr. Phil:	I didn't know about that, but I have to ... I feel stupid just standing here in the door.
Kyle:	You're not stupid, you're a grown-up. (Looking at me for the first time)

Kyle and I became friends in no time. He taught me that he really believed he was stupid. He was sure that he messed up everything and was too stupid to see how. He believed his uncle molested him because he deserved to be humiliated. He also taught me that everyone in his family called everyone else in the world stupid when they were upset for any reason. (After a year of family therapy Kyle was proud to be himself.)

LABELING IS DISABLING

Dr. Haim Ginott makes it clear with his saying, "labeling is disabling" that placing a character label on a child's behavior lowers that child's self esteem. What this means for parents is that we must be very careful when judging our children. Let me be very clear, I am not saying that we do not judge, I am saying that we must focus on judging behavior not character. Children need limits set for them. This helps a child to learn what is expected of them. We show our love by setting limits and following our own structure.

Most parents get into trouble when they confuse setting limits (judging behavior) with judging character. For example, Kyle was told he was stupid for any mistake he committed. No matter the size or the degree of inconvenience. Dropping a fork or missing one math equation was proof to his family, and eventually himself, that he was stupid. In fact, if he was really a slow learner, his parents would have protected him from being called stupid. It would have been seen as cruel. Kyle incorporated the word stupid into his definition of "self." When anything went wrong he just consoled himself with his belief, "I'm stupid so it must be normal for me to do stupid things." With this attitude Kyle became self defeating. How could he learn from his mistakes if he was, due to a character flaw, stupid and unable to learn?

When a child is not labeled, she will tend to explore ways to solve problems. This exploration builds self esteem.

Children seem to be able to get into trouble naturally. By helping children figure out ways to deal with conflict we assist them in learning how to work their way out of trouble. We serve our children best by teaching them problem solving skills. With problem solving skills your child is being prepared to enter the world with high self esteem.

My family was once invited to Christmas Eve dinner at a friend's home. The home was warm and welcoming. At the kids' table, their five year old child did what young children do well, she spilled her milk. Her father slammed his hands on the table and thundered ... "Clean that up, you're so clumsy!" His five year old looked shocked. She froze with eyes wide. Her mother came over, "It's okay honey, I'll clean it up."

In a few minutes calm settled over the table. The children's voices were back to spirited tones. Then, the real world crept in. My son, also five, did what five year olds do. He spilled. He didn't just spill a little, he really spilled. His glass slipped from his fingers, hit the table on an angle and hosed down three children across from him. The world stopped spinning. Everyone looked at me. The children held their breaths. "Josh, what are you going to do?" I asked calmly. "I'm going to get a sponge and clean up my mess." He announced with a smile. (Smarty pants older brother added in the background, "And give Rickey a bath.")

A few hours later, out on the back porch, my host asked how I stayed so calm. He was very apologetic for yelling at his daughter with so many people around. I explained that I wasn't calm. Inside my thoughts were racing to an explosion. I was furious that Josh spilled the milk at someone else's home. I also knew the big picture. I expect my children to get into and out of trouble all by themselves. I pointed out, gently, that he judged his daughter by saying, "Clean that up, you're so clumsy!" That for him, the spilled milk became a character issue (proof of clumsiness, incompetence). I, on the other hand, advocated for my son, "Josh, what are you going to do?" I assumed that he understood the problem and that he would have to, with my support, solve it. (I also joked that his daughter was not a very good spiller and that my son was able to stain three new Christmas outfits.)

By advocating for our children we let them grow and learn. This is a process. I remember, in the privacy of our home, when Josh wanted to leave spilled milk for the cat or use the vacuum cleaner to suck it up. In those cases we looked at the options and discussed the outcomes. In time we got to the sponge idea. Raising children spills a lot of milk.

When we advocate for our child we are future oriented. We are developing in our offspring life skills such as:

Problem solving

Cooperative behavior
Creativity
Brainstorming
Responsibility
Caring
Job completion
Communication

Isn't this the stuff we all put on our wish list of things we wish to give to our children?

When we judge we put our children on the defensive. We focus on the character of our child not on the solution to the perceived problem.

When we judge we give the solution. When we advocate for our child he creates the solution to his problem. We support by gently guiding his solution.

When we judge we tell our child what to think. When we advocate our children learn how to think.

This is a major difference. I want your child to think as a caring individual. At age thirteen when your child is very upset with you for whatever reason, I want him to be involved with his solution solving process. Let's look at two scenarios.

THE JUDGED CHILD

Cliff has a heated argument with his mother. On his way to school he is fuming. He runs into Tim. Tim is sympathetic to Cliff's plight. He explains that he has a little pill that makes him feel better when his life becomes unbearable. Cliff shows some interest in solving his problems with drugs. Tim offers to introduce him to his supplier.

THE ADVOCATED CHILD

Dan has a heated argument with his mother. On his way to school he is fuming. He runs into Tara. Tara is sympathetic to Dan's plight. She explains that she has a little pill that makes her feel better when her life becomes unbearable.

Dan: You take a pill to feel better?

Tara: Not every day, just when I need it.

Dan: I ain't that upset. It is just an argument. I'll figure out a way to solve it, I just need time.

Tara: Why bother, in ten minutes you'll have no prob-

When we disclaim praise, it is only showing our desire to be praised a second time.

François de La Rochefoucauld

lems.

Dan: I can handle my problems. How can you put that stuff into you, don't you worry about your health?

Tara: Naw. I just don't think about it.

Dan: I would if I was you ...

Tara: Don't be a jerk ...

The big difference is that Dan has a history of solving problems. He knows that he has the skill and plans on using it. Tara, Tim and Cliff are judging themselves as incapable of dealing with their world.

THE POWER OF PRAISE

Praise is a powerful two edged sword.
One edge builds self esteem slowly,
the other destroys it quickly.

Most people see praise as one hundred percent positive. "If I praise my child he will grow up feeling good about himself." On the surface this makes sense. But in the real world praise is not as easy to use. For an example let's go to Thanksgiving dinner at the Hamilton's home.

Mary Anne Hamilton is a happy go lucky fourteen year old. She is usually easy to live with. Her family works together quite well. On this festive occasion, with the family all around, Mrs. Hamilton praises Mary Anne for her help in getting the dinner prepared.

Mom: Mary Anne was so helpful, I just don't know what I would have done without her. I bless my lucky stars that I have such a wonderful daughter. You know honey, you are such an angel.

Mary Anne: Moooom, stop!

Mom: No, it's true. You are the joy of my life.

At this point, mild mannered Mary Anne exploded. She pushed

by her mother knocking the mashed potatoes out of her hands. When Mrs. Hamilton consulted with me she was very concerned. "My Mary Anne never would act like that. She is an angel. Do you think it could be (whisper) drugs? I can't believe my baby would use drugs."

When I met with Mary Anne it was apparent that overall she was doing wonderfully. But, the pressure had just become too great.

Mary Anne:	You wouldn't understand. My mom is just a, you know– a perfect person. She is always happy. She is soooo loving, all the time...
Dr. Phil:	And the point is?
Mary Anne:	I just lost it. All those people and she was calling me her "angel". You know, as if I was perfect or something.
Dr. Phil:	Being perfect is a bad thing?
Mary Anne:	Well, yeah ... No. (pause) I was having, you know, thoughts.
Dr. Phil:	I'll know when you tell me ...
Mary Anne:	I was thinking of (whisper) boys.
Dr. Phil:	So?
Mary Anne:	(Blurting it out) All morning I was thinking of boys. All I could think about was boys. Then my mom, in front of everyone called me "her angel." If she really knew me she would hate me ... she would think of me as a slut.

Praise is a two sided sword. If praise is focused on character it tends to be dangerous. Mary Anne is a caring and wonderful person, but she is mainly a person, with all the positives and negatives that go with person-hood. The well intentioned praise of her mother was perceived by Mary Anne as painful.

If we praise character we are labeling our child. If we label we disable the creativity of our children.

I was invited to a preschool to talk with the teaching staff about ways to deal with aggressive behaviors with three to five year olds. While I was waiting for all the teachers to arrive, a little tot bounced over and asked me if I liked her watercolor finger painting.

Dr. Phil:	Well, let's take a look at this. I see red, green and a little blue.

Tot:	I did it with my fingers.

Dr. Phil:	I enjoyed looking at it. Thanks.

A few seconds later a little boy came over to the teacher standing next to me and showed off his finger painting.

Teacher:	Boy is that great ... You are so good at this.

Little boy:	I did it myself!

Teacher:	You're the best little artist ...

At this point the little boy got upset. He walked back to his area and sat down with a huff.

"You see," said the teacher. "I have a class of little angry kids."

The teaching staff and I spent the meeting discussing the role of praise in the classroom. When the teacher told the little boy that he was "the best little artist" I can only imagine his internal dialog.

"I'm not the best, Sammy is the best..."

"This teacher is teasing me because I don't paint as well as Timmy."

"What a dumb teacher, she thinks this is good, I did good yesterday, this is just okay."

The teacher, meaning to be supportive, made the painting a character issue by calling it great and labeling the child as "the best little artist."

I don't know for sure, but the little boy's behavior showed that the praise he got was not a positive.

The little girl that I met painted me a picture and gave it to the classroom grandmother to give to me. What I did was simply <u>define</u> what I saw and gave my opinion on how it effected me.

"I see red, green and a little blue."

"I enjoyed looking at it."

By defining what we see the child knows we are interested in them. They feel the implicit difference between <u>being seen</u> and being <u>looked at</u>. By defining your observation, your child feels your involvement without feeling that you are telling them what to think. Even in the adult world it is hard to receive praise. Many adults have a difficult time hearing praise about themselves. Many will feel obligated to disagree with the praise or immediately return a compliment. On lists of psychologically stressful situations you will find categories like, "received an award " or "earned a promotion at work." It is difficult for children to be showered with praise. Having to live up to the praise of another is virtually impossible. The more valued the praise giver the harder the praise is to accept.

Let's take a look at the positive sounding list from earlier..

THE POSITIVE SOUNDING LIST: REVISITED

You're so good
You're so beautiful
You're so smart
You can do it if you try hard enough
You're so creative
You could do anything you put your mind to
You can be anything you want to be
I didn't have the breaks you will have
You're an angel
You're a gift from God
You've got such a pretty face
You're so kind to others

On the surface the above list looks very positive. However, in the real world, these positive sounding pats on the back erode self esteem. They are all labels. Each tells the child about what you believe to be their character. Everyone of the praises in this list were given to me by children who found these positive sounding words to be a negative, painfully negative.

Connie (age 17) put it simply, "From about 13 until I left home, every time my mom uttered the words, 'You're a gift from God' I wanted to kill myself. How dare she tell me that God cared for me. If God cared for me my dad wouldn't have died."

I am sure that Connie's mother had only the best intentions. Unwittingly, she was hurting her daughter when she thought she was helping. I asked Connie what words her mother could have spoken that would fit her mom's needs while still feeling helpful to her. Connie thought for almost fifteen minutes, "I feel better knowing God loves me." She explained, "That way I could see that God was helpful to my mom and not feel that God hated me." What Connie stumbled upon was defining versus labeling. By defining we share what we know, by labeling we tell the other person what we think. Or, what we think they should think.

Let's take the positive sounding list and fix it so it actually is a positive list. We want the same feelings to be shared but we want the outcome to be self esteem building.

▼ = Positive Sounding List
　　▲ = Positive List

▼ You're so good
　　▲ I liked the way you acted today
　　▲ The way you treated Tommy seemed caring
▼ You're so beautiful
　　▲ I enjoy looking at you smile
　　▲ Being with you makes me feel good
▼ You're so smart
　　▲ I'm impressed with how well you understood that chapter
　　▲ You did that math homework in no time
▼ You can do it if you try hard enough
　　▲ I'm concerned that you aren't trying your hardest
　　▲ What plan do you have to finish your homework
▼ You're so creative
　　▲ Wow! Where did you get that idea from
　　▲ Did you feel creative when you solved that problem
▼ You could do anything you put your mind to
　　▲ It doesn't seem to me that you want to...
　　▲ How would you like to see it get done
▼ You can be anything you want to be
　　▲ I find myself wondering what you will be doing in...
　　▲ When you let yourself dream what do you dream about?
▼ I didn't have the breaks you will have
　　▲ I worry that you are not taking advantage...
　　▲ I'm happy that you have choices in your life
▼ You're an angel
　　▲ I enjoy spending time with you
　　▲ Spending time with you helps me feel special
▼ You're a gift from God
　　▲ I am thankful that I know you
　　▲ I thank God that I know you
▼ You've got such a pretty face (concern over weight gain)
　　▲ I'm worried that you have gained weight
　　▲ I didn't buy any cookies this week
▼ You're so kind to others
　　▲ Your friendship is very important to me
　　▲ When I see you acting kindly, I feel proud to be your mom

There's an old joke that goes like this: "What did the kindergartner say when asked his name? "Billy, no"

As you can see from the above, the word "I" is very important. You are sharing a part of yourself without telling your child how to think. Because your child cares for you, what you think is very important to him. He is constantly comparing himself to what he thinks you want him to be. By sharing your thoughts in a "positive" esteem building manner, both you and your child benefit. Your child feels your love and you know your love is felt. Life can be truly wonderful.

HOMEWORK REVISITED

At this point I suggest you take a few minutes to revisit the homework from Chapter One. I advise you to look at the words from your past. Evaluate the innuendo and subtleties of control. Look for the verbal pokes and prods. By looking at the nesting material you used to build your own self esteem, you may find insight into the building materials you make available for your children to use in the formation of their self esteem.

Please, do not overdo this look backwards. Keep perspective on the enormity of words that make up your life. I advise you to observe trends rather than placing blame. Look for what you can learn. Keep guilt at bay. Simply put, look back so you will not repeat what you believe should not be repeated. Go easy on yourself and your family. Advocate for your parents, too.

TEACHING RESPECT

The title of this section is somewhat misleading. We do not truly teach respect. We actually earn it. I am contacted regularly by parents who say, "My kids do not respect me!" My first question tends to be, "Do you respect them?" This is a difficult question. Mrs. Elmira put it bluntly, "I expect respect, I put food on the table ... I am the mother. I expect to be respected."

Behavior counts. In fact, behavior counts more than words. Your children watch you closely. They pick up most of their social cues from you (until high school). One parent told me the following story:

> I walked into the living room. My three girls were playing with their dolls. I paused at the door and watched. My eleven year old was running the play household. Every few seconds she had the mommy doll complain and hit the other dolls. Not hard hits, just constant hits. She kept saying, "Let's go honey, mommy is in a hurry." Or, "Hurry, you're making mommy late!" The part that hurt the most was that my daughter was using my words with a tone of hate. She sounded so put out by the children dolls.
>
> I asked the children over dinner about the game, and my eleven year old said, with an innocent smile, "I got to be you, I bossed everyone around and clob-

You must look into people, as well as at them.
Lord Chesterfield

bered them for not listening."

This parent was astonished to discover how she sounded through the ears of her children. She never thought that she "clobbered" her children. What she learned was that her children did not feel respected by her. What she thought was prodding, the tapping, motivating pushing behavior of her own childhood, was a regular example of disrespect.

We, as parents, need to model respectful behavior. This is easier said than done. Our children are around us 24 hours a day. Fortunately for us, teaching respectful behavior is a slow process. It only takes a few long years for a child to learn to read, but it takes many more for a child to internalize self respect and exhibit it outwardly.

We teach respect by using "please," "thank you," "I don't know," and "I'm sorry" on a regular basis. We exhibit respect by not shrieking or over powering our children with words. We share the love of respect by talking at eye level to a young child. We respect by directing children *to do* versus *not do*. A child feels respected when a parent directs him away from misbehavior versus telling him to stop doing the misbehavior.

Which sounds more respectful to you?

"Billy, stop bothering the cat!" or "Billy, will you help me in the kitchen?"

"Sally, I told you not to tease your sister!" or "Sally, please let the dog out."

"What are you up to, put that hammer back!" or "What do you need a hammer for?"

Children will "test" behaviors out on their parents that they see others doing. Mrs. Story was upset,

Carl (age 14) walked into the house and plopped himself on the sofa putting his shoes on the coffee table. I was shocked. "What are you doing young man?" I asked him. He told me to, "@$#$%^ off." I couldn't believe he would talk to me like that. My husband and I don't use such language.

Carl was practicing what he saw at his new friend's home. To Carl's surprise, his parents' reaction was not the same as his friend's parents. Carl was trying out behaviors "modeled" in another's home. This is normal. Children will try behaviors seen elsewhere. Even two dimensional TV and movies are influential in your child's life.

We need to use clear messages when a new behavior is not acceptable. When there is no character assassination, kids tend to make quality choices. For example, a few years ago a movie showed the tough gang bangers sucking on baby pacifiers and reprimanding their parents. Lots of kids in my area started carrying pacifiers around. The fad lasted a few weeks then ran its course. (I guess the idea sucked.) Many parents had to learn how to *support* their children during this fad.

Judging: What are you, a baby?

Advocating: You can suck on a pacifier if you need to, but I'm not comfortable with you sucking it around me. Please put it in your pocket.

Judging: If you talk to me like that again I'll wash your mouth out with soap!

Advocating: I do not allow such language from my children. Please respect my wishes.

Teaching respect is a long process. Mrs. Columbia called to thank me about a family session almost two weeks prior.

Dr. Phil, I just want to let you know that Bethany is trying. She asked me if I had time to fix her jeans. She was polite. She said, "Mamma, would you be able to fix my jeans? I would appreciate your help." This is nice, she usually says, "Fix this, I need them after school."

As parents we need to demand respect while we show respect. This way we can teach our children that some behaviors are acceptable while others are not. This is not only in our home. I have received appropriate respect from rude acting children and adults alike by firmly stating, "I do not allow people to talk to me like that. How can I help you?" This firm but respectful statement has avoided many uncomfortable situations.

LOOKING FOR THE POSITIVE

Most parents are much too hard on themselves. They expect perfection out of themselves and their family. This expectation is very hard to live with, as well as unrealistic. As a society we honor a baseball player who bats 300. We do not notice that seven out of ten times that same baseball player failed. With a batting average of 300, the hero baseball player only did his job, getting on base,

Quick Reference Guide

Temperament: The characteristic way of thinking, behaving, or reacting of a specific person.

three out of every ten times.

If a football quarterback was able to throw 14 of 20 passes for completion it would be a great accomplishment. A consistent 14 of 20 passer is a multimillionaire. But, in the real world, 14 of 20 is only 70%. If you only picked up your child from school 70% of the time your child would be living in a foster home.

I hear daily from well meaning parents that they are not living up to their own and society's expectations of parenting. This is usually much worse for moms than dads. During a father/son lunch at a family restaurant, we boys were having a great time making a mess and laughing it up. (This is normal behavior, even when mom is around.) A kindly older woman interrupted our mayhem and said, "It's so nice to see a father baby-sitting." What?! Baby-sitting? I didn't say anything at the time but, I was a little offended. I do not think of myself as a *baby-sitter.* I was simply *parenting.* All too often our society allows fathers to "baby-sit." I have had well meaning fathers sit in my office and complain that on their day off they have to baby-sit. How unfortunate for the family when a father disregards his importance as a parent to his children.

One mom told me that she was upset that she didn't spend more time with her preschooler. Between work and momming she had no time for anything else, but she was telling me the truth when she shared her feelings.

We have to be more reasonable with ourselves. Parents need to have adult lives also. If you are a mom or a dad all the time you will go bonkers. Parents need adult time. This need must be respected. I advocate for all the parents I work with go on dates. That's right, dates. Parents set up a little time every week and have adult time. This is very difficult to do but important for the sanity of the individuals and the emotional health of the family.

In the real world we need to focus on the "squeaky wheel." The problems tend to be louder than the positives. Usually we have no choice but to focus on the negatives. If there is a criminal stalking my community I need to know about it. If there is danger I need to protect my family. But, in the home we need to nurture a tiny world of safety. A tiny world of loving interactions. I know for myself that on some days the only sunny spot on my planet is my little world called home. I want the same sunny spot for my children too.

As parents we need to focus on the positives whenever possible. If Jimmy has spilt milk eleven meals in a row, let him spill grape juice so that the stains are more interesting. Use humor to help you wade through the swampy parts of life. Notice the little positives and define them. "Tommy, your homework looks interesting tonight; is it?" Let's not focus on the homework, let's focus on Tommy's feelings and thoughts about his homework.

As discussed earlier, "relationships are built on small moments." We need to seek out these small moments and cherish them.

It is our hypothesis that differences in temperament in the newborn and the very young are biologically determined, but then the infant's temperament is influenced by her interactions with her parents, which may either intensify or modify her original temperament. And as the child grows older, other environmental factors may accentuate, modify, or even change one or another temperamental attributes.

Stella Chase, M.D.
Alexander Thomas, M.D.

YOUR CHILD'S TEMPERAMENT

Mrs. Darting was in tears when I first met her. She sat down on the couch. I asked her why she made the appointment (she refused to tell anyone when she made the appointment). Then it happened, more tears. I handed her some tissues and asked if I could help.

Mrs. Darting: I hope so. I just don't know what to do. My son is slow.

Dr. Phil: How did you come to that conclusion?

Mrs. Darting: His teacher said he was "slow." She said he was "slow in math and reading." My baby is slow ... how will he ever take care of himself? What am I to do? Will he ever make something of himself?

As it turned out Mrs. Darting's son, Kyle, was slow. In fact he read very slowly. He computed his math very slowly. Everyone that knows Kyle knows he is slow. He does his chores slowly. He speaks very carefully and slowly. He also is intelligent, caring, and sensitive. He is an easy child to like. He is an easy child to teach. He is a loving child. But, boy is he slow. Kyle's temperament is easy going. He seldom gets upset and when he does it is hard to tell.

When Mrs. Darting heard from Kyle's teacher that Kyle was "slow" she got herself all worked up. She thought that Kyle's teacher was telling her that Kyle was retarded. "All I could think of was how bad a mother I was," she explained, "For all these years I knew Kyle was physically slow but I didn't know he was unable to learn. I kept kicking myself for not helping him more." Kyle was not retarded. He had an easy going temperament.

In the early part of the 1900s it was popular to believe that children were born as a "blank slate." It was touted that the newborn was born to be molded and taught by its mother. This led to the mid 1900s when all negative behaviors in a child were the result of the mother consciously or unconsciously writing the wrong stuff on her child's "slate." It was popular at that time for behavioral psychologists to state, "Give me a baby at birth and I will mold it into a scientist, a teacher, or whatever you want." Other psychotherapists developed grandiose theories of "id" and "ego" interactions. It was postulated that all behavior was an intricate interaction of conscious and unconscious processes. All this is well and good, but very confusing for most parents.

Research in the 1980s and 90s has shown us that newborns are born as individuals. They each have a "pre-wired" personality. They are, in short, individuals. This "pre-wire" is their temperament. As parents, we can influence our children's temperament but we cannot

Every piece of marble has a statue in it waiting to be released by someone of sufficient skills to chip away the unnecessary parts. Just as the sculpture is to marble, so is education to the soul. It releases it. For only the educated are free. You cannot create a statue by smashing the marble with a hammer, and you cannot by force of arms release the spirit of the soul.

Confucius

It is not what they profess but what they practice that makes them good.

change it. Also, as we influence our children, our children influence us. Parenting is a two way street. Your temperament is influenced by your child. (As our children get older others will influence our children.)

What is most important about all this psycho-babble theory are your *expectations*. For example, let me tell you about the Sandel family. Mrs. Sandel has three children. She is a single mom. She came to my office concerned that her daughter, Robin (age 14), was having a problem getting out of bed on school mornings.

Mrs. Sandel: Every morning the same old thing. Robin is impossible to wake up. I shake her, I scream at her, I've even thrown cold water on her. It is a huge battle every morning. I just can't take it any more.

Dr. Phil: How do the boys do in the morning?

Mrs. Sandel: It's like night and day. The boys hop out of bed with a smile and start running. We joke about how I have two hares and one tortoise. Robin just doesn't move. She is a real couch potato.

Dr. Phil: Robin, what do you think is going on?

Robin: Not much, I'm just sleepy in the mornings. No matter how much sleep I get, I'm sleepy until noon.

In this family, the two boys and the mom got tired at about 8 PM. It was rare that they could stay up past nine without passing out. Robin, on the other hand, started her day slowly but when the rest of the family was ready for bed she was reving up for her evening. She watched TV and talked on the phone until 2 AM most nights. If she was allowed to she would sleep until noon.

Mrs. Sandel told me about how hard Robin was as an infant. That she seemed to never sleep. She was quiet and calm but always awake. Both of her boys, she joked, "You could set a clock by them. As babies they went to sleep at six, had a meal and diaper change at two and then slept again soundly until six in the morning. Not Robin. She never slept and only snacked. Twenty times a day for over two years. I was exhausted." Mrs. Sandel had described her children's temperament. Her children did not learn their sleep patterns. Robin's temperament was that of an owl, her brothers' temperaments were more like roosters. At this point, the discussion was focusing on *expectations*. Mrs. Sandel was very frustrated when she came to my office. She was concerned that she was a bad mother and that her daughter would never amount to much. "How could she keep a job if she was late every morning?" she once told me.

What Mrs. Sandel needed to learn was that Robin's temperament was not a problem. It was a fact. It was Robin. And Robin had better learn how to fit into the world. Notice the focus. Robin had a problem. She had to get along in a world that doesn't care if you are tired. Robin had to figure out a way to get her temperament to work for her, not against her. (And she did. What a great kid!) When I first met Mrs. Sandel she had a problem. Soon there after, she learned that Robin had a problem. And, that only Robin could solve this problem. This change in view helped Mrs. Sandel gain her life back. She went back to being "loving mom" and stopped being "nagging alarm clock." She was there to support her daughter, but she was not there to solve her daughter's problems. That was impossible. Her goal was to advocate for her daughter's needs and to support and guide her daughter. Wow! She got to be mom. The role she wanted in the first place.

As parents we have an enormous amount of influence when it comes to our children. But, we can't change our child's basic temperament. If our child is a square wooden block in a family of round rubber wheels we can't magically change wood to rubber. But with time, love and organized caring we can help our child roll through life. At first every roll of a wooden block is thump, thump, thump. Then slowly, over time, the sharp corners get rubbed away until the block is mostly round and rolling through life quite well. One of our jobs as a parent is to help sand the rough edges off our children, helping them to roll through life easier.

By keeping in mind that our children have individuality, their own temperament and personality, we help ourselves deal with the frustration of bumping into the rough wooden edges while they get sanded down.

CARETAKER VERSUS CAREGIVER

I confess, I have a pet peeve. A little something that really bothers me. In fact, it bothers me more that it probably should. Which, I guess is the definition of a pet peeve. My pet peeve is parents who are caretakers versus caregivers. Please allow me to vent. A caretaker is a person who makes sure that their charge is taken care of. Their charge is well fed and protected. But the relationship tends to be superficial. A caregiver is a person who sees the whole child. The caregiver makes sure that the child's needs are met but, that is only the beginning. The caregiver opens themselves to a true emotional relationship with the child, the ups and the downs. The caregiver takes the chance to feel the whole spectrum of emotions. The joy and the sorrow. The caregiver puts their needs on hold for a moment and focuses on the other. For the time they are together, the child knows, at their core, that they are very important to the caregiver. They know that they, as an individual, count.

Don't confuse caregiver with *giving*. A caregiver is not all giving. This is not the materialistic form of giving. It is an emotional form of giving. Caregivers keep the big picture in mind. The word "no" is very easy for them to say. The caregiver focuses on the child's needs, what is best for the child.

I once was fortunate to observe a very minor interaction that illustrates care giving quite well. When my oldest son, Ethan, was in second grade we went to visit his mother at school where she was a new second grade teacher. While we were helping decorate mom's new classroom another second grade teacher popped in to say hi. Mrs. McCarthy was a 49 year veteran of the elementary school. That's right, she had taught school since the invention of the printing press.

A few minutes later Mrs. McCarthy asked Ethan if he would help her carry some paper. As they walked out of the room Mrs. McCarthy said softly to Ethan, "Teach me your name." This request caught my attention. This veteran teacher was asking this little boy to *teach her.*

Later, as we were driving home, I asked Ethan what he thought about mom's new classroom. He said, "It's OK, Mrs. McCarthy thinks I'm great!" "How do you know?" I inquired. "I just do," he continued, "She likes me."

In just a few moments, Mrs. McCarthy was able to impart to Ethan that he was important, that he was lovable. This is care giving. Letting your children know, at the core of their being, that they are lovable and special to you is the cornerstone of their self esteem.

Many of Dr. Copitch's cartoons are available at www.zazzle.com/copitch*
You can get them in full color on lots of stuff such as a shirt, mug, or apron.

Chapter 3

Time Out
is not punishment

3. TIME OUT IS NOT PUNISHMENT

IT IS A STOP GAP MEASURE

As parents it is our responsibility to help our children develop into responsible and caring adults. There are lots of obstacles in the way. Our children are influenced by many people and circumstances. I am sure there are more influences outside of our control than ones we can manufacture to assist our children.

The family management skill of **Time Out** was developed to empower our children to make age appropriate choices, while at the same time allowing caring parents to be people. Many parents feel that they become jailers to their children. They feel that their children choose to disobey because their children dislike them. This makes for a rough relationship for both parents and children.

Probably, the most important single skill we can nurture in our children is the skill of making *informed decisions*. This is not a simple task. Most adults find that they tend to react to their world verses interact with their world. When one interacts with their environment they take in information, control their initial emotional reaction and then evaluate their options. This process is often a rare commodity, even in adults. It is much more common for people to react to the situation, to get caught up in the moment, to view only the immediate, the short term.

When I was at the gift shop of a large amusement park, I witnessed families overpaying for all sorts of "must have it now" stuff. I imagine that these same parents are more price conscious at their local department store. But, with all the excitement, the bells and whistles, I saw $57 sweat shirts and $28 tee shirts flying off the shelves. I'm not saying this is bad, I'm just observing this phenomenon. Most local department stores could not sell a $28 cartoon tee shirt.

It is important that we teach our children to make informed decisions. To take the time to think of *what* they really want and *why* they want it. And, to take into account the consequences of their choices, the consequences of their behaviors. Unfortunately, many well meaning professionals are teaching Time Out procedures as a form of punishment. "If you do not sit in your seat and focus on your math sheet, you will have to go to the Time Out area."

I was asked by a school principal to observe a few classes and suggest some topics for the school's in-service program. The principal was happy overall with his school but he was concerned that over the last few years the students were getting more violent. He told me, "Five years ago, when I took over, the biggest problem was foul words exchanged on the playground. This very month I have sent four children home for fighting. Not pushing matches mind you, down and dirty drag out fights." The principal went on

At a PTA meeting:

"Dr. Phil I can't give my fifteen year old a Time Out, even though he needs one more than my two younger children.

"Why not?" Dr. Phil responded, "I give myself Time Outs, I just call it 'going for a walk." With teens, you can define it as, *"Please go to your room* until you are calm and able to talk to me calmly."

Quick Reference Guide

Punishment: The presentation of an aversive stimulus following an undesired response that decreases the likelihood of the undesired response.

Discipline: Learned choices, self control.

Kids *do* better when they *feel* better. We don't motivate kids to do better by making them feel worse through punitive Time Outs.

Jane Nelson
Lynn Lott
Stephen Glenn

to explain that Time Outs were not working any longer. "Even the younger children do not respect the teachers. I heard one first grader scream at his teacher, 'I don't have to do a !@#$% Time Out, you can't make me!'"

Earlier, we discussed the definition of punishment. For something to be a punisher it must decrease the likelihood of the undesirable behavior in the future. At the school mentioned above, the principal was frustrated that Time Outs were not decreasing the likelihood of an undesired behavior. This is true, a little nothing Time Out cannot decrease the likelihood of an undesired behavior. Time Out is not punishment. Time Out is a procedure to help a child regain self control. When the basketball team calls for a Time Out to devise its last second play, the Time Out does nothing for the score. It simply allows the team to get its composure back, to build a plan, to develop options. When a child earns a Time Out, the Time Out itself solves nothing. It is simply a way for the child (and parent) to build a plan and develop options. If need be, the parent or teacher can assist the child, once all is calm— to look at choices. Time Out does not control a child's behavior; the child must do that. Please note, at the point that the child earned a Time Out, his behaviors were working for him or he would not have been acting that way. Maybe in the long run the behavior was dysfunctional, but not at the time he was doing it. Kids act out because it works for them. It gets a need met. This need does not have to be understandable to us, but we must understand that the child is getting a need met.

PUNISHMENT VERSUS DISCIPLINE

Punishment is the presentation of an aversive stimulus, following an undesired response, that decreases the likelihood of that undesired response. **Discipline** is learned choices, self control. With punishment we force our demands on our child, but when we teach our children to be disciplined we teach them how to make choices and let them build character.

Over the years I have seen many children in my practice who understood right from wrong, but chose wrong to prove to themselves that they could. These children tended to be from families that used punishment as their main parenting tool. As these children developed into adolescence, disobeying parental authority was their measure of their own budding adulthood.

Ruby is a good example of how punishment can backfire. Ruby was 16 years old when I first met her. She had run away from her family but had no specific reason for doing so. Ruby told me, "They don't understand me. My dad just tells me what to think. He is so mean." Mr. and Mrs. Stein were at a loss. "Ruby was a good girl. She never gave us any trouble," Mrs. Stein said. "Then she started to argue about everything. It was as if she wanted us to punish her.

She went out of her way to cause problems."

As Ruby got older she had a need to voice her opinions. When this happened, her parents tried to talk calmly and logically about the case at hand. For Ruby this was belittling. She was a cauldron of feelings. She wanted to change her parents' thoughts. She didn't want to discuss, she wanted to be _right_. When things got out of hand, Ruby would be sent to her room. "It used to make me so mad! They would just dismiss me like I was a servant. I would go to my room fuming. I would think of all sorts of hideous things that should happen to my parents. I even prayed to God to smite them for their insensitivity." (As you can tell, Ruby was a dramatic child.)

When Mr. and Mrs. Stein sent Ruby to her room, their goal was to teach her to calm down and talk to them in a civil tone. But, instead, the reason for the punishment was lost on Ruby. All she learned was to hate her parents for punishing her. Then she felt guilty for her hateful feelings. In the long run, Ruby ran away from home because she was angry at herself for having mean thoughts about her parents. Punishment misdirected the issue. What Ruby needed was to share her feelings without her emotions alienating her parents. Mom and dad wanted Ruby to learn how to argue sociably. An important life lesson for Ruby to learn.

As parents, we want our children to be disciplined, to possess self control. By using Time Outs with a child we help that child develop personal monitoring skills, internal checks and balances that will serve the child for a lifetime.

Time Out is not just for children. On a regular basis I find a "long walk" or "sitting on the porch" to be good for my decision making skills. Most adults find that _ponder time_ is important in keeping perspective. I have also used Time Outs to help negotiate business deals.

To illustrate this I get to tell a story. I was once asked by a company to help them finalize a deal that they were desperately trying to broker. Acme Company wanted to buy what Beta Company had to offer. The problem was that Beta Company wanted about forty percent more for its product than the going rate. Usually, this is not a problem. Acme would just find a different company to buy from. But, life being what it is, challenging, there were problems. There was a nationwide courier strike. So, even though Acme could find the product at a much better price they had no idea when the product would be delivered. Also, Acme had let Beta know that they really needed the product by next Thursday or they were going to default on a big contract with a retailer. This was a problem. Acme was up the creek and on the way to a waterfall and Beta knew it. Beta liked the idea of selling at such a high profit. My job was to get the deal closed within forty-eight hours, and cost was not the primary motivation. The middle managers at Acme did not want the upper managers at Acme to know that their actions cost the company an

Peace comes not from the absence of conflict in life but from the ability to cope with it.

additional 40%. The concern was not the money, the concern was saving face.

The table was set. Their negotiator was a well dressed, well educated attorney. I point out the dress because I think her outfit cost as much as my mortgage. I was escorted to the Beta corporate conference room. The table was adorned with piles of papers and French bottled water. I surmised that my fellow negotiator was planning to sit at the far side of the table. So I sat at her spot and started to thumb throgh her notes.

When their negotiator entered the room, flagged by a staff of four, she was outwardly unhappy with my invasion of her space. She used her eyes and nose to direct one of her teammates to gather her belongings. She sat across from me. Her staff sat behind her against the fabric covered wall. (No kid was ever allowed into this room, that was for sure.)

Following the pleasantries we got down to business. She talked about product and price. I asked questions about protocol and Diet Coke. (All they had was fancy water.) After about ten minutes, I relocated to the chair next to her. She was not at all comfortable with my lack of corporate manners or sophistication. Over the next two and one half hours, whenever the topic did not go my way, I politely excused myself to the bathroom. I went eleven times in two and one half hours. Each time taking at least five minutes.

At the end of our meeting, Mrs. Fancy Attorney said, "I'm glad that we agree. We will sell lot number 123456 at the fair market price as stated in our July sales sheet. I will draw up the documents and have them delivered by 9 AM." I thanked her for her assistance and wished her and her staff well. The July sales sheet was the price sheet before the 40% increase.

As I was walking out, one of her staff members escorted me to the lobby. In the elevator he handed me a small scrap of paper with a telephone number on it. He softly said, "Mrs. *Fancy Attorney* is concerned about your prostate. This is the number for her father-in-law. He is the best urologist in the state."

So, what happened? I gave myself a Time Out every time I got off track. When my behavior was not correct I earned a Time Out. I have to be in control of my behavior or no one will be. So, when the conversation turned to money, I earned a Time Out. If the conversation turned to limited options, I earned a Time Out. Boy, I was a bad little negotiator. I earned a lot of Time Outs. Oh, I also used the teaching process of shaping and shaped Beta's negotiator away from certain topics. I only talked about appropriate topics such as "fair market" and "working well together." The negotiation was never heated. In fact, the only way she could win my presence in the room, was to talk about us working well together. My leaving was a mild punisher. My return a soft reward. My presence was down right frustrating for her. I personally, my body, became a negative

Adversity has the effect of eliciting talents, which, in prosperous circumstances, would have lain dormant.

reinforcement. The Beta team wanted to remove this adverse stimulus, lovable old me, and the only way they could was to close the deal fairly. What they thought was a prostate problem was my way of not getting caught up in the emotions of the moment. Time Out is your child's way to help himself not get caught up in the emotion of the moment. It builds self discipline. It gives your child choices. [I later found out that the Beta team had planned to camp out at their offices. They laid in provisions for four days, expecting to finalize the deal late Sunday night. The way I found out was that Beta hired me to teach a seminar called "Negotiating The Close." Mrs. Fancy Attorney turned out to be a wonderful person to work for, but to this day she has never asked me if I went to see her father-in-law. I hope she doesn't read this book!]

THE GOAL OF TIME OUT

The goal of Time Out is to assist your child in becomming cognitive of her behaviors. Our children should be taught that there are positive and negative consequences for their behaviors; and that they, as individuals, must be in control of their behaviors. Thus, they are responsible for their positive behaviors and should be proud of such. But, they are also responsible for their negative behaviors and accept the consequences for them.

Throughout the Time Out procedure, a child is <u>always</u> treated in a respectful manner. She is taught that she is responsible for her behaviors — <u>all</u> of her behaviors.

Our children need support to learn that there are many possible behaviors that they can exhibit and that if they choose a negative behavior there is an appropriate negative consequence. If they choose a positive behavior then there is a positive consequence.

DEFINING "TIME"

Many people use Time Out and a timer. I find this to be dysfunctional. A teacher may say, "Go to the Time Out area for ten minutes and think about your behavior." This is fine, but it is a punishment of ten minutes in duration. It is not a Time Out. A Time Out is not timed. A Time Out is experienced. My children get as much time as is needed for them to get themselves under control. It may only take twenty seconds. So I see no reason for my child to have to sit for twenty-one seconds. It may take fourteen minutes, so a ten minute Time Out would not be enough for my child's needs. When I go for my walk to calm myself down, I walk until I am no longer in need of walking. The time it takes for me to walk is not relevant, it is the *self work* that takes place that counts. By **self work** I mean the internal dialog that I use to deal with the world outside of my thoughts. It is during self work that we make life decisions, ponder

They are able because they think they are able.
Vergil

Moderation in temper is always a virtue; but moderation in principle is always a vice.
Thomas Paine

Quick Reference Guide

Self work: Internal dialog one uses to question one's own thoughts.

our needs, and prospects. It is with self work that we develop and define our self-discipline and the rule book that we use to govern our own behaviors. This personal rule book is never completed. We update it regularly and check our behaviors against the ideals we have developed for ourselves. During a Time Out your child starts to develop his self worth, his identity, his personal rule book.

At this point, most parents ask the basic question, "Well, when does my child get off a Time Out?" This will be discussed in a few minutes in the section entitled, "Ending a Time Out."

ROUTINE COUNTS IN TIME OUT PROCEDURE

Using Time Out is both easy and tricky. The easy part is the basic ritual of the Time Out procedure. The tricky part is our desire to do more, e.g. to teach our children lessons, to fix stuff. This is not the time. Remember, time is out. The game is put on hold. The parent team has to wait until the kid team is back on the field. It makes no sense for the parent team to play if the kid team is not playing (paying attention).

The Time Out procedure is <u>very, very, very</u> ritualistic. The process is the same old boring process time, after time, after time. I cannot emphasize this enough. You as a parent have to say the same words with the same tone with the same facial expression every time. Why? Good question. It is because of the learning process we discussed in the first chapter called, reinforcement. Your child will try to get you to back down, change your mind, or just down right quit as parent. Anything you do aside from the routine, no matter how unrewarding it may seem to you, your child will interpret as a reward. A reward for them not being under their own control. Thus, you shoot yourself in the proverbial foot. If your child wins you by controlling your behavior you are reinforcing his out of control behavior.

Routine counts. Next you will learn the ten second routine you will need to memorize. Relax, in no time you won't even think about it, you will recite it as the old family saying that it is.

HOW TO START A TIME OUT

When your child breaks a rule he earns a Time-Out. (Please note the word "earn." You didn't give it to him. It is not a gift. He earned a Time Out by his behavior. You are assisting him to make cognitive choices.)

The ideal procedure is:

> Parent: "Wendy, I asked you not to run in the house (define the infraction); "Please tell me when you're starting your time."

Please note: When told to take a Time Out the child has no choice. The child must go to the Time Out chair (area, couch, bench, tree, etc.) and state, in a reasonable voice, "Starting."

To this, you respond in a rewarding tone, "Thank You."

Once the child is told to take a Time Out, <u>there is no discussion</u>. Once a Time Out is given, the child has no choice but to comply.

"Please tell me when you're starting your time," is the only response your child should hear. It is said in a calm, relaxed, matter-of-fact tone.

I know at this point most of you are saying, "What? Must comply! Oh sure, my kid isn't going to comply, he is going to ... !" For the moment just stick with me. For our example we have some unknown, perfectly behaved child that is falsely accused of an infraction. Relax, I'll show you how to deal with a real kid. But first we must learn what the ideal Time Out looks like.

For example, if the child screams ... "Starting!" You, as a loving and caring parent respond...

Parent:	"Please tell me when you're starting your time."
Child:	"How much time do I have?!!!!"
Parent:	"Please tell me when you're starting your time."
Child:	"@###**&&#``//?!!!"
Parent:	"Please tell me when you're starting your time."
Child:	"I hate you and your MOTHER!!! Blank-e-ty blank blank growl growl hiss!"
Parent:	"Please tell me when you're starting your time."

"Please tell me when you're starting your time," is always stated in a calm supportive voice. <u>Always</u>. You do not want your child to be reinforced for his antics. So I mean it, ALWAYS!

Child:	*calmly,* "Starting."
Parent:	"Thank you."

We judge ourselves by what we feel capable of doing, others judge us by what we have already done.

Longfellow

We should always thank our child for making the appropriate choice. This is very important and rewarding to our children. We need to say it and mean it. By saying "thank you" we are acknowledging that our child made a choice that we wanted them to make. Out of all the things they could choose to do, they chose to let you parent. When I thank a child for letting me parent I am truly honored with their choice of me. (Unfortunately, I have known many teenagers who have disowned their parents. I cherish the role of parent that my children allow me to have.) In the classroom the teacher's thanks is very important. The child is letting you be their teacher.

Remember, without a meaningful relationship you have no way to influence.

DOING A TIME OUT

On the surface a Time Out is very simple. Your child is responsible to sit calmly and think about the how's and why's that lead up to the Time Out. He knows that for the Time Out to end he will have to explain what led up to the Time Out.

The child's age and temperament determines what *calmly* looks like. You know your child. Is he calming himself down? Is he open to talking about his choices?

ENDING A TIME OUT

When your child has sat calmly and shows you through his behavior that he is ready to talk, your child should hear:

> Parent: "[child's name] why are you doing a Time Out?"

Your child must explain, at his level of ability, what his misbehavior was. Following a reasonable explanation your child should hear:

> Parent: "Thank you, your time is up."

If your child doesn't remember why she is sitting:

> Parent: "I will tell you why you had to sit, but you will have to do your Time Out over..."

If a child doesn't recall why they were doing the Time Out they

The future is that time when you wish you'd done what you aren't doing now.

did not do their self work. They are calmly informed and asked:

> Parent: "Please tell me when you're starting your time."

Our children must learn that they are responsible for their behaviors. Expecting our children to remember why they are doing a Time Out helps them focus on their responsibilities for their behaviors in the family or in the classroom.

ADVOCATING FOR GOOD CHOICES

The end of the Time Out procedure is the crucial moment when you get to help your child develop new thoughts and practice making informed decisions.

When you ask your child, "...why are you doing a Time Out?" you are opening up a dialog for your child to experience these new thoughts. Remember, the goal is not to tell your child what he did to get you to give him a Time Out. We want our child to share his thoughts on what his choices are, now that he is calmer and open to looking at choices. Our goal must be looking towards the future. What else could be done in the same type of situation. But, with a better outcome.

The way we support our child's choice development is to allow her to tell you her thoughts and explain how she made those choices. Our role is to advocate for her, and to present a warm and safe relationship for her to practice her choice development.

Lester was a happy go lucky child of seven. He tended not to think before he acted. This caused Lester to spend many hours sitting in the office of his school. His mother told me:

> Lester is a sweet little boy. He is almost always happy. But, it seems he is constantly getting into trouble for small stuff. He was sent to the office just this morning for wandering around his class and touching stuff. Mrs. Moscowitz, his teacher, seemed almost apologetic for having to send him to the office.

Lester's mother learned about Time Out and implemented its use with her three children. The following week she told me this story:

> I was picking up Lester at school and having a friendly chat with his teacher. I was so happy to hear that he had a good day when, he walked up to the teacher's desk and took a big bite out of her apple. He put the apple down and walked away. I was shocked. I gave him a Time Out right there. It was wonderful,

It is easy to be critical. The real test is to develop constructive alternatives.

after his Time Out we talked...

Mom:	Lester, why are you doing a Time Out?
Lester:	Because I ate Mrs. M.'s apple.
Mom:	What does that mean for you.
Lester:	I just wanted a bite. But it wasn't mine. I shouldn't put my germs on her apple.
Mom:	How could you do it differently?
Lester:	I could have waited until no one was looking?
Mom:	You could have waited until no one was around. How else could you have done it differently?
Lester:	I could have asked Mrs. M. if I could have a bite of her apple.
Mom:	You could have asked Mrs. M. How else could you do it differently?
Lester:	I could have bought it off of her for money.
Mom:	Yes, you could have paid for the apple. If you asked to pay for the apple then what would happen?
Lester:	Mrs. M. would want lots of money. I wouldn't get the apple.
Mom:	That could happen. If you asked Mrs. M. for a bite of apple, then what might happen?
Lester:	She might say yes or no.
Mom:	If you waited for no one to be around then what might happen?
Lester:	I would go to jail for being a bad guy. With bars and everything!
Mom:	So, what do you think would work for you?
Lester:	I could say, "Mrs. M. can I have the apple ... my germs are all right for me."

What Lester's mom did was advocate for her son. She set limits and then helped him look at the consequences of his behavior. She used the question, **"What could you do differently?"** and then followed up with an **If/Then** statement. In this way she helped Lester look at his options. She held her opinion to herself concerning the appropriateness of her son's choices. She allowed (respected) her son to figure out the right and wrong or the usefulness, for him, of his options. This three minute conversation brings parent and child closer and allows the child to comfortably talk about how he sees the world. I have seen thousands of families use Differently/If/Then conversations to replace parental lectures that the child only turns a deaf ear to. It is very common for a child to turn to his parent and ask, "How would you ... ?" Then listen carefully as the parent outlines their thought process through the use of Differently/If/Then internal conversations.

In the next chapter, FAMILY RULES, we will look more closely at how we help our children use their internal dialog to solve their personal conflicts.

HOW CHILDREN TEST THE TIME OUT PROCESS

The heading of this section is actually a misnomer. Your children are not testing the "procedure" of Time Out, they are testing you. That's right, **you**. They are testing your honesty and your word. They are testing your character. And, as I have pointed out many times, no one likes to have their character tested.

So, first things first. Do you mean it when you say, "Please tell me when you're starting your time." Are you sure in your soul, that you are willing to presently confront your child so your child, in the long run, can develop discipline. Are you willing to help your child learn discipline? Or do you need to punish your child for his "bad" behavior?

This is important. If you need to punish your child, to personally let off steam, your child will easily escalate the Time Out into an argument. A screaming match where you both lose.

If your child believes that he has to take the Time Out **he** earned, then he will. Moments later, you and he are discussing his options and you both are feeling wonderful about your close relationship.

But, if he doesn't believe in you, he will test this disbelief by acting out. He will do things that have worked in the past to escalate the situation. He may yell, scream, throw stuff, knock over stuff — whatever it takes to get you to lose your self control. Then, once you have lost your composure, the focus will be on your anger and your hurt feelings and off his responsibility for his behavior.

So, be forewarned. Your child knows all your hot buttons. This is her job. She stays up late at night organizing her data base on you. She has your number. You're in the cross hairs of her attack

Laugh at yourself before anyone else can.
Elsa Maxwell

Quick Reference Guide

Secondary Gain: When your child gets a rein-forcement that is not your intention. Often it is the power of controlling

and you have no place to run.

However, there is reason for hope. If you say what you mean and mean what you say, your child will quickly learn that you will not back down or allow distractions.

I find I say to myself on a regular basis, "This kid is worth it, keep your cool." While I say outwardly, "Please tell me when you're starting your time."

To follow, I will share with you some tricks of the trade.

WHAT TO DO WHEN YOUR CHILD REFUSES TO START A TIME OUT

Rule number one. Relax, take it in stride. Understand that what your child's behavior is really saying is, "I don't trust you." As pain-ful as it is you need to know it. Now you do. Wonderful. Teach your child that you are an honest person who cares for them. Say, "Please tell me when you're starting your time," and really mean the word <u>please</u>. Let your child *feel* that you want them to let you parent them.

Remember that parenting is a long process and *the process counts*.

TRICK #1: TAG TEAM

If at all possible get help from another adult. It is amazing how often parents tell me that, "When his mother walked into the living room, our son went over to start his Time Out, as if he wasn't all worked up." What tends to happen is that the second parent (adult) changes the believability factor in the room. It is hard for the child to disbelieve you when another adult in the room is believing you.

Other times the other adult simply says, "Please tell me when you're starting your time." and the child smirks in your direction and goes off and does a great Time Out. Let the disrespect go for the moment. When the Time Out is over and feelings are calm is the best time to discuss your child's disrespect. ("Bobby, earlier today my feelings were hurt when you ...")

TRICK #2: FOR EVERY MINUTE ...

At first, it is common for children who are angry to prolong starting their earned Time Out. Most often this looks like *I don't care* behavior on the part of the child. Mrs. Montgomery said it this way, "Jonathan plopped himself on the floor and screamed "You can't make me do a Time Out!"

Jonathan is correct. You cannot make him do a Time Out. He has to allow you to parent. He has to choose to take a Time Out.

If you think about it, Jonathan is setting up a challenge, The *make me* challenge. A game a parent cannot win. And, if you as a parent back down, Jonathan also loses by not feeling that you care about him. So, no one wins, everyone loses. This is not a game that is worth playing.

In this situation, Mrs. Montgomery needs to make Jonathan *feel* responsible for the down side of his behavior, not starting a Time Out. The up side of the above scenario is that Jonathan feels power over his mother. This feeling of power, secondary gain, is a positive reinforcer. A reinforcer that Jonathan can give to himself instantaneously. As we learned in Chapter 1, this makes the reinforcer very powerful. I have seen children play the above family dynamics out for years, until the parents could not deal with the degree of conflict and sought professional help.

Mr. Robinson said:

> My son will cut his nose off to spite his face. When he gets a Time Out, he explodes and trashes his room. He gets himself so worked up that he cries himself to sleep. After his nap he is calm and we talk about the problem. But honestly, he never does a Time Out. Marge (mom) and I are afraid to give him a Time Out.

This is a great example of **secondary gain**. By definition, secondary gain is when your child gets a reinforcement that is not your intention.

Four year old Salvador had a great way to get secondary gain. Whenever he was told to do something he did not like, which was often, he would start scratching at his face. His face was covered with scratches in different degrees of healing when I first met him. His parents were frazzled. They were afraid to say "no" to anything little Salvador wanted, fearful that he would injure himself. One would think that the pain of scratching one's own face would be a punisher, and I would have to agree. But, the secondary gain of controlling one's parents is a very powerful reward. Powerful enough for Salvador to offset the pain of scratching his own face.

The three families above added one little twist to their family's Time Out procedure and the negative behaviors went away in short order.

When rejecting the ideas of another, make sure you reject only the idea and not the person.

When your child is in the *I don't care* mode, you need to make him responsible for his poor choices (lack of caring). This is accomplished by calmly stating, "You need to make better choices, for every minute it takes you to start your Time Out it will cost you four minutes of room restrictions." Then you simply take care of keeping track of time.

If your child believes your word, she will run to the Time Out area and say "starting." If she does not believe your word she will need to test you. At the end of the Time Out, whenever that might be, as part of the discussion, you remind your child that she earned *X* amount of room restrictions. (Four times the number of minutes it took her to start her Time Out.) It usually takes only two or three testing situations for a child to stop showing a behavior that is no longer working for her.

The number four is my suggestion. With younger children I may use two minutes, with older children as much as ten. I find four times works well, it is encouraging without the child feeling that you are throwing your weight around. Avoid going over ten minutes for every minute. Remember, you will have to enforce the room restriction. So, make it easy on yourself. Do not set yourself up to feel cruel or overbearing. Also, do not allow yourself to become overly punitive. Your goal is for your child to focus on their own behavior, not on the punitiveness of your behavior. This is a tough situation which must be experienced and practiced by parents. It is part of the *art* of parenting.

The little four year old above, who scratched his face, was very indignant when his parents implemented this technique. He said, "That's not fair, you have to play by the rules!" He stopped scratching his face within two hours and only four Time Outs. The very next day he had to relearn this change with his daycare provider and again on Sunday with Grandma at Grandma's house. Without the secondary gain, the scratching became just a punisher. And as you recall, we all dislike punishers.

TRICK #3 TEASING OTHERS WHO ARE ON TIME

It is common for a second child to tease another child who has earned a Time Out. The child on the Time Out is stuck. If he reacts he is probably going to have to restart his Time Out. The "captive audience/victim," is sometimes too irresistible a situation for other children to resist.

If this is an every now and then problem, I advise that you deal with it by giving the second child a Time Out for teasing. Then talk about picking on the underdog and ask how he would feel. If it is an ongoing problem you need to reward the first child for trying to deal with someone picking on him. What I advise you to say is, "Billy, you should not be talking to someone on a Time Out. If Sally's Time Out is so important to you, you can do it for her." Then let Billy finish Sally's Time Out. This switch-a-roo does let Sally off, so to speak, for her Time Out, but it stops the malicious teasing dead in its tracks.

This problem does not come up much, but if it does you need to nip it in the bud.

OOPS! WHAT TO DO IF YOU MAKE A MISTAKE

Sorry, but it is true, you are going to make mistakes. When you make mistakes with your children it is also a blessing in disguise. If you take responsibility for the mistake, honestly apologize and forgive yourself, you are teaching your child a valuable lesson. The lesson of taking personal responsibility.

This is a Dr. Phil confession, it happened a long time ago and I still feel a little guilty about it. So please, do not tell anyone that I did this. Once, after bedtime, I put a child on a Time Out. He was up running around, bothering the other children. He had a hard time starting his Time Out. It was just too exciting to be up when everyone else was in bed. His Time Out went on and on. I finished up some stuff in the kitchen then watched the news. Yep, you guessed it. I forgot about him as he sat in the overstuffed chair no more than ten feet from me. At a little after 2 AM he came into my room, woke me up and asked, "How long do I have to do this Time Out for anyway?"

When you make a mistake show your children how to deal with making mistakes.

WHO'S RESPONSIBLE?

There is an old joke which goes like this: hundreds of people are sitting around a casino praying to God for a particular card. One person wants an eight, another wants a queen. St. Peter looks to God and says, "I have a headache, I can't keep track of these requests, what do you want to do?"

God decrees in a booming voice, "Bust everybody!"

This joke is often given as the reason you don't get the card you ask for. It is also the way to deal with a crowd of confusion. If you walk into the living room and six kids are all pointing fingers and yelling their version of what happened, "Bust everybody!"

If the class is out of control, "Bust everybody!"

If three kids are sliding down the stairs on their bellies and two more are waiting upstairs, "Bust everybody!"

Then sort out the pieces in a few, calmer moments. I find asking the question following the Time Out, "Do you folks need my help to solve this problem or can you solve it yourselves?" tends to solve half of the excited conflicts kids get into.

So, all things being equal, "Bust everybody!"

BUT WE ARE NOT ALWAYS AT HOME!

I was once at Sears buying shoes for my boys, then two and five. As is the rule with shoe shopping, it is frustrating and thankless for the parent. My boys were having a blast. Shoes are way too much fun for little kids. Finally, the antics had gone too far. As they trotted through the clothes rack I gave their feet a Time Out.

To my surprise, three little children walked out from between the clothes and sat down calmly on the small bench in the shoe department. None of the three children were mine. A woman came over and crossed her arms. "Thank you mister," she said turning to her children, "One more minute of this foolishness and we were going home without new shoes!" Wow, I busted a stranger's kids ... and it worked! Then I went looking for the correct little feet to bust. I found my boys in the women's shoe department dancing around in patent leather, fluorescent yellow and pink high heels.

So I, "Busted everybody!"

When you are away from home your Time Out procedure goes with you (thankfully). If you're at the park, designate a tree or a particular bench. If you're at a friend's house, designate an area or a chair.

Many parents find that by designating a Time Out area they are actually giving 1/2 a Time Out. Designating an area when you first get to the park, reminds the children of their personal responsibilities in controlling their behavior.

When in a car, have your children put their hands under their thighs as a symbol of a Time Out. This procedure of sitting on their hands is very effective and keeps us away from the, "Do you want me to turn this car around?" statement that your kid doesn't believe anyway.

"I WANT TO TALK CODE"

Often children will act out to get attention. Sometimes it is just kid stuff other times it is "child needs adult" stuff. Your children need to know how to get your attention, or the attention of other adults. This is where we need to give our children an opening line that gets an adult's attention, even if the adult doesn't know it is a code.

The code sentence is, "If you have a minute can we talk?" What this does for your child is to open a helpful conversation with an adult. Almost any adult.

If a teacher is very busy, "If you have a minute can we talk?" lets her know your child has a need. When a police officer is approached with, "If you have a minute can we talk?" the officer is able to shine attention on your child. If your child says to you, "If you have a minute can we talk?" you know your child needs a child parent talk.

"If you have a minute can we talk?" lets adults see your child as respectful. Most adults will bend over backwards to help a respectful child. Even busy adults, will work out a time to help your polite child.

Time Outs are a very effective way for you to teach your child self discipline. When you punish your children, you are trying to control their behavior. This leads to resentment and anger on their part. Through Time Outs children learn to control their own behavior. They take on the responsibility for their own choices. The results may not be immediate, but they are long lasting.

Chapter 4

Family Rules

4. FAMILY RULES— THE DIFFERENCE BETWEEN A HOUSE AND A HOME

I must admit that as a family therapist I have a pet peeve. It is a large purple funky life-form that makes me initially feel upset and then feel pity. My pet peeve is when a parent says, "I do it for the kids" or "I do it for the family." For example, the Michaels family is in disarray. Their seventeen year old son spends most of his day avoiding the family. Their fifteen year old son is failing every class and was arrested while breaking into neighborhood homes to use their phones and computers. Their daughter, eleven, is in an emotional daze, numb due to the constant bickering between her siblings and the hateful words between her parents. Mr. and Mrs. Michaels have been married for almost twenty years. Mrs. Michaels explains, "In the last twenty years we have learned how to look like a happy family. On the outside we show well. But, inside the walls of our house, we hate each other. We argue constantly, if we talk at all. Most days I wish I could just run away from home."

When I first met Mr. and Mrs. Michaels they were scared and angry. Their fifteen year old son had been accused of $60,000 worth of destruction to a neighbor's home.

> It is curious that physical courage should be so common in the world and moral courage so rare.
>
> Mark Twain

Mr. Michaels: I don't know what to do ... our son must hate us. He says he 'just lost it' and destroyed the inside of a neighbor's home. He tore the sheet rock off the wall and poured paint all over the carpets and furniture.

Mrs. Michaels: I just can't believe he would do this sort of thing. It was just evil. He must just hate me ...

Mr. Michaels: No! He doesn't hate you, he is crazy! It must be that he is just mad, there was no reason to destroy the neighbor's home.

> The real test of a parent is to possess power without abusing it.

Dr. Phil: Where were you folks when it happened?

Mr. Michaels: We were at work. We usually get home around six-thirty or seven. It seems that he has been breaking into neighbors' homes for months ... after school and on weekends. The police say they have phone evidence that he has been using other neighbors' phones too.

Dr. Phil: Your children are unsupervised from after school until around six?

Mr. Michaels: Sure, it has never been a problem until now. We both work long hours ... we try to get as much overtime as possible. We are a little behind on our bills. WE DO IT FOR THE KIDS! And they treat us like !@#$%.

There's my pet peeve, "WE DO IT FOR THE KIDS!" Mom and dad Michaels love the concept of being in love with their children, but they had to say that their children were hard to love. The behaviors in the family were so abrasive that no one could chance showing love or affection because of the fear of being hurt by other family members. If you parked your car on the curb in front of the Michaels' home you would see a beautiful, four bedroom, freshly painted, house. The lawn is well kept. The windows are covered with warm curtains. The rooms are well appointed with newer furniture. Three cars fill the driveway. A boat is in the garage. A motor home is along side.

My problem is with the misguided belief, "WE DO IT FOR THE KIDS!" I have found that many parents use these words to justify their chosen behaviors. They use these words to justify not making time to properly parent.

The word **parent** is a noun. But the act of parenting, to parent is a verb. Parenting is an action word. A doing word. The primary role of a parent is *to parent*, to participate and direct the upbringing of their children. Don't get me wrong, I know that money makes the world go round, but I am adamant that paying the bills is not enough. It is a part of the adult world, but it is not the primary role of a parent in the life of their children.

Parenting is a full-time (plus) job. It has no pay and only non-tangible rewards. And, let me be very clear ... most of the time it is time consuming!!! Yep, it takes time to parent. Lots of it. Period. It is your responsibility to care for and protect your children from the real world and sometimes even from themselves.

THE ART OF DISCIPLINE

I would like to take a moment to further investigate the relationship between two words: punishment versus discipline. As we initially discussed in the first chapter, punishment is something that decreases the likelihood of a behavior. In Chapter 3 we explored both punishment and discipline.

Punishment is the presentation of an aversive stimulus, following an undesired response, that decreases the likelihood of that undesired response. Discipline is learned choices, self control. With punishment we force our demands on our child, but when we teach our children to be disciplined we teach them how to make choices and let them build character.

Now we look at the essence of our choice to use punishment verses develop discipline within our children. Both punishment and discipline have their place in child rearing. What I would like to look at is the art of parenting that allows us to know when we should punish and when we should develop discipline.

In Chapter 1 we looked at the negative side effects of punishment:

> *Punishment is a powerful teaching tool. However, it has two major drawbacks to its efficiency. First, for punishment to be effective it must be severe. If not, its efficiency is only temporary. Second, punishment brings to the relationship powerful feelings such as anger and revenge, which can destroy a positive learning situation.*

These side effects can severely undermine the parent/child relationship. Thus, I advocate that we use punishment sparingly.

The definition for discipline is often misunderstood. Many people think of it as authoritarian, such as the way a Marine drill sergeant treats a new recruit. This is a very narrow view of the word. Discipline comes from the Latin word *discipulus* for "learner." It is related to disciple, doctor, and document. In Anglo-Saxon times the Latin root and Old French merged to become *deciple*, meaning instruction or knowledge. Over the centuries the meaning developed into "*maintenance of order.*"

For me, I perceive discipline as "self control." The act of my child learning to accept personal responsibility for his behavior. The act of taking individual responsibility for emotional and behavioral self regulation. It is my goal as a parent to systematically relinquish my external control over my child, while my child systematically takes over his own self control.

This systematic release and acceptance of control is the art of parenting that most of us find so difficult. We want to protect our children from harm or even discomfort. Unfortunately, this virtuous goal tends to allow us to be overly protective and, in the long run, we inadvertently hinder our own children.

When I was an undergraduate student, I watched a rat experiment that some graduate students were conducting. The experiment consisted of teaching two

I'm going to define a new word as a dictionary might define it: *to parent*— "to use, with tender loving care, all the information science has accumulated about child psychology in order to raise happy and intelligent human beings."
Fritzhugh Dobson, Ph.D.

Taxi?

groups of rats how to find food at the end of a maze. The large maze was constructed out of wood in the basement of the psychology building. The experiment was interesting as well as hilarious to watch. The graduate students had two groups of rats. Both groups were treated the same in all aspects, except one.

Group 1 members were placed at the starting point of the maze and then observed. Each rat nosed around the maze eventually finding the "reward" food at the end of the maze. Each member of Group 1 experienced the process of finding food twenty times. Each time the rats got faster at finding their way through the maze. Basic rat learning in progress. Then the funny stuff happened. Group 2 also got 20 trips through the maze. The graduate students had concocted a little "rat wagon" that the rats got to ride in. Twenty times each member of Group 2 was pulled along through the maze and was rewarded with food at the end. (The rat, not the student.)

The graduate students were investigating passive versus active learning. They wanted to see which group could run the maze the fastest, which group learned the maze the best. The next day, (so the rats would be hungry and motivated to play maze with the graduate students) each of the rats were timed as they ran the maze. The rats in Group 1 were very fast. They dashed through the maze and gobbled up their reward. The rats in Group 2 just sat there at the starting gate. Most didn't even explore much. They just sat there, hungry, waiting for a ride. When they finally did start to explore they were very tentative. They were substantially slower than Group 1 rats were their first time through the maze. How interesting, helping the Group 2 rats through the maze subsequently hindered their ability to learn. But it sure was funny to watch.

I assure you that I am not equating our children to rats. But, we can learn a lot from experimental evidence.

Albert was a small framed, angelic looking boy of nine. A few minutes into a therapy session, Albert's watch fell off. He picked up his watch from the carpet and stated, "Dr. Phil, put this on for me." When I explained that he was able to put his own watch on he matter of factly marched off to the waiting room and barked his order at his mom. "Mom, put my watch on!" As I got to the waiting room door I got Mrs. Warren's attention and nodded "no" to her. She understood and politely told Albert, "I think you can put your own watch on," and handed it back to him. Albert took the watch and threw it on the ground screaming, "I want you to put it on for me! I want you to put it on for me!" I motioned to mom to come with me and we went back to the therapy room and sat down. I reminded mom about last week's session when we discussed that she should have more age appropriate expectations of Albert. The week prior we had discussed how she was not truly helping Albert if she did everything for him. We had the following conversation:

Mrs. Warren: (looking worried) If I don't put his watch on he may lose it.

Dr. Phil: That may be so ...

Mrs. Warren: If I don't help, he may think I don't love him.

Dr. Phil: That may be so ...

Mrs. Warren: He will have a temper tantrum. (She put both hands on her head and rocked it in despair.)

Dr. Phil: That may be so ...

Mrs. Warren: Albert loses everything!

Dr. Phil: That may be so ...

At this point Albert found his way to the therapy room. He was calm, collected and just a little red faced from all of his screaming. "You guys left me out there ... I was having a temper tantrum you know!!!"

"That may be so," smiled Mrs. Warren, "but you haven't put your watch on." Albert looked at his feet. "I broke it when I threw it on the ground," he said softly.

Over the next few weeks Albert trotted into session excitedly telling me all the new things he could now do. "I took out the garbage, I made my bed, I walked to the store." He quickly started to act like a nine year old.

At the end of three months the family didn't need therapy any longer. Mrs. Warren wrote me a nice thank you letter. One part caught my attention. "It is nice to see Albert playing with the neighborhood children. I saw him pulling the neighbor's six year old in a wagon this morning. He was so happy. He is getting so big. Thanks for making me stop pulling Albert in the rat wagon." (I always get warm fuzzies when people remember my stories.)

In this section we are going to explore the process of developing a home that encourages individuals to develop discipline and self control. Only when our children have self control, can we stop being police officers, judges, and probation officers and be what we are ... loving parents. Our goal should be to provide a *home* not just a *house*.

If you ask children what they want, they sing out, "Freedom," as it should be. As your children grow they should want to be adults. Through the eyes of minors, adults have it made. We can do whatever we want to. We go to bed when we desire. We eat whatever crosses our fancy. We can say and do whatever we want. Boy, are

Correction does much, but encouragement does more. Encouragement after censure is as the sun after a shower.

Goethe

kids uninformed. They don't know about taxes, bosses, and adult responsibilities. They don't know that we go to bed so we can get up to go to work. That we eat cardboard fiber and low fat, tasteless stuff because of our waist lines and our clogging arteries. In fact, kids have it made. We protect them. But, nonetheless, kids want freedom.

As parents we really want realistic freedom for our children. Our long term goal is for our children to develop self control so we can relinquish our limited control over them. We want our children to have respect for themselves and others. We desire that our children use good judgment to direct their lives. When babies enter the world they are, by design, self centered. They know nothing about the rights and self responsibility of others. As they grow and mature, they build awareness of others and eventually respect for self and others. Within the limits of our society, children learn how to be free.

I like to think of degrees of freedom as the size of the envelope our children live within. By envelope I mean the limitations within which our children can perform safely and effectively. When our children are very young, the envelope is the crib, our arms or the area that has been made safe on the living room floor. As our infants grow into toddlers, the envelope may be the "baby safe" living room and the car-seat. Preschoolers get the run of part of the house or the enclosed playground. The size of the envelope grows with the child. School children expand to the classroom, most of the house, and parts of the neighborhood. The envelope is the limitations we place on our children.

The size of this envelope is very important in helping our children learn what freedom is. As our child teaches us that they can handle more freedom — we enlarge the envelope. If they teach us that the freedom is more responsibility than they can control, we limit the envelope. The art of parenting is "knowing" when to enlarge or reduce the envelope.

I advise that parents help children (especially teens) to see growing up as proving that they can handle increases in freedom. This leads us to four major factors.

1. **Parents need to define, within themselves and their marriage, what they believe the size of the envelope should be.** Parents need to talk openly about what is and is not allowed within each child's envelope of freedom. This process will be mapped out for you in the following pages.

2. **After the parents have defined the size of the envelope for each child, the limitations must be clearly defined for that child.** Children need well defined limitations to feel safe and secure in their lives.

In giving advice I advise you, be short.
Horance

3. **Parents must give more freedom when their child teaches them that they have mastered the present limitations of their envelope.** As your child develops you can only challenge her to grow with further freedoms.

4. **If your child teaches you that the envelope is too large, you must respect your child's need for limitations.** If your child breaks a rule that forces you to implement a consequence, you must respect your child's needs. When your child again teaches you that she is ready for an enlargement of the envelope, you can again give your child more freedom.

I often tell the following story to teens to help them see their involvement in the size of the *envelope of freedom*. Unfortunately, this story is sad, but like all the stories in the book, it is true. The lesson it teaches is important.

Mr. and Mrs. Peabody came to my office to talk about the stress their family had recently undergone. The problem centered around their sixteen year old son, Scott. Scott was a wonderful child and a respectful and talented teenager. He was on the high school football team and was interested in studying anthropology in college. As the Peabodys told me about their son I was impressed with his talents and social skills.

Six weeks prior to my first session with Mr. and Mrs. Peabody, a terrible thing happened. Three classmates were angry with Scott. They were jealous of his sport talents and his ease in social situations. So, as a prank (their words), they thought that they would bring Scott down off his high cloud. They wanted to publicly embarrass Scott and get teachers to not like him as much. The three boys conspired to put phencyclidine (PCP) in his drink. Scott drank the spiked drink and had a massive seizure. Scott suffered permanent brain damage. He now had the mind of a three year old. [See Chapter 5, WHAT DO I NEED TO KNOW ABOUT STREET DRUGS? for more information about PCP.]

I tell this story to teens and ask them how Scott's parents should treat him. Should they treat him as a sixteen year old or as a three year old?

Mr. and Mrs. Peabody had to learn how to treat Scott correctly. They had to learn to protect Scott from himself. They had to hold his hand when he was near a street. They had to "child proof" their home. I can honestly say that Mr. and Mrs. Peabody taught me much about compassion and parental love. I am honored to have known them.

We have to respect the needs of our children. The needs of our children define the size of the envelope of freedom we allow them to practice their lives in. The envelope is defined by the needs of

Every artist was first an amateur.

Emerson

the individual child.

If your child teaches you that he should be treated like a twenty-two year old, it would be disrespectful to treat him any other way. If your child teaches you that she should be treated as an eleven year old you must treat her like an eleven year old. Please note that we must treat our children as their behavior teaches us, not based on the chronological date of their birth. It would be unfair to treat Scott as a sixteen year old. It would endanger him to have the freedom of a sixteen year old. Conversely, it would be unfair for a parent to treat their fourteen year old as a ten year old if he is acting sixteen.

Now, let's look at how we can fairly and respectfully treat each other in the family.

MUST, MAYBE AND MINOR RULES

Most families have too many rules. Yep, that's what I said, too many rules. So many rules that the members of the family can't even keep track of all the rules. So many rules that parents become law clerks trying to keep track of the family's laws. Kids say it, usually loudly, "I didn't know that," or "You never said that," or "You said this or that." What a mess.

Most families don't really have well defined rules. What they really have are "preferences." Parental expectations based on lots of unmentioned factors. The following conversation is typical of one heard during the first session with an acting out teenager and his mother.

Mom:	Johnny just won't behave. He is in trouble at school all the time.
Son:	I'm not in trouble all the time ...
Mom:	See, he argues about everything ...
Son:	Sure I do, you lie about me all the time.
Mom:	As an example of his uncooperative behavior, I asked him to come home right after school today because we had this appointment. He never showed. I had to go to school and pick him up.
Son:	I would have been home in plenty of time to make it to this stupid appointment.
Mom:	I'm here because of you ... Do you know how much this is going to cost?
Son:	Just give me the money. I wouldn't get into

trouble if I had cash to do stuff with.

Mom: What, to buy drugs? You're never going to go to college with your attitude.

Son: I'm going to college, you just don't believe in me...

Mom: I love you so much (tears start flowing). That is why I'm worrying myself sick over you.

Dr. Phil: Do you believe your mom?

Son: Sure, most of the time.

Dr. Phil: Is it OK if I ask you about how honest your mom is?

Son: Sure man, it's your office.

Dr. Phil: If your mom says 'come home after school' what does she mean?

Son: What? She means come home after school, I guess.

Dr. Phil: Sometimes you come right home after school?

Son: Sure, if my mom means it, I come right home.

Dr. Phil: What does that mean?

Son: Look, if she says, "I need you to watch your brother right after school," then I know she needs me to be home right after school.

Dr. Phil: Other times ...

Son: Sometimes she says, "Be home after school, I'm bringing pizza home after work." So I know that as long as I'm home by five thirty she won't be too mad.

Dr. Phil: Too mad?

Son: Yeah, you know ... She will just growl at me for a minute then we eat pizza.

Mom, in this type of situation, is always in shock. She sits speechless. Then says something like, "Why can't he just follow

The size of the envelope is defined by the child when the limitations are not clearly defined.

Never assume anything except a 41/2 percent mortgage.

the rules!"

My belief is that he is following the "family rules." The rules as he has learned them to be. In this family the rules are actually preferences. If mom needs you to watch your baby brother, then after school is 3:45. If mom is bringing home pizza after work and won't be too upset, then home after school is 5:30. Please note, <u>the size of the envelope is defined by the child when the limitations are not clearly defined.</u>

Please take a few minutes and complete the following exercise. We will use the information later in this chapter. Don't even think about skipping this homework assignment. This assignment is mandatory for you to get the most out of this book. Remember, process counts and the process of doing this assignment will really help you to learn a lot about your parenting skills.

Please fill in the following form (Dr. Phil's Three M's of Rule Types) with the rules of your family. Your family rules as they actually are, not your dream family rules, your <u>actual</u> family rules. There are three categories to be filled in.

1. **Must Rules:** Rules you make sure are followed <u>100%</u> of the time. Not 99% or less of the time. For example, you will miss work to make sure this rule is followed. You would stop watching the end of a great movie to make sure this rule is followed. You would put up with public embarrassment to make sure that this rule is followed.

2. **Maybe Rules:** You really want these rules to be followed but you know that they are not followed 100% of the time. Often your kids follow these rules, especially when you beg, nag, or are angry, but the kids do not follow these rules 100% of the time. (This is a long list usually, use extra paper if need be.)

3. **Minor Rules:** Rules that are followed by your child (a minor) so well that you don't worry about it anymore. For example, you no longer check your fourteen year old's underwear to see if he needs changing. When he was two you needed to. But you no longer find a need to monitor your "big boy's" bowel movements. At this point your child is 100% responsible and capable of following this rule.

WHERE ARE WE TODAY: HOMEWORK ASSIGNMENT #1

Please complete the following form as completely as possible.

Please <u>do not read on</u> until the three M's form is completed.

FAMILY: _____

DR. PHIL'S THREE M'S OF RULE TYPES

DATE: _____

MUST	MAYBE	MINOR
Must Rules are followed through by parents 100% of the time	Maybe Rules are not followed through by parents 100% of the time	Parents are comfortable with minor's ability to follow these rules independently

Thank you for completing the assignment before you continued on. Most families find that the Three M's form is somewhat skewed. They usually find that there are a few Must Rules (if any) and a few more Minor Rules and a whole encyclopedia of Maybe Rules. To tell you the truth, I don't think you would be reading this book if that was not the case.

Many parents bring back the list after taking many hours to fill it out. Often I hear, "Our rules are so simple ... how come my kids fight them so much?" or, "I can't believe my family is this out of control. I knew it was uncomfortable but as I wrote up this list I found myself getting angry. Why do my children make our family life so difficult?" One couple proclaimed, "As we worked on our homework assignment, we found ourselves getting angry. The more we talked the more we came to the conclusion that our kids just hate us. We never acted like this with our parents!"

The three M's list tends to point to the symptom of the problem in many homes. It points to one simple but powerful fact: Your

A TYPICAL 3M LIST

The first rough draft of the 3M list tends to be a snap shot of the present family rule structure. As Mr. and Mrs. Smith talked about their family conflicts it quickly became apparent that most of the Must Rules were actually Maybe Rules. This is to be expected at first.

Until there is a clearly defined consequence associated with a family rule it is most likely destined to be on the Maybe pile of want-to-be rules.

Family: Smith **Dr. Phil's Three M's of Rule Types** First Draft **Date:** Jan 1997

Must Must rules are followed through by parents 100% of the time	Maybe Maybe rules are not followed through by parents 100% of the time	Minor Parents are comfortable with minor's ability to follow these rules independently
No name calling	Follow all rules of the apartment complex	Pick out appropriate clothes for school
No hitting / hurting		Keep room clean
No damaging other's belongings	Do homework before playing	Do your best in school every day
Do not answer the phone	Pick up own clothes & toys	
Do not go to other people's	Wash hands before eating	Seat belts
houses without permission	Shower every other day	Keep track of homework
No playing in the street	Be considerate and kind	and school books
	Help with laundry	
	Bedtime is 9pm	

children do not believe you. If they did believe you, your Must Rule list would be the long list followed by the minor list. The Maybe list would be empty. That's right, empty. Over the next few pages this should become evident to you.

MAYBE RULES CAUSE CONSTANT CONFLICT

Your children are people, yep, people ... with all the human nature that people possess. I point this out because over the years I have noticed one consistent thing about people. All people, irrelevant of race, creed, sexual orientation, economic status, or parenting, have one, huge, binding consistency. A same-ness that binds us throughout the generations and history of mankind. One undoubtable fact that proves humanness. We all know it to be true, but hate to believe it:

All things being equal, people do what they want to do!

Humans, including children, possess rational and logical thought, at least from their perspective, from their point of view. People always have clear and plausible reasons for why they did whatever they did. (Later they may believe, "Well, at the time it seemed like a good idea.")

I once read in the paper about a man in his twenties who shot his hand gun from the parking lot in the direction of a small store. When asked why he shot a man as he was walking out of the store, the shooter answered, "I didn't shoot the man, he walked in front of the bullet."

All things being equal, people do what they want to do! So let's get down to brass tacks. Your children, from their point of view, have excellent reasons for getting their needs met. For example, let's look at a real life situation <u>from the child's point of view</u>:

You are a fourteen year old girl who wants to fit in with the "cool" group at school. Would you rather wear the appropriate dress your aunt bought you, or the rad jeans and tank top (or less) that your boyfriend said makes him think only of you? As a kid, which would make more sense to you?

You are sixteen years old and your dad tells you to clean your room. Would you rather comply and build a deep meaningful relationship with your father or blast heavy metal music throughout the neighborhood to express your individuality and impress your old man with your lack of concern about his imperial rule? As a kid, which would make more sense to you?

Never let your authority blind you to the need for leadership.

John Luther

The rules are defined by the children when the limitations are not clearly defined.

You're a fifteen year old boy and constantly noticing rumblings in your pants. Would you rather split participles and evaluate sentence structure for your English teacher or go over to Bob's house and evaluate "babes" in super slow motion on the VCR? As a kid, which would make more sense to you?

You're twelve years old and starting to hate school. The same, boring stuff again. Your best friend offers to let you try pot for the first time. She tells you it helps her deal with the lame stuff in school. Do you sneak off to the bleachers or go to class? As a kid, which would make more sense to you?

You're a ten year old girl and you believe you can never please your parents. Whatever you do they always nag you to improve on something. Now dad wants you to clean up the kitchen. You could get the job done as quickly as possible or you could take control and work at a snail's pace. You know it will really get his goat, and it feels good to make his life as miserable as your life is. As a kid, which would make more sense to you?

You're a fifteen year old girl and you just had a nuclear blow up with your parents. You run away from home to the arms of your stud muffin. He assures you that you have been seriously wronged and that your parents will never understand your maturing needs and they only think of you as a little girl. Stud muffin holds you safely and agrees that you are an adult. In fact, you are very mature, even womanly. He helps you feel safe and tells you that he loves and respects you. He touches you in a very exciting way and lets you know that he too has mature needs. Do you tell him that you need to go and talk things out with your parents or do you fall into his arms and mask your pain with your fantasies? As a kid, which would make more sense to you?

All things being equal, people do what they want to do! Our job as parents is to influence our child's thoughts so that they include our choices in their behavioral options. This is done by implementing consistent Must Rules into the family. We need our children to internalize our values.

Maybe Rules are a waste. They lead to nagging, anger, and dishonesty. Families tend to have 90 percent of their conflict around the Maybe Rules. This conflict weakens the ties within the family. If you are not going to be consistent with your rules, why should your children?

NORMAL FAMILY INCONSISTENCIES

Please allow me to be a fly on your wall. It is 7:00 PM and your family is just finishing up dinner. "Whose turn is it to do dishes?" you inquire. "I've got dishes tonight" Dana moans (place your child's name here). You explain, "I've got a lot to do, boy am I behind on my stuff." You plead, "So get the dishes done as soon as possible. I still want to make brownies for Tommy's class tonight."

"Sure," Dana moans again.

Now you're off and running. You have a load of laundry to start in the garage and papers to find in your bedroom for the meeting tomorrow. (Plus Tommy's class brownies) "No more procrastination, it all has to get done," you tell yourself.

At 7:05 you are on your way to the garage and you spy the empty kitchen. "Dana," you bellow, "Get to work on your chore."

"OK mom, I'm on my way," she yells back sounding innocent.

At 7:06 you can't believe you have to go out to the car to get the laundry soap. At 7:10 you are rushing back to your room to find those damn papers, "Dana, you never brought in the laundry soap from the car ... Do I have to do everything?" Your voice echoes around the house.

"OK mom, I'll get it right after the dishes are done."

At 7:15 you're up to your elbows in boxes of papers when the phone rings. With teenagers in the house, you long ago learned that the phone is rarely for you.

"Mom, it's Aunt Sara ... she needs to talk with you."

You pick up the extension phone. You tell your sister that the number she needs is on the bulletin board in the kitchen. But you will happily get it for her, implying that she should have copied it down yesterday when she was visiting. You dash to the kitchen. To your surprise you are alone in the kitchen. Your kitchen help is parked on the couch watching TV. "Hold on Sara, Dana!" you yell, "get on the dishes, I still need to make brownies for Tommy's class tonight."

"In just a minute, the show is almost over," Dana replies.

Not wanting a scene, you already have enough to do, you try to be reasonable, "OK honey, right after the show, I'm counting on you." You give your sister the number you tried to give her yesterday.

7:20 and you're back to the paper chase. The sound of sibling abuse catches your ear. You drop everything to investigate.

"Mom, Tommy is in the way of the TV. You said I could watch the show before I go do the dishes."

Tommy is not happy with anything, "You always let Dana pick the show, how come she always gets to hog the TV?"

"Tommy are you done with your homework?" you ask pointedly. "Almost, mom. But I need help ..." He whines.

"You don't need help Tommy, you go take a look at your homework, and I'll come help you in a few minutes, I have to find a very important paper and still make brownies for your class."

"Mom shhhhh, I'm trying to watch the TV, it's almost over."

"I'm sorry honey, Tommy go to work on your homework. We're bothering Dana ..."

Tommy throws a pillow at Dana.

"Mom!" Dana erupts.

Your voice is harsh towards Tommy, "You go to your room <u>right now</u> before I get angry, I have too much to do to play this silly game tonight." You are muttering as you head for the garage, "I still have to make brownies ..."

The garage is a quiet sanctuary. Moving laundry along seems comforting.

It is 7:35 and back through the house you go. You're astonished. "Dana, what are you doing?"

"I'm looking in the TV paper, why?"

"You can't watch TV. You have the dishes to do." You're feeling your blood pressure rise behind your eyes.

"I know, I'm not stupid you know!"

"How come the dishes aren't done, I still have brownies to make tonight!"

"I don't care about any stupid brownies, I'll get the dishes done," Dana snarls.

"When?!!!" You scream.

"I'm going right now, why are you so upset. You are always doing stuff for Tommy, why yell at me?"

At this point you head for your boxes of papers. You are so angry you could bust. Dana is in the kitchen slamming pots around making sure you know she is mad at you. Tommy is in his room yelling over and over, "Don't get this, I need help!"

Wow! Just writing this down tired me out. I have told this type of story to thousands of families over the years. Regularly I hear, "Were you at my house?"

This story is an example of how many people live their family life— conflict to conflict. Only when mom gets angry *enough* does Dana go and do her chore. What a mess. There is no discipline. Dana knows that she can push her mom only so far then she may (or will) get punished. *Dana does not believe her mother until her mother is angry. This is a major point, Dana does not <u>believe</u> her* *mother until her mother is angry.*

After pushing the limits of the envelope for thirty-five minutes, Dana feels like a victim. "I'm going right now, why are you so upset. You are always doing stuff for Tommy, why yell at me?"

We will return to Dana in a few moments, but first let's learn that only parents can break rules.

ONLY PARENTS CAN BREAK A MUST RULE

When I bring this up in a family therapy session the kids love this and the parents look concerned while they reevaluate my clinical skills. But, I am positive ... only parents can break a rule.

What is a rule? It is an equation that looks like:

One Rule = Child's Behavior + Parent's Behavior

A rule is an If/Then statement. If you do [Child's Behavior] then this will happen [Parent's Behavior].

Almost every family has this (maybe) rule: "No running in the house."

One Rule = *No running in the house* [Child's Behavior] + Parent's Behavior

If your child runs in the house what happens? One mother was very frustrated during an early family therapy session. "Look Dr. Phil, I just don't understand why it is all that hard. I should be able to say, "Don't run in the house," and the kids should just do as they are told!"

I understand the sentiment, but the reality is that, *All things being equal, people do what they want to do!* So, if your child wants to run in the house and only sometimes they earn a negative consequence, why wouldn't they continue getting their needs met? (running in the house) Our job is to influence the *all things being equal* part of the statement. We need to impart information that makes our rules become their rules.

Most parents try this through logical nagging. "Don't run in the house or you will fall and hurt yourself!" or "Don't run in the house or you will knock something over!" For those of us who have internalized the rule, this makes lots of sense. But, to a child who uses their own envelope of understanding, "If I want to get there quicker, run!" Our nagging makes little sense to them.

With, "No running in the house," you really have only half a rule, the child's part. We all know that a child will interpret this to their advantage.

"But mom, I was in a hurry."

"Dad, you don't understand, I had to answer the phone."

"You never yell at Tommy for anything, why me!"

"Mom told me to go right to my room and do my homework." (This kid is good!)

For the rule to be effective it must have the child's part and the parent's part. In long hand it looks like this: If I catch you running in the house, you are breaking a Must Rule. I as a loving parent follow Must Rules 100% of the time. So, if you run in the house I must send you to your room for ten minutes. Even though I would like to explain my well founded parental decision, I will keep it to myself, for now, and give you what you have earned.

Boy, what a mouthful! In equation form it is much easier to see:

No Running in the house = **If** you run in the house, **Then** you earn ten minutes of sitting on your bed.

One Rule = Child's Behavior + Parent's Behavior
One Rule = **If** (child action) + **Then** (parent action)

This makes it very simple to understand. If you run in the house you earn time sitting on your bed. Who is responsible? Who initiated the rule breaking? The child is responsible. Did the parent have a choice about the consequence? Not one bit. The parent honors the child by being honest. The parent honors themselves by being honest.

If you throw a rock straight up into the air and it comes straight down on top of your skull, are you mad at the rock? Maybe at first, but it is a very easy leap of thought to get from, "I threw the rock up in the air and it came down on my head" to "I hit myself on the head with a rock." In the same way, it is very easy for your child to learn that, "My mom tells me that if I run in the house, she will send me to my room for ten minutes," to "I earned ten minutes of restrictions because of my behavior." The child gains nothing by being mad at the rock or the mom. However, the child gains something very important from the If/Then. It is important that she learns that her mother is an honest person. This is no small point. If your child knows that you are an honest person then she knows that she can count on you and your wisdom.

Must Rules are followed through 100% of the time. So, we need to be very careful about what the Must Rules are.

No Running in the house = **If** you run in the house, **Then** you earn ten minutes of sitting on your bed.

One Rule = Child's Behavior + Parent's Behavior
One Rule = **If** (child action) + **Then** (parent action)

At this point in a family session, a bright child usually smirks out, "But what if the house is on fire, do I have to go to my room and DIE?" At this point we have to teach children to weigh the If/Then statement. "Are you willing to earn ten minutes of room restrictions in exchange for running out of a burning house?" This is not as silly as it initially sounds. We have to make this type of decision on a regular basis. If I speed in my car I can get a speeding ticket. Am I willing to get a speeding ticket in order to get to work five minutes earlier? Am I willing to get a speeding ticket to get my beloved to the hospital to deliver a baby?

If I go over the speed limit, do I expect myself to look down at the speedometer and say, "oh golly whizz, I'm going four miles over the speed limit, I better skedaddle to the police station and pay my fine." (I doubt if the police even have a form to fill out in the event that someone turns themselves in for a speeding ticket.) The real question is, do I monitor my own behavior and place limits on myself? If I find myself going over the speed limit, do I take responsibility for my behavior and reduce my speed? Have I internalized the rule? Is it a rule that I have agreed, within myself, to follow? Many adults have not truly internalized the rules. An example is the driver who is angry with the traffic cop who issued the ticket. Assuming the cop didn't lie and just gave out a bogus ticket, why are adults angry with the cop? He was being honest about the rules:

45 Miles per hour = **If** you are caught driving over 45 miles per hour, **Then** you earn a speeding ticket.

One Rule = Driver's Behavior + Traffic Cop's Behavior

Who is being honest and who is not? I point this out because over the years I have seen many adults that blame the rock for falling on their head. They have not learned their own responsibilities. The following statement came from adults during initial sessions:

I hit her (wife) because she didn't listen.

My boss is always telling me what to do!

I didn't mean to wreck the car, I just had too much to drink.

I didn't call my mother on Mother's Day because she always nags at me for not calling.

It is imperative that we teach our children that they are responsible for their behaviors. By doing so we give them life tools that will make the rest of their lives easier and more creative.

DANA AND THE DISHES

A few moments ago we were flies on the wall of Dana's house. Her mom had lots to do. Find some lost paperwork, move laundry along, and make brownies for Tommy's class. But what a mess occurred from 7:00 to 7:35 PM. The time line went as follows:

7:00 PM	The family dinner finished with this conversation. "Whose turn is it to do dishes?" "I've got dishes tonight." Dana moaned. You explained, "I've got a lot to do." You pleaded, "So, get the dishes done as soon as possible. I still want to make brownies for Tommy's class tonight." "Sure," Dana moaned again.
7:05 PM	"Dana," You bellowed, "Get to work on your chore." "OK mom, I'm on my way," she yelled back sounding innocent.
7:06 PM	You're at the car bringing in the laundry soap.
7:10 PM	"Dana, you never brought in the laundry soap from the car ... Do I have to do everything?" Your voice echoed . "OK mom, I'll get it right after the dishes are done." Dana stated.
7:15 PM	Sister called. "Hold on Sara, Dana," you yelled, "Get on the dishes, I still need to make brownies for Tommy's class tonight." "In just a minute, the show is almost over," Dana replied. Not wanting a scene, you tried to be reasonable, "OK honey, right after the show, I'm counting on you." You gave your sister the number she should have gotten herself yesterday.
7:20 PM	The sound of sibling abuse caught your ear. You dropped everything to investigate.
7:35 PM	"Dana what are you doing?" "I'm looking in the TV paper, why?" "You can't watch TV. You have dishes to do." You felt your blood pressure rise behind your

eyes.

"I know, I'm not stupid you know."

"How come the dishes aren't done, I still have brownies to make tonight!"

"I don't care about any stupid brownies, I'll get the dishes done."

"When?!!!"

"I'm going right now, why are you so upset? You always are doing stuff for Tommy, why yell at me?"

Let's look at this scenario from the stand point of a Maybe Rule. In a Maybe Rule, the child knows that their parent's mood has a lot to do with the letter of the law. If mom is in a good mood, then the letter of the rule is, "it is OK to push the envelope." If mom is in a bad mood, you better straighten up and fly right. The child also knows that they probably have very little to do with mom's moods. Work, spouse, and the rest of the family influence mom much more then any one kid. So, if mom is in a bad mood and making you fly straight, it isn't because she cares or loves you as much as it is because she is pissed! In the mind of the child, they have no responsibilities, they are just the victim of mom's (or dad's) sour mood. The child sees Maybe Rules as:

One Maybe Rule = Child's Behavior + Parent's Mood

In the above story, Dana got her needs met, watching TV. All things being equal, would a child rather watch TV or wash the dishes? Then, when mom's mood went sour, Dana felt unjustly persecuted but went and did the dishes before her mother did something rash and unreasonable like, give her dishes for a week or remove her TV privileges. Dana saw herself as the victim. If her mother took away her TV privileges she would be upset and say something like, "What, am I your dish slave? All I ever do around here is work!!!"

Mom would also be upset. All she wanted to do was get the long list of stuff done that she was responsible for. She doesn't like fighting with her daughter. And, on top of everything else, now her daughter was going to make everyone miserable for a day or two because she felt so misused.

So, where did it all go wrong? At 7:10, 7:20, or 7:30? Actually it went into the giant family dumpster of inconsistency right from the beginning. Right at the beginning? When mom *lied* and allowed her daughter to *lie*.

Let's review the first moments of the problem:

It is 7:00 PM and your family is just finishing up dinner. "Whose turn is it to do dishes?" "I've got dishes tonight." Dana moans. You explain, "I've got a lot to do, boy am I behind on my stuff." You plead, "So get the dishes done as soon as possible. I still want to make brownies for Tommy's class tonight." "Sure," Dana moans again.

Now you're off and running. You have a load of laundry to start in the garage and papers to find in your bedroom for the meeting tomorrow. (Plus Tommy's class brownies) "No more procrastination, it all has to get done."

At 7:05 you are on your way to the garage and you spy the empty kitchen. "Dana", you bellow, "Get to work on your chore."

"OK mom, I'm on my way," she yells back sounding innocent.

This five minute period is a tissue of Maybe Rules. Unclear rules lead to conflict. You read the rule your way while your children read it their way. You are trying to be easy going and reasonable, while your children see you as weak minded and naggy. The problem is that mom is not saying what she really wants to say. Mom's words are open to interpretation by the child.

If this family had a Must Rule that read something like (child's behavior defined), "Chores are done before anything else is done," or "After dinner, the kitchen chore must be done within 20 minutes." This takes the interpretation out of the picture. Of importance here is that a Must Rule defines acceptable behavior, decreasing family conflict. When mom states, "I've got a lot to do ... so, get the dishes done as soon as possible. I still want to make brownies for Tommy's class tonight." This is nagging. It tells the child that you do not believe that they are up to the task at hand. It is a subtle attack on their character. This statement lowers the expectations your child has for herself.

Your life is much less complicated if your children believe you when you talk to them. Unfortunately, many parents actually teach their children to "read between the lines" when they talk. In a grocery store I observed a mom say the following statements in a five minute period.

"I know you want a candy bar but you can't have one today, OK?"

"Stop running, OK?"

"You will have to hold my hand ... Are you listening to me when I speak to you?"

Her two children paid very little attention to her. They did not believe their mother's words. By using the word "OK" she was asking permission, from her children, for the rule to exist. What kid would give such permission? The statement, "You will have to ..." is a threat. If the mother meant the rule it would have been an <u>action</u>. "Please hold my hand, your behavior is not acceptable." Ordering, even politely, by using the word "please," is an action that restricts the child's behavioral envelope. Parents who use threats lose their children's respect. If the family's basic trust is constantly undermined, members of the family will feel unsafe.

MUST RULES BUILD A FAMILY

Must Rules define for our children the limitations that we expect them to adhere to. These limitations, the envelope, help our children feel safe. One young lady of fourteen summed it up clearly:

> I told my boyfriend that I wouldn't have sex with him. He was very upset with me. He told me that he loved me and that he thought that I loved him. I do love him, you know? At first I told him that I couldn't sleep with him because my folks have a Must Rule about sex. The rule is *No sex until marriage*. I think it is a dumb rule, but I figure that I live with them so I have to follow the rules. I told them that I would. Well, my boyfriend broke up with me. He said it wasn't about the sex, just that he had to date other people. Then, one night I was thinking, he didn't really love me, if he did he would want me to be safe. My parents are kind of old fashioned but I know they love me. They want me to be safe.

Must Rules empower children. The Must Rules set the limits for the child to feel safe within. Over the years I have worked with lots of gang kids. One thing about gangs that has always impressed me is their steadfast rules. Most of the kids I have met in gangs are lonely lost souls. The restrictiveness of the gang makes the kids feel safe. And the rules of the gangs are amazingly restrictive.

Rebecca was fifteen years old when I met her. She was a referral from the emergency room of the local hospital. She was admitted to the emergency room with a broken sternum and three broken ribs. Her left lung had collapsed. Rebecca never told anyone who beat her. The police were pretty sure it was the fellow members of

Home is home, though it is homely.
English proverb

Home is where the heart is.
Pliny the Elder

the gang she hung out with. Following weeks of care in the hospital she was released to the custody of her parents.

<u>During our third session:</u>

Dr. Phil: Your parents seem very worried about ...

Rebecca: Not really, it's just an act. They have to worry about me.

Dr. Phil: Are you in any danger?

Rebecca: No, I don't think so ... why?

Dr. Phil: I read the hospital report, you were in pretty bad shape.

Rebecca: Yeah, I thought I was going to die ... The doctors put me back together. I'm OK now.

Dr. Phil: How come you got so beat up ... Aren't you protected?

Rebecca: Sure I am. I'm full in ... But I really @#$%-up!

Dr. Phil: What does that mean?

Rebecca: You know, I'm not ratting on anyone.

Dr. Phil: I'm not asking for evidence, I'm just trying to understand your world.

Rebecca: I slept around and the sergeants found out. I was so stupid. With AIDS and all, I know better. I can't believe I @#$%-up!

> A consequence is an **If-Then statement**. **If** you are a member of the family **Then** you get the positive effects, consequences of being a member of the family

As it turned out, Rebecca's gang had a "Must Rule." *You can only sleep with fellow gang members.* If you break the rule you are punished with a line beating. In a line beating you pick six gang members to punch you or kick you in the chest. If you wish to show the gang that you are really remorseful you stand with your back to a wall so the beating is intensified. Rebecca was so concerned that the gang would disown her for her transgression she stood against a brick wall after picking the biggest kids to punch her in the chest.

When I asked Rebecca's mother about her daughter's problem with the family, she said, "Rebecca is just out of control. She hates to follow even the simplest of rules." Over six months of family therapy Rebecca "bought" herself out of the gang and returned to her home and school. Rebecca and her mom did wonderfully with consistent Must Rules at home.

With discipline we restrict behaviors to teach true freedom to our children.

POSITIVE CONSEQUENCES OF BEING A MEMBER OF YOUR FAMILY: HOMEWORK ASSIGNMENT #2

For every behavior there are consequences. Some of these consequences are positive and some are negative. But, there are always consequences. Some small, some gigantic. But, there are always consequences. This fact is usually difficult for children to comprehend. Often kids will tell me, "My parents have to love me," or "Mom has to let me play basketball." Most children see the world as very black and white, with them right in the center of everything. But, when I ask them about how other kids live they are able to pull from their memories sad stories of unfair parental misconduct.

Kent was fourteen years old when I met him. His parents were concerned about his attitude concerning school and job completion. Overall he was doing relatively well. When I asked him about his world he said, "My parents are boarish. All they want to talk about is me getting into college." When I asked him about the worst family life he had direct knowledge of he became soft spoken, "I know this girl, her parents drink every night. She told me that she has to put her dad to bed all the time because he passes out on the couch."

Children as young as three notice what they have. One little tyke squealed with joy as he told me about his bedroom. "I got a bed with superman sheets. My dresser is white and I'm not allowed to color on it. The floor is soft. When I fall out of bed I don't break my head much."

What do your children get for just being a member of the family? What are the positive consequences for being lucky enough to be a member of your family? Please rack your brain, then list the positive consequences below:

Quick Reference Guide

Consequence: Something that logically or naturally follows from an action or condition.

If-then statement: A statement of cause and effect.

_____
_____
_____
_____
_____
_____
_____
_____
_____
_____
_____
_____
_____
_____

Second marriage is the triumph of hope over experience.
                                    Samuel Johnson

In my office I have a large blackboard. Early on in family therapy I ask the family to brainstorm on this question of positive consequences. At first the families are hesitant, "You mean like special stuff, like a trip to Disneyland?" But I explain that I am talking about the stuff that makes membership in the family comfortable and safe. The "what you get from the family, just for being a part of the family." Most families easily fill the large blackboard with positive consequences.

The Knapp family consisted of mom and dad and their two children, a girl fourteen and a boy nine. They brainstormed the following positive consequence list:

> Food, love, help with homework, mom's spaghetti, rides to soccer, a bed, living room furniture, a bathroom, toilet paper, electricity, a refrigerator, a nice home, friendship, movie night with popcorn, soda pop - sometimes, clothes, medical insurance, hopefully a car when I'm sixteen, hugs, grandparents, a pet rabbit, two cats and a dog, soccer cleats, birthday parties, birthday presents, Christmas, special food, back rubs, laughs.

This is a pretty typical list. All the good stuff that makes being a member of the family worthwhile. A consequence (positive or negative) is an **If/Then statement**. **If** you are a member of the family **Then** you get the consequences of being a member of the family. Most parents are surprised at how many positive consequences there are for simply being a member of the family.

MUST RULES SHOULD BE WRITTEN DOWN

All things being equal, children do what they want to do. To help them survive this fact we need to make the limitations on our children's behavioral choices clear cut. We need to make these limitations so clear cut that there are no loop holes for our children to strangle us, or themselves, in.

If a rule is so important to your family that you are going to insist that it is followed 100% of the time, write the rule down. All Must Rules should be written down. The act of writing the rule down causes two major things to happen.

1. Parents force themselves to think clearly about their objectives while planning the rule.
2. All family members have a ready reference to the rules.

The Armondo family consisted of a mother and her eleven year old daughter, Allison. Mrs. Armondo was adamant that she did not want to keep a written list. "I work for the state," Mrs. Armondo explained, "All day long I have half-wits quoting regulations to me, I don't want my daughter exposed to that." Three weeks later Mrs. Armondo's opinion had changed.

> Over the weekend Allison and I had an awful argument. Last session I made it very clear that she could not watch TV if her homework was not done. Well, Saturday afternoon she was watching some stupid television program when I asked her about her homework. To make a long story short, we both got very angry with each other. She said that she could watch TV if it was a weekend, and I became furious. She was manipulating my intentions. Believe it or not, this argument went on until Monday night!

It was Allison's contention that homework was a school day limitation. Mrs. Armondo saw homework as very important, no matter what the day. She expected homework to be completed before any entertainment. Mrs. Armondo found that if the rule was not written down and clearly understood, Allison remembered the discussion to her advantage. All things being equal, children do

There are those who understand everything till one puts it into words.
Francis Bradley

what they want to do.

Mr. Depue was insistent that writing the rules down was a waste of effort. His four teenage sons thought it would be a good idea. Following a long family discussion it was clear to all, that the sons were concerned that their father arbitrarily manipulated family rules to get his way. All things being equal, parents do what they want to do.

Initially, writing the rules down, usually in a family meeting or over a relaxed meal, lets it be known what the family expectations are for each member of the family. The Must Rule list is a living document. A rule that may be very important when Bobby is three, is irrelevant when he is eight, and down right silly when he is thirteen.

I advise that parents post family rules in a centralized location. Most use the refrigerator or the family message board. Some families feel that the family rules are a private matter and "post" them inside a cupboard or in a binder. One very artistic family made a papier-mache mock up of two biblical tablets and mounted it by the kitchen table. The family had a running joke, "God gave us ten commandments and mom and dad added eight more." One family used the family rules as a screen background on the computer. It was labeled, "Rules to Live By." Their son changed it one day to, "Rules that Byte." Find a place that works for you. Life will become easier the moment you post your family rules.

WHO WRITES THE MUST RULES?

Parents write the family rules. Most families find that if the process includes the children, family harmony is heightened. But, parents write family rules. Parents run the family.

Let's take a moment to define what I mean by parents. It is not as simple as you might think. With divorces and step families, live-in lovers and roommates, it can be a little tricky to decide who is the writer of the family rules. The rule of thumb is, "Involve all adults who take on the responsibility of caregiving for the minors of the family." It is important that all parental types agree to work together to enforce the family rules. Without this agreement, the children are in an emotionally unsafe environment. I am very adamant about this. If your co-parent is not participating in the process of developing and implementing family rules, then they are undermining the process.

HOW DO YOU WRITE A MUST RULE?

This is not a simple process. I have never seen a mother and a father just sit down and write out a list of rules. Family rules define who we are as a unit. Who we are is constantly growing and chang-

The very bond of love.
Shakespeare

ing. The family rules list is a snapshot of where we are at this moment in time. Most families find that the family rules list is relatively consistent over the years, once it is developed.

To start writing a family Must Rules list you have to ask yourself when does your family need a rule? As you recall, most families have millions of preferences (Maybe Rules) that work most of the time. Not everything needs to be, or should be spelled out to the final period. That would be too confining for the family. It would crunch individuality and creativity.

When do you need a Must Rule? The simple answer is when you have a problem that is not being remedied by a preference. For example: If your son leaves his towel on the bathroom floor, a simple reminder is probably sufficient. But, if after numerous simple reminders the towel on the bathroom floor has become a problem that is building into conflict, you need a Must Rule.

You need to write a Must Rule to keep yourself from getting into the situation of nagging, yelling, sulking or vengefully punishing your beloved child. You write Must Rules to build family harmony, security and safety. You start by looking inward and openly talking with your co-parent(s). What do you worry most about for your children? What limitations do your children need placed upon them at this time to protect them from themselves or others? These worries are the seed of your Must Rules. There are two basic reasons for a Must Rule:

1. A problem has developed that is causing unnecessary conflicts within the family.

   Examples: Rules about sibling arguments, personal property rights, and sharing common areas of the house.

   ·Usually developed following a problem.

2. To prevent endangerment to health and safety of family members.

   Examples: Rules about drugs, sex, and swimming pools.

   ·Usually developed prior to a problem raising its ugly head.

Once you need a rule, the rule must be written down clearly. Remember, all things being equal, children do what they want to do, so Must Rules must be written clearly. Rules must be written at the level of understanding of each member of the family.

Must Rules are written about behaviors. Parents cannot control thought, they are only able to influence behaviors. Must Rules must be enforceable. You and your co-parent must agree to enforce the

Must Rule. If you do not, you do not have a Must Rule.

A Must Rule has two parts, the kid part and the parent part. The kid part is a concern you have for the health and safety of your child. The parent part is the negative consequence that will be earned if the kid commits a rule breaking behavior. As you recall from earlier, One Rule = Child's Behavior + Parent's Behavior. We start writing the Must Rule from the concern, the Child's Behavior side, the problem. In a few pages we will look at an actual parental concern from my home. I will go through the actual process of how my wife and I developed a usable Must Rule.

Let's look over the shoulders of two families. One with young children, one with teenage children. The behavior problems are very similar. The Must Rules will have to be worded differently, but the central parental concerns are the same. At the core, each family is developing similar family values. However, with toddlers, the Peachtree family is worried about potty training, while the Swartz family is worried about pot smoking.

Mr. and Mrs. Peachtree have been married for seven years. Both work in sales and have a difficult time juggling their work schedules with their home life responsibilities. Mr. and Mrs. Peachtree have two active and healthy boys, Chuck, age 3 1/2 and Barry, age 5. Their biggest complaint about their home life is the never ending need to juggle their lives to meet the needs of everyone else in their world.

Peachtree Family Main Parenting Worries:

Barry bites Chuck when he is angry.

Chuck kicks Barry as retaliation or just because he wants to.

Both boys are rough on the family cat, Kat.

Both boys fight naps.

Both boys fight going to bed.

Chuck still needs a diaper when he sleeps.

Barry is a very picky eater.

Chuck cries when he is dropped off at the preschool.

Mr. and Mrs. Swartz have been married for seventeen years. Both work in sales and have a difficult time juggling their work schedules with their home life responsibilities. Mr. and Mrs. Swartz have two active and healthy boys, Gary, age 13 1/2 and Larry age 15. Their biggest complaint about their home life is the never ending need to juggle their lives to meet the needs of everyone else in their world.

Swartz Family Main Parenting Worries:

Larry punches Gary when he is angry.

Gary kicks Larry or breaks Larry's belongings as retaliation.

Both boys are rough on the family cat, Silvester the Lame Hearted. (Named by the boys three years ago. The cat has still not adjusted to his name.)

Both boys fight homework.

Both boys fight bedtime.

Gary still needs reminders about hygiene.

Larry is a very picky eater.

Both boys complain a lot about school.

Both boys have a bad attitude about household responsibilities.

When asked to complete the 3M's list both families had no Must Rules and over sixty Maybe Rules. The Swartz family had two Minor Rules, one for hygiene, another for piano practice.

Next, the two families went over their worry lists to formulate the Must Rules "first draft." The concept of writing a must list was new to both families. So, the first draft was a learning experience for the parents to start defining what they believed their families should ideally look like.

Peachtree family Must Rules: First draft (Child Behavior):

No hitting

No biting

No kicking

Must take a nap

Must eat all your food

Must go to bed

Must do what you are told the first time you are told

Swartz family Must Rules: First draft (Child Behavior):

No hitting

No kicking

No pot in the house

Must do what you are told the first time you are told

Must go to school without complaining

You must do your chore everyday

No complaining about your food

Must go to bed when told to

In my office I find the number one concern parents have is about the "attitude" their children exhibit.

> My kids fight all the time!
> The kids are in constant competition for our (parental) attention.
> My child's attitude just irks me, he acts as if he was put on this earth to be catered to!
> Whatever I say ... it's always an argument!

I assume these statements hit a cord with you too.

What is the seed of these parental concerns? Most parents start with words like "attitude," or "grumpiness." But if you dig a little deeper, we get to *choice*. Our children *choose* to act "grumpy," "angry," and/or "mean." This fact of choice is very important. If my son screams, "Josh is driving me crazy!" I can advocate for him and softly question, "What did you choose to do?"

Hopefully he says something like, "I walked away so his immaturity did not negatively influence my behavioral choices."

On the day he states such a wonderful thing I will know that I

All violence, all that is dreary and repels, is not power, but the absence of power.

Ralph Waldo Emerson

am a *good* dad, but unfortunately, that day has not yet come, so I am left in the caring teaching mode of dad.

Ethan usually states something like, "I told him he was an idiot and went back to my room!"

This allows me to parent with expansive questions such as, "You chose to call him names?" or "Did that help you get your needs met?" (Remember, parenting is a long process made up of many little steps.)

What we are talking about is how our child *chooses* to interact with his world. Must Rules should be written from the concern, the parental worry.

Poorly worded (Child's Behavior) rule:
   (pointing out what not to do)

      No Yelling at your brother
      No acting mean
      No rolling your eyes
      No being mad at your brother

This focuses on what not to do. Your child already knows what not to do, but finds that it is kind of working to solve their present situation. Our goal should be to expand their behavioral choices, giving them more options to try in similar situations in the future.

Well worded (Child's Behavior) rule:
   (pointing out choices)

   For younger children:

      If you hit ...
      If you bite ...
      If you kick ...

   For older children:

      If you choose to hit ...
      If you choose to act disrespectfully ...
      If you choose to not care about another's feel-
   ings...

This form of rule wording leads your child to look at options. As discussed earlier, your child needs to ask himself, *What can I do differently?* This is empowering your child to channel his creative thoughts towards solving a problem. This is a character building, self esteem developing, emotional growth process. (See, ADVOCATING FOR GOOD CHOICES in Chapter 3 for further discussion.)

**You are or you will become
what you think about the most.**

I wish for our children to think the most about personal choices, and self control. Our children can only build this skill by practicing it over many years with the aide of our parenting.

WHAT REALLY COUNTS FOR YOU: HOMEWORK ASSIGNMENT #3

Often I meet families that are in crisis over stupid stuff. I am not being flippant, it is a fact. Many families fight over stupid stuff. The Sewell family were at each other's throats about curfew. Mrs. Sewell believed that her children needed to be home at 8 PM on school nights and 10 PM on non school nights. The three Sewell children ganged up together and were adamant that 8 and 10 were just arbitrary times. "It makes no sense to be home at 8 o' clock. It's just a number. Why should mom care if I come home safe, even if it's 8:15?"

By the time I met the family the feud had grown into a civil war. Mrs. Sewell resigned from office saying in anger one night, "I give up, you kids just come and go as you please, see if I care!" During the first session I explained about perspective, what really counts. This family was only looking at the clock on the wall, not the big picture of what mom wanted for her family.

Mrs. Sewell started the meeting stating, "I said 8 o' clock, it should be a simple rule to follow, 8 o'clock." By the half hour mark mom was talking about individual responsibilities. "It is important that my children are honest. If they need to be home at 8 o'clock, I expect them to be home at 8 o'clock. It is a trust factor." When Mrs. Sewell moved the focus away from the time to the "meaning" of the family value, her children saw her love and concern. Prior to that point the teens only saw parental domination.

Must Rules need to be written with your family values in mind. Our goal is to write rules that develop internal values within our children, not just blind obedience to parental power. Our goal is to develop individuals with discipline.

Homework assignment number three is for you to write a list of the values you want to "instill" in your children. For example, Mrs. Sewell was having difficulty getting her teens out of bed on Sunday. It was important to her that her children go to church every Sunday. While struggling to write a Must Rule for church attendance, the Sewell family wrote the following Must Rule variations over a six week period.

Week 1: You must go to church on Sunday.

Outcome: Yelling and bad feelings, little compliance.

Week 2: You will go to church. If you do not, then you do not get your allowance.

Outcome: Yelling and bad feelings. The kids chose no allowance.

Week 3: Mom wants you to go to church every Sunday. If you do not, you have to do chores around the house from 8 AM to noon on Sunday.

Outcome: Yelling and bad feelings, chores throughout the week became a family sore point. Teens who went to church acted angry.

Week 4: Mom wants you to go to church every Sunday. If you do not, you have to do chores around the house from 8 AM to 3 PM on Sunday.

Outcome: All teens went to church. Time at church was uncooperative and behavior sullen.

Week 5: You only have to attend church if you want to.

Outcome: Mom spent her time at church concerned that she was not helping her children's souls.

Week 6: Sunday night is family dinner. Each member of the family brings God to the table in the form of a story, picture, or through a poem.

Outcome: Mom went to church alone. Sunday evening was warm family time.

Over the next month, one at a time, the children asked their mother if they could attend church with her. Sunday dinner became an event. Skits were performed, songs were sung.

By the sixth month point, Mrs. Sewell told me, "I used to get so angry. The more I pushed church, the more my children protested. I

There is no better test of a person's character than their behavior when they are wrong.

Quick Reference Guide

Arbitrary
1. Determined by chance, whim, or impulse, and not by necessity, reason, or principle.
2. Based on or subject to individual judgment or preference.

Logical
1. Of, relating to, in accordance with, or of the nature of logic.
2. Based on earlier or otherwise known statements, events, or conditions; reasonable.

Consequence
1. Something that logically or naturally follows from an action or condition.
2. The relation of a result to its cause.
3. A logical conclusion or inference.

have good children. When I let them make the choice, in their own way, they each made a good choice. We now talk about church as a family activity. I think I was getting my kids to resent God by forcing church on them. My girls are talking about working at the summer church camp.

If we share our values, our true beliefs, without forcing our thoughts down our children's throats, our children will examine our beliefs. This examination is the starting point of self discipline.

In Chapter 2 we first saw the following list:

-to be happy
-to be safe
-to be smart
-to go to college
-to grow up and have a great life
-to be whatever he wants to be
-to have a better life than my parents
    could give to me
-to do well in school
-to be self confident
-to be thoughtful and kind
-to give to people less fortunate than herself
-to know and love God
-not to get into major trouble
-to have integrity
-to be honest

HOMEWORK ASSIGNMENT #3:

As you recall this list was compiled when I asked parents, "What do you want for your child?" Over the last 80 or so pages you have gathered a lot of information about your children and your role in their caregiving. So, I ask you now to take a pause and ask yourself this question again: "What do you want for your child?" What values do you want your children to learn from you? Please write your answers below

_____
_____
_____
_____
_____
_____
_____
_____
_____

_____
_____
_____
_____
_____
_____
_____
_____
_____
_____
_____
_____
_____
_____
_____
_____

It is a wise child that knows his own father.
Homer

The above list is your "guide" to the values you wish to impart to your children. This list will help you to focus on the "big picture" of what you want for your family.

CHILDREN LEARN BY CONSEQUENCES

Silence is sometimes the severest criticism.
Buxton

Two year old Cody is playing in the sand box. He throws the toy truck into the air and, without warning, he is taught one of life's lessons. We all had to learn it. No, it is not that gravity suck; It is that for many behaviors there are natural consequences. Little Cody learns, to his amazement, that the natural consequence of throwing a toy truck straight up into the air is that you will be hit on the head by that same truck. The cause and effect along with their punishment (discomfort) teaches Cody not to hit himself in the head with toy trucks. This is usually learned quickly. It takes much longer for a child to learn that hitting her playmate in the head is inappropriate.

A child psychiatrist named Dr. Rudolph Dreikurs pointed out the importance of consequences in child rearing. Dr. Dreikurs wrote widely on how parents can use consequences to help their children develop healthily. He defined consequences as being either Logical or Arbitrary.

Logical consequences are the outcome of a particular behavior. Throwing a toy truck straight up causes a pain on the top of your head. There are two forms of logical consequence, **natural** and **parent made**. A logical consequence that naturally occurs is by far the easiest for a child to understand. It makes sense even to young children, that if you leave your bike in the front yard, a "bad guy" may steal it. A parent made logical consequence is one devised by the parent to teach a lesson in a cause and effect fashion. This cause and effect is not as easy for a child to comprehend.

If nine year old Samantha leaves her bike in the driveway and someone steals it, that would be a natural logical consequence. The problem with it is its severity when it does occur. Samantha may leave her bike in the yard for years, rain or shine. She may get a smaller natural logical consequence way before the bike is stolen, rust. Natural is wonderful, but not always practical. Her parents may implement a Must Rule that reads: *If Samantha leaves her bike anywhere other than in the garage or school bike area, then her bike will be grounded for one week.* This is a parent made logical consequence. Her parents believe that Samantha will learn the value of her bike if they simulate her bike being stolen for one week.

An **arbitrary consequence** is imposed by an outside force (i.e. parent). It is not a logical consequence for a particular behavior. In this example an arbitrary consequence would be if Samantha earned an extra chore for leaving her bike in the front yard. Arbitrary consequences are not logically based. It is often very difficult for children to comprehend the cause and effect of an arbitrary consequence.

With an arbitrary consequence it tends to be much harder to elicit cooperation from children, and it is usually down right impossible to get cooperation out of teenagers. For example, Allen was very upset that he had to pay part of his allowance for bickering with his sister. This caused the family great turmoil. Allen felt so wronged by the arbitrary consequence that his overall behavior deteriorated. Because Allen felt that the arbitrary consequence was "unfair" he felt persecuted by his parents. Allen's mother and father accidently opened a hornet's nest. When the rule was reevaluated, Allen's mother and father saw that their arbitrary consequence felt extremely harsh because he was trying to save money for computer camp. The "no bickering" consequence was changed to, "**If** you use words as a weapon **Then** you owe the family a chore to make the world fairer." This change in the consequence encouraged family harmony and it worked well for this family. When Allen "bought into" the arbitrary consequence, the consequence worked.

Because arbitrary consequences lack logic, they should be the last choice when developing consequences. Family harmony and cooperation is greatly increased with natural consequences. The goal of imposing a consequence is to teach cause and effect. This is made more likely when your children feel that they are being treated "fairly."

PUTTING IT ALL TOGETHER

Over the last thirty or so pages we have covered the process of making a *home* out of a house. At this point most parents find the information interesting but less than practical. How do we go from the theory to the reality of daily living? In this section we will put it all together.

First, a quick overview. If any of the following statements are not clear to you, flip back and reread that section. Our job now will be to take this mass of data and form it into a usable tool.

- Parenting is a full time job.

- The primary role of a parent is *to parent*.

- Punishment has limited value in parenting.

- Discipline builds character.

- Children learn better through active learning.

- As parents, we want realistic freedom for our children.

- Limitations, the envelope, is very important in helping children learn what freedom is.

- Must Rules are followed 100% of the time.

- Maybe Rules are parental preferences.

- Minor Rules are under the control of your child.

- Maybe Rules cause most of the conflict in daily family life.

- All things being equal, children (people) do what they want to do!

- Parental inconsistencies are viewed by you, the parent, as times when you are trying to be reasonable and understanding.

- Parental inconsistencies are viewed by your children as a parental mood disorder that can often be manipulated by them.

- Children who live with Maybe Rules tend not to believe you really mean what you say until you are approaching feelings of anger.

- Only parents can break a Must Rule.

From a Christmas card:

Dr. Phil,
Hope all is well with you and your family. Things are good for us. Sally is still testing the waters of adulthood. I had to pick her up from school the other day because she had thrown up all over her 2nd period class. Come to find out the alcohol she had for breakfast didn't sit well with her.
Thank God for <u>Must Rules</u>!
Thank you for all you have taught us!

Philip Copitch, Ph.D. 139

- One Must Rule = Child's Behavior + Parent's Behavior.

- One Must Rule = If (child's action) + Then (parent's action).

- Must Rules build a family. These limitations, the envelope, help our children feel safe.

- The positive consequences of living in your family and following the rules are one-heck-of-a-good deal.

- A consequence (positive or negative) is an If-Then statement.

- Must Rules should be written down.

- Parents write the Must Rules. Having your children involved in the writing is a wonderful way to teach your children about the thought process that went into developing them and your reasons behind the rules.

- Writing a Must Rule list is difficult. It is a living document that grows and changes as the family grows and changes.

- Must Rules are written with the parental concern as the focal point.

- Must Rules reflect your family values.

- Logical consequences are the outcome of a particular behavior.

- There are two forms of logical consequences, natural and parent made.

- An arbitrary consequence is imposed by an outside force (i.e., parent).

- Arbitrary consequences are not logically based. Because arbitrary consequences lack logic, they should be the last choice when developing consequences.

Chapter 5 looks at specific problem areas and how to deal with each of them. In Chapter 5 we will "solve" many specific problems, some that will seem very close to your own personal situation. For now, I want to tell you a story about my boys.

THE DEVELOPMENT OF A MUST RULE

I am blessed with two happy and healthy boys, Ethan is nine and Joshua is six. About five weeks ago school started. Ethan was looking forward to fourth grade because he would finally get letter grades. He saw the switch to letter grades as an elementary school rite of passage. No longer would he be a little kid getting checks and pluses, he would now be a big kid, earning real grades. Joshua was looking forward to first grade with great expectations. He liked the idea of having a full day of school. He liked the idea of two recess periods and a lunch period. He didn't talk much about academics, focusing mainly on recess and lunch.

During the last week of summer, my beloved, Geri, brought up in passing, "School's almost here. Summer, went by quickly, I really dislike school mornings." When I didn't hear the importance of her statement, she stated, "Phil, have I ever told you how hard Ethan is to get up on school days?" She had despair in her voice. She sounded resigned to her belief that Ethan was hard to wake up on school mornings.

I slipped into my Dr. Phil role and asked, "What is the Must Rule on getting up?" She thought for a moment and explained, "I wake him up at seven o'clock. He is very hard to wake up. At 7:05 I try shaking him, I tickle him, I beg him to get up. Some mornings he is just so tired he can't wake up. Other mornings he pretends to be sleeping. I can't always tell. (She started to get angry) I find myself harping on him to get up, then he moves slowly ... I find myself getting frustrated and angry most mornings. School mornings are a real battle, I hate them!"

"Ger, it sounds like you have a real problem." I noted.

"I sure do." She pointed out, "Ethan is so hard to wake up on school mornings. And when it gets cold, he is even harder. He gets all rolled up in his blankets and pretends he doesn't really hear me! It makes me so angry when he pretends that he doesn't hear me!!!"

In my mind I was thinking:

> Define the problem
> Whose problem is it?
> What are the rewards and/or punishments for the person involved with the problem?
> Is it a real problem? And if so, do we have a Must Rule to cover it?

"Geri, I can't deal with it right now, let's deal with it on Friday (family night dinner)." The real world has demands on Geri's time and mine. So, the only thing that could be done was to "appoint" the problem. For now, "the problem" was resting on my back. I would carry it until Friday night's dinner. It is important to note that not every problem needs to be attacked at the moment you become aware of it. At the same extent, you can't let problems linger with open ended statements like, "Let's deal with it later," or "Not now, I'm busy." By making an appointment to start to deal with the problem, I kept the importance of the problem alive, but postponed the needed diagnosis and treatment. It was now my responsibility to initiate dealing with the school morning problem. My wife knows that I am an honest person and I would follow through with dealing with the problem on Friday. This allowed her to put the problem on hold and to feel my love and respect for her.

Friday dinner arrived and the family sat together for a little bit longer to make it more of a special meal. It is a family norm that we linger on Fridays, enjoying good food and good fellowship. Often we have a guest or two. It is not unusual for Friday night dinner to be two or more hours long with dinner being a small portion of the time.

For me, the best family dinners end with books piled on the dining room table, scraps of paper strewn around. I like it when dinner becomes a search for information. When one family member disagrees with another, and a search for knowledge ensues. Then out come the reference books and the fun begins. "How much does a rhinoceros' horn grow in a year? What is the largest building in the country? What is meant by largest building? Are you talking tallest, usable floor space, or cubic feet of a building? All these and many more have been postulated and "proven" around our dinner table.

It is common for a family member to say on Wednesday, I have a great trivia question for Friday night ... I'll stump everyone!" This looking forward to the warmth of the family is very important. It allows warm family feelings to go with us all throughout the week, even on the most hectic school mornings.

This Friday night I announced that I had a few questions to bring up. As the plates began to empty I postulated, "What do you get for being a member of the Copitch family?" This is the "positive consequence list" we discussed earlier.

I had pencil in hand and a scrap piece of paper. After a few moments the answers started to fall like snow flakes. Each family member reminded others of the positives of our family. Each of us looked at the question from our own perspective. This was the list we wrote:

> School, a house, our dog, food, allowance, live on a mountain, my rat, great cooks, bedroom, warmth, bikes, enough money, TV, refrigerator, tree house, band aids, telephones, medical insurance, help with homework, silverware, a kitchen, Grandma, vacations,

camping equipment, pictures, camera, books, computer, watches, I don't have a watch, telescope, loved by mom and dad, talk with mom and dad, presents, soccer, JuJitsu.

I continued: "We get all this great stuff," holding up the list, "When we are on target and living fairly as a family. Mom and I have a concern. Next week we start school and we are worried about how the school mornings should go. We can remember that some school mornings were less then fun last year. I don't want to have anything other than wonderful mornings for us this year."

Then came the barrage of "it's other people that cause me a problem."

Ethan:	Mom gets me up too early.
Josh:	Ethan is a meanie in the morning.
Ethan:	It's mom's fault, she gets me up too early.
Mom:	I don't get to decide when school starts.
Josh:	Let's not go to school, OK?
Ethan:	School is fun! I just can't get up in the morning.
Josh:	School is funner for me. I get two recess and a lunch!

Interrupting I proceeded, "That may be so, but ... it is not fun for Mom when she has to get you two up and on target every school morning. Last year mom and I made a mistake, we shouldn't have let mom be in charge of your behavior."

Ethan seeing where this was leading, rolled his eyes and slumped into his chair. "But, mom gets me up too early!"

"That may be so, but who is responsible for getting you up and downstairs for breakfast?" I questioned.

"Mom is." Ethan whined back.

"How can mom get you to do something you don't want to do?"

Ethan's face got stern, "I knew it. I have to get myself up in the morning."

"Makes sense to me, you're going into fourth grade," I encouraged.

"I think I should still wake you up," mom stated. "Between me and your alarm clock you should be able to know it is time to get up, but I can't stand over you and *nag you awake.* You must hate that as much as I do."

I was planning to post the new Must Rules on the refrigerator. But, there was so much art taped on the doors, along with soccer snack lists, and honey do lists I thought the index card I rewrote the new rule on would not get noticed.

I also knew that I was scheduled to write this section in a few weeks, so out of curiosity, I made copies of the new rules and gave a copy to each child.

I was curious to see what the boys would do with their copy.

It's been five weeks and both boys still have the rules posted. Josh placed his in a position of honor, by his bed, "So I can see it when I need it," he explained.

Ethan's list seems to migrate around the house. When I asked him why he keeps moving it, he explained, "I don't want Josh to forget it." I don't quite understand this statement, seeing Josh is so happy and easy going in the morning. I guess it's a big brother thing.

In late January, Ethan had a writing assignment from his fourth grade teacher. He was charged with writing a paragraph about, something he considered stupid.

Stupid

The stupid rules are having 25 minutes. I have 20 minutes to eat and 5 minutes to get in the car. If I am not down the steps by 7:25 I get early bed. If I'm not in the car by 7:45 I get 1 chore a minute. I think they are stupid because I like to sleep late and I am not a morning person.

Ethan's teacher gave him 10/10 for his homework assignment. His mom commented that his penmanship still needs improvement and I noticed that he took responsibility for his behavior.

Ethan looked surprised, "No ... I didn't mind you waking me up a hundred times a morning. I really hated you pulling my covers off when it was cold." Then he smiled and said, "What time do I have to get up by? <u>What's the last second?</u>"

At this point we were taking the problem off mom's shoulders and we were looking for appropriate shoulders to place the responsibility on.

I explained:

We all have to figure out how we get ourselves downstairs to breakfast our own way. I find that my morning shower is very helpful in finding the "on" switch to my brain. Some people, like Josh, just seem happy to wake up in the morning. I wish I could wake up as easily as you do Josh.

We all have to do it our way. But, we have to do it. Let's work backwards from when school starts and let's see the time line that we have to follow.

The family calculated the following school morning facts. (Note, the kids really got into this. At age six and nine, organizing and estimating skills are growing. Flexing their newly developing skills was fun for the boys):

School starts at 8:20 AM.
Car needs to leave house at 7:45 AM to get us to school on time.
It takes at least 20 minutes to comfortably eat breakfast, clean up your place setting, and put shoes on.
Boys need to be downstairs by 7:25 AM.
It takes at least 25 minutes to get up, get dressed, comb hair, and wash up.
Mom needs to wake up boys at 7:00 AM.
Growing boys need about 10 hours of sleep to grow healthy and learn lots at school.
Bedtime should be no later than 9:00 PM.
It takes an hour to get ready for bed, get story time, and hugs and snuggles.
We head upstairs at 8:00 PM.

This led to the If/Then discussion. We focused on the behavior. Who needs to do what and when. The new Must Rule that we started the first day of school was:

School Mornings

[School night Bedtime: 9:00 PM]

Mom wakes boys at:	7:00 AM
Boys must be downstairs, dressed and hair combed:	7:25 AM
All in car, seat belt on:	7:45 AM
Goal is to get to school by 8:10 AM. School Starts at:	8:20 AM

[Note: The above is a list of parental preferences. It only looks at the child's side of the "rule," so technically there is no rule as of yet.]

Two new Must Rules:

[Written by mom and dad but openly discussed with all involved.]

If not downstairs with hair combed and dressed by 7:25 **Then** 1/2 hour early bed next school night.

[A logical consequence (parent made) for being too tired in the morning. If you are tired in the morning, you need to get more sleep.]

If not in car, seat belt on by 7:45 AM **Then** for every minute you're late you earn 1 chore.

[A logical consequence (parent made) for forcing a parent to take responsibility for getting a child into the car. It seems fair that a parent should get "repaid" with a little help for having to "work" to get a child on target.]

Over the first two weeks of the school year a few notable things occurred. The night before school started, Geri confessed to mixed feelings about our new, untested Must Rules. She sheepishly said, "I know this (Must Rules, advocating) works at your office, but Ethan is so tired on school mornings ... What if he can't wake up?"

"He seems to be pretty smart, I think he will figure out a way to get his needs met," I advocated.

Over the first few days, Geri was very happy with how the morning routine was going. Still she questioned, "I like that the mornings are going so well, but ... what happens when the boys aren't as excited about getting up?"

"They seem to be pretty smart, I think they will figure out a way to get their needs met," I advocated.

By the second week both kids had earned an extra chore for being late getting their seat belts on. Geri raved about how well the boys handled their consequences.

Tuesday of the third week, "it" hit the fan. Ethan was late getting down to breakfast. Later on that day, Geri called me at the office. "Ethan is furious with you, well us. He was 23 seconds late for breakfast. He says he is going to talk with you.

"Really," I tried to joke scared.

"Yeah, he said you never said that 23 seconds counted. He is really upset, he is sure that I am not following the Rule. I told him that 23 seconds is late."

Later that day, Josh called me at the office. (With mom's permission.) "Dad, Ethan is really mad at you. He said that you wrote a stupid rule. He is very mad. He said that you forced this dumb rule on him. Dad, he is really mad at you."

"Josh," I questioned, "are you having a problem with the new Must Rule?"

"No."

"Great," I reassured, "I'll see you later ... Bye."

When Ethan and Josh got into the car following JuJitsu class the next day, they talked nonstop about their day. (Josh mostly talked about recess and lunch.) After fifteen minutes I asked Ethan, "I hear you missed part of soccer practice."

Ethan:	Yeah, I had to leave early, I had early bed.
Dad:	How did it go?
Ethan:	Mom said that I had a choice, I could skip soccer practice or go until 7:00.
Josh:	Did I tell you about the hot dogs at school? They are small, like half hot dogs, but you get two.
Dad:	Two? Wow ... Ethy, I hear that you're mad at me.
Ethan:	Yeah ... but I know what you're going to say.
Dad:	What am I going to say?
Josh:	Ethan said "stupid" a lot ...
Ethan:	Josh, I'm talking to dad now ... I know you're going to tell me that 23 seconds past 7:25 is 23 seconds late, even if it is just a little late.

Dad:	How do you know me so well?
Ethan:	Mom told me.
Dad:	Mom seems to be pretty smart. (I advocated.)

What Ethan didn't know was that Geri and I talked about early bed and soccer practice. We talked about how at this soccer practice the kids were going to scrimmage another team, and that it would be fun for Ethan. We discussed that 23 seconds was only 23 seconds. We discussed that if Ethan earned early bed on a JuJitsu night, he would have to miss his JuJitsu class. We talked about how all of this was important. We also talked about the fact that Must Rules are not preferences. That 100% of the time is very clear. If school mornings were not a problem we would not have written a Must Rule to deal with them. We discussed our choice to be honest people and our desire for our children to know that our word is important to us. We talked about how our children need to be responsible for their own behavior. What a wonderfully loving time we spent talking about our "big picture" for our family.

I cannot emphasize it enough, write as few Must Rules as you can and follow each Must Rule 100% of the time.

MINOR RULES BUILD CARING ADULTS

A Minor Rule is a Must Rule that the child is solely responsible for. It is the enlargement of the behavioral envelope that allows your

Chapter 5

Controlling Chaos: Basic Parenting 101 In Action

"Why don't I get it back till I'm 18... Does it take you <u>that</u> long to read it."

5. CONTROLLING CHAOS: BASIC PARENTING 101 IN ACTION:

Now we can get down to brass tacks. In this section we will roll up our sleeves and look at the specifics of dealing with some common problems within families. This section is not self contained. It is built on the information contained in the first four chapters of this book. The intent is to give you usable examples of how you can actively deal with a full range of common problems.

Not every problem or conflict can be covered in the following pages. I have tried to show a diverse cross section of problems, with the intent of letting the reader see the How's and the Why's of parenting. I encourage you to read all the subsections of this chapter so you can experience ways to implement the first four chapters of this book.

The assumption is made that you have read and understood the first four chapters. As you will see, only with that understanding will you be able to get the most out of this section.

Before we get started, I want to take a moment to talk about the process of intent. In this section it is important to keep our focus on the child's needs while at the same time we try to build cooperation within our parent/child relationship. Recently I was reading, at bedtime, *The Little Prince* to my boys, I came across the following:

> He (the Little Prince) found himself in the neighborhood of asteroids 325, 326, 327, 328, 329, and 330. He began, therefore, by visiting them, in order to add to his knowledge.
>
> The first of them was inhabited by a king. Clad in royal purple and ermine, he was seated upon a throne which was at the same time both simple and majestic.
>
> "Ah! Here is a subject," exclaimed the king, when he saw the little prince coming.
>
> And the little prince asked himself:
>
> "How could he recognize me when he has never seen me before?"
>
> He did not know how the world is simplified for kings. To them, all men are subjects.
>
> "Approach, so that I may see you better," said the king, who felt consumingly proud of being at last a king over somebody.
>
> The little prince looked everywhere to find a place to sit down; but the entire planet was crammed and

I am only one, but still I am one. I cannot do everything, but I can still do something. I will not refuse to do the something I can do.

Helen Keller

A conflict is the moment of truth in a relationship — a test of its health.

Thomas Gordon,

It is always helpful to learn from your mistakes because then your mistakes seem worthwhile.

Garry Marshall

The word mentor is an example of the way in which the great works of literature live on without our knowing it. The word has recently gained currency in the professional world, where it is thought to be a good idea to have a mentor, a wise and trusted counselor, guiding one's career, preferably in the upper reaches of the organization. We owe this word to the more heroic age of Homer, in whose *Odyssey* Mentor is the trusted friend of Odysseus left in charge of the household during Odysseus's absence. More important for our usage of the word mentor, Athena disguised as Mentor guides Odysseus's son Telemachus in his search for his father.

American
Heritage Dictionary

obstructed by the king's magnificent ermine robe. So he remained standing upright, and, since he was tired, he yawned.

"It was contrary to etiquette to yawn in the presence of a king," the monarch said to himself. "I forbid you to do so."

"I can't help it. I can't stop myself," replied the little prince thoroughly embarrassed. "I have come on a long journey, and I have had no sleep..."

"Ah, then," the king said. "I order you to yawn. It is years since I have seen anyone yawning. Yawns, to me, are objects of curiosity. Come, now! Yawn again! It is an order."

"That frightens me ... I cannot, any more ..." murmured the little prince, now completely abashed.

"Hum! Hum!" replied the king. "Then I—I order you sometimes to yawn and sometimes to—"

He sputtered a little, and seemed vexed.

For what the king fundamentally insisted upon was that his authority should be respected. He tolerated no disobedience. He was an absolute monarch. But, because he was a very good man, he made his orders reasonable.

"If I ordered a general," he would say, by way of example, "If I ordered a general to change himself into a seabird, and if the general did not obey me, that would not be the fault of the general. It would be my fault."

The Little Prince
by Antoine de Saint-Exupery
Harcourt, Brace and World, 1943

What is the intent that you have for parenting? I hope that you are able to look at the big picture of family life. Only by looking at the big picture will you be able to keep your perspective during the trials and tribulations of your real minute to minute life.

Parents are not their children's "bosses," we are their mentors.

The king on asteroid 325
by Ethan Copitch, age 9

ANGER, YOUNG CHILD

My son is only three but he seems to be very angry. He hits other children and sometimes bites. The preschool uses Time Out but he doesn't seem to be getting any less angry.

Young children tend not to have the words to express their feelings. So their feelings are played out as actions. It is every parent's goal to teach their children to deal with life's conflicts. To that end the following word list has been devised by Dr. Myrna Shure, a developmental psychologist. These word combinations have been found necessary for your child to understand prior to being able to teach her about the consequences of her behaviors. These words, on the surface, look simple to understand. However, I have found that many children, as well as some adolescents and adults use the words freely but do not understand the concepts that these word combinations represent.

Section one: Basic word examples

Is/Is Not

"Mr. Thompson <u>is</u> a man"

"The ball <u>is not</u> square."

Or/And

"Is the cat a boy <u>or</u> a girl?"

"The puppy is small <u>and</u> fuzzy."

Some/All

"Are <u>some</u> of the flowers green or are <u>all</u> of the flowers green?"

"Did you clean <u>all</u> of your room or <u>some</u> of your room?"

To handle yourself, use your head; to handle others, use your heart.
Donald Laird

Same/Different

"Does the truck look the <u>same</u> as the car or <u>different</u> than the car?"

"Is a rat the <u>same</u> as a guinea pig or <u>different</u>?"

Might/Maybe

(The words <u>might</u> and <u>maybe</u> are combined with <u>if</u> and <u>then</u> to clarify consequential thinking. The words <u>might</u> and <u>maybe</u> are used to help children define other people's likes and dislikes.)

"<u>If</u> I hit Susie she <u>might</u> slug me in the head."

"<u>Maybe</u> Bobby likes apples. <u>If</u> I ask him he <u>might</u> tell me."

Before/After

"Is dinner <u>before</u> bedtime or <u>after</u> bedtime?"

"Would you like to take a shower <u>before</u> dinner or <u>after</u> dinner?"

If/Then   (If/Then are the most basic consequential words.)

"<u>If</u> you go to the store <u>then</u> you will not be able to go to the park."

"<u>If</u> you break the plant stem <u>then</u> what will happen to the plant?"

Why (How come)/Because

"The rock hurt my toe <u>because</u> I dropped it."

"<u>Why</u> do you think we should go to the library?"

"<u>How come</u> you are crying?" (<u>How come</u> is easier on the listener to hear than the word <u>why</u>.)

Fair/Not Fair (Unfair)

"What is a <u>fair</u> way of giving out the cookies?"

"It is <u>not fair</u> to do it that way."

"It is <u>unfair</u> to me if you talk when it is my turn to talk."

SECTION TWO: DEALING WITH INTERPERSONAL CONFLICT.

There are four steps that people use to deal with conflict. Each step allows the child to use consequential thinking to deal with a conflict. These same basic negotiation skills are used in million dollar deals as well as on the playground to get a child's personal needs met.

1. Define the problem (conflict).
2. Note own and others' feelings.
3. Brainstorm solutions to the conflict.
4. Evaluate consequences to brainstormed solutions.

Following you will find a few examples of how parents inadvertently get caught up into solving their child's problems. This takes away conflict management practice from their child.

Common parent trap #1:

Child: Tommy hit me with a rock!

Mother: When did he throw the rock at you?

Child: During recess.

Mother: I'll talk to your teacher tomorrow. She should be watching her class during recess.

In this small example we see a caring mother helping her child. Without knowing it, she is limiting her child's conflict management skills. This mother solves the problem for her child. The child is not involved in taking care of himself.

Common parent trap #2a:

Child: Tommy hit me with a rock!

Father:	Did you hit him back?
Child:	No. He would kill me.
Father:	He won't kill you. You have to stand up for your- self.

Common parent trap #2b:

Child:	Tommy hit me with a rock!
Mother:	What did you do?
Child:	I kicked him in the knee.
Mother:	It's not nice to kick people. Only bad people kick or hit. I don't want you to act like that. Don't you want to have friends?

The parents in #2a and #2b imposed consequences on their children. By telling their child what to do or what not to do they ignore their child's point of view. Both children were told what to think. They were not encouraged and supported to think for themselves. Without this practice, children are limited in consequential thinking skills.

TEACHING CONSEQUENTIAL THINKING (CAUSE AND EFFECT)

I now, years later, have fond memories of my children learning to tie their shoes. At the time however, I believe I hated shoes. I remember having non positive parental thoughts of "How long can it take to put on a shoe," or "Once your shoes are on, KEEP THEM ON!" The core of the problem was that learning to tie one's shoes is a long process and my schedule never seemed to have that much time in it.

Recently, I was at the roller rink, another seven year old's birthday party. After my sons laced up and were gone, I noticed three different moms lacing up their children's roller skates. One mom was upset and told her eight year old, "Let me do that for you, you're so slow ... the party will be over before you get to skate." At that moment I was glad I took the time to let my children learn independent shoe tying. If I had tried to tie my childrens' shoes, the oldest would say, "Hey dad, what are you doing? I don't have Corn Flakes for brains," while the youngest would say, "Dad, I'm not a baby, why don't you go play with the adults."

I bring this up because it takes time to teach consequential thinking to your child. But it is time well spent. Most parents mis-

Retribution breeds retribution. Shun it, and you will live beyond you tormentors.
  Hebrew proverb

takenly believe that their children will learn consequential thinking as they grow up. The fact is, <u>consequential thinking is learned</u>. Part of what we can do for our children to help them traverse life's conflicts, is to teach them cause and effect earlier than later.

There are four parts to the process:

1. Define the problem (conflict).

Help your child find words that define how he feels about the problem. Resist telling your child what he should think. Let him tell you his thoughts. Let him mull his thoughts over outside of his mind without you judging his thoughts.

2. Note own and others' feelings.

Ask your child to teach you what *he* thinks are his and the other person's feelings about the conflict. Resist telling him what to think. Resist judging his thoughts.

3. Brainstorm solutions to the conflict.

Brainstorm with your child about alternative ways to deal with the situation. The use of the question, "How could you do it differently?" has served me well over the years to help elicit additional thoughts.

4. Evaluate consequences to brainstormed solutions.

Go over each brainstormed idea in a cause and effect process. "If you did (idea) then what would happen?" Let your child try each If/Then cause and effect on for size. It is more important for you to focus on how your child is thinking rather than the specific outcome. Our goal is to teach our children to develop the technique of conflict resolution.

The most positive side effect of this conflict resolution process is that your child will find your counsel helpful. As he gets older he will choose to come to you to ask for your counsel. In this way you get to teach your child when he is really ready to learn, when he is asking for your emotional support and direction. This is a long term process. You can't teach a dolphin to jump out of the pool by dangling a rope twenty feet above his head. Children learn conflict management by successive approximation.

BED-WETTING

Quick Reference Guide

Enuresis: Voiding into the clothing or bed not due to a general medical condition. Bed-wetting.

My six year old son is fighting going to summer camp. He really wants to, but he is fearful that he will wet the bed. He tends to have one or two accidents per week and summer camp is for two weeks. What can I do to help my son stay dry throughout the night?

My family has a huge secret. My son is sixteen years old and still wets the bed. We went to the doctor when he was eight or nine, but received little help. We have tried everything! When my son is upset he says that he sees himself as a freak and that he hates himself. My husband and I used to tell ourselves that he would grow out of it, but it hasn't happened yet.

Let's start our discussion by dispelling some myths. The following statements are parental myths that I have heard over the years. None, I repeat <u>none,</u> are based in medical or psychological fact:

"Children who wet the bed are less intelligent." Not true.
"Children who wet the bed are lazy." Not true.
"Children who start to wet the bed after having nighttime bladder control have been sexually molested." Not true (but extreme emotional stress can lead to problems of bed wetting).

There are four major reasons for bed-wetting, each will be discussed individually:

1. Medical conditions that influence bed-wetting.
2. Emotional conditions that influence bed-wetting.
3. Developmental conditions that influence bed-wetting.
4. Behavioral conditions that influence bed-wetting.

WHAT IS BED-WETTING?

Enuresis is the medical term for voiding into the clothing or bed not due to a general medical condition. Most children begin to stay dry throughout the night between the ages of 24 and 36 months. A large portion of children are unable to stay dry throughout the night until age five. It is not unusual for nighttime "accidents" to occur until age twelve. In most cases this should not worry parents. If an accident happens, parents should encourage their child to take age appropriate responsibility for their hygiene and their bed. It is best to be supportive but non-concerned. Most children are very uncomfortable if they have an accident. Many children are worried about their parents' reaction, while others are very hard on themselves for many internal reasons. A few children are very frightened that they are physically ill, reverting back to infancy, or "broken" in some way. Warm assurance is by far the best way for their parents to help them.

Bed-wetting is a common childhood problem. It is imperative that parents do not ridicule their children about bed-wetting. Over the years I have counselled numerous adults that relate their present (low) level of self esteem directly to being ridiculed for bed wetting. On the opposite side of the coin, parents should not alienate the bed-wetting child. Treating your child with disgust or anger can harm his emotional stability.

It is common in our society for us to blame the child for bed-wetting. This is unfortunate and narrow minded. Research shows us that only 75 percent of four-year-olds and 85 percent of five-year-olds stay dry at night more nights than not. It is common for adolescents and even adults to wet the bed occasionally. Researchers have reported that 4 percent of adolescents and 1 percent of adults wet the bed. Over the course of childhood, 1 out of every 4 children between the ages of four and sixteen have a problem with bed-wetting. It is more common for boys to have bed-wetting problems than girls. When we look at the population of children who wet the bed after the age of four we find two groups, continuous and discontinuous bed-wetters. **Continuous bed-wetters** continue to wet the bed from infancy. **Discontinuous bed-wetters** re-initiate bed-wetting following at least three months of dry beds. Eighty percent of bed-wetters are continuous.

MEDICAL CONDITIONS THAT INFLUENCE BED-WETTING

Research shows us that 1-2 percent of bed-wetting is caused by a medical condition. Some medications as well as physical ailments can influence the urinary nerves and/or bladder capacity of your child. The most common medical cause of discontinuous bed-wetting is a urinary tract infection. A urinary tract infection can be easily diagnosed by your child's medical doctor. Even though medical conditions are rare, it is a good practice to start with a general physical by your child's medical doctor. In rare instances your child's doctor may refer you to a pediatric urologist.

EMOTIONAL CONDITIONS THAT INFLUENCE BED-WETTING

Research shows us that approximately 20 percent of discontinu-

Think of the bladder as a water balloon

To keep the water in the balloon you have to hold the opening very tightly.

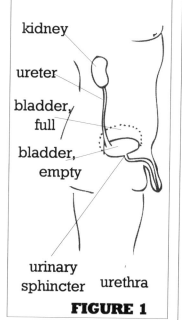

kidney

ureter

bladder, full

bladder, empty

urinary sphincter   urethra

FIGURE 1

ous bed-wetting is do to an emotional problem. Most of the time, the emotional trauma to the child is readily noticeable. Changes in the family such as a new baby, moving, or starting school are common causative agents. It is common for this type of emotional baggage to elicit nightmares and anxiety at bedtime. Often the child will be "extra" clingy during the day. Many children will outwardly verbalize their concerns, "You don't love me now that that baby showed up." Or, "It's scary to sleep in this new house!"

Parental assurances go a long way to solving this transitory problem.

DEVELOPMENTAL CONDITIONS THAT INFLUENCE BED-WETTING

Developmental conditions are the most common cause of bed-wetting. In this situation we are specifically talking about your child's physical bladder development. Although your child may have no medical condition that causes bladder control problems, the bladder, like all parts of the body, grows and develops at its own pace. Many children, simply put, just do not have the storage capacity to hold what their kidneys can make throughout the night.

Think of the bladder as a water balloon. The balloon expands as more liquid is placed into it. To keep the water in the balloon you have to hold the opening very tightly. The same is true with the urinary bladder. It expands as the kidneys send it more urine to store. There are a ring of muscles at the bottom of the bladder that keeps a tight squeeze on the urethra, the tubing the urine travels through to exit the body. See Figure 1, top. Rather than injuring the urinary bladder, the body voids itself.

The bladder is made up of elasticized tissue. Because of this the capacity can be stretched over time to allow for greater storage capacity. The urinary sphincter is mostly muscle tissue. As with all muscles of the body, the urinary sphincter can be strengthened over time. See Figure 1, bottom.

Most children have a urinary bladder capacity of about 12 ounces. With a capacity of 12 ounces a child tends to have little trouble storing urine throughout the night. Many children with a urine capacity of 4-10 ounces will have difficulty storing urine throughout a normal night's sleep.

I will discuss a bladder training method later in this section.

BEHAVIORAL CONDITIONS THAT INFLUENCE BED-WETTING

We have spent a lot of time discussing the individuality of your children. When children are awake they "show" us their personality and temperament. Children also sleep like individuals. Some children are light sleepers, others can sleep through a train wreck. This individuality is known as your sleep pattern. If your child's sleep pattern is such that he sleeps deeply, he may not notice the internal mechanism that tells him to wake up and go empty his bladder. The problem is often confounded when a deep sleeper is equipped with a small urine storage tank and/or a weak sphincter.

There are two major behavioral conditions that influence bed-wetting. Children who do not notice the internal signal to wake-up to use the toilet are the first kind. The second are children who manipulate the family with their bed-wetting. It is rare, but second-ary gain can be a powerful reinforcer if the child is controlling the family situation with her bed-wetting.

The good news is that there is help for children and adults with enuresis.

SOLVING THE PROBLEM OF BED-WETTING

There needs to be a two prong approach to solving the problem of bed-wetting. The first prong is the possibility of a medical solution. The second is a behavioral approach to solving the problem.

MEDICAL INTERVENTION

I have read research studies that have found that 1-10 percent of bed-wetting is due to a medical condition. In my experience the 1 percent finding seems more likely. But, we need to rule out a medical cause first for the simple reason that, if it is a medical condition, our behavioral intervention cannot work. It is important to note that bed-wetting often continues after the medical condition is effectively treated.

If your child has a urinary tract infection your child's medical doctor will most likely prescribe an antibiotic or antiviral and some cranberry juice. Make sure you follow the prescription. It is important that the medication is taken for the prescribed period of time, even if your child is feeling better before you are out of the medication.

If your child is the anxious type, many medical doctors will prescribe tricyclic antidepressants with Imipramine. Research shows us that tricyclic antidepressants work well for 1 in 3 children. Unfortunately, when the antidepressant is discontinued, the bed-wetting tends to return quickly.

BEHAVIORAL INTERVENTIONS

Parents have had great success in stopping bed-wetting by using behavioral interventions. There are four parts to this process. Your child may need all four or just one or two.

1. Your child needs to feel safe within the family.
2. We need to enlarge your child's urine storage capacity.
3. We need to strengthen your child's urinary bladder sphincter.
4. We need to teach your child to notice the "wake-up and go to the bathroom signal" even in a deep sleep.

YOUR CHILD NEEDS TO FEEL SAFE WITHIN THE FAMILY.

I cannot over emphasize the fact that your child needs to share his problems with others within the family. I advocate that your child hear that "we" have a bed-wetting problem. Parents need to advocate for their children. I am sure he feels deep shame due to the bed-wetting. This shame tends to be exhibited as an "I don't care attitude" for older children and adolescents.

I advocate that parents focus on how their child is dealing with the problem versus the problem itself. Depending on the emotional maturity of the child, dealing with the wet sheets and remaking the bed should be a Minor Rule. If your child is not ready for the Minor Rule, the process of taking care of himself should be a Must Rule. One family found the following Must Rule very helpful:

Must Rule: If a bed is wet, the sheets and PJ's must be taken out to the garage before breakfast.

Consequence: If the sheets are not in the garage before breakfast, 1/2 hour chore of folding laundry to help mom with her work.

Must Rule: If you wet the bed, you must shower, using soap, and wash your hair before breakfast.

Consequence: 1 hour of room restrictions for not caring about yourself.

After three years of morning fighting and family anger the above family implemented these Must Rules. After three weeks their teen son asked for the Must Rules to be made into Minor Rules. The parents agreed to try this. After two months of bladder training, described below, this teen went on his first sleep over. This family moved from blaming to advocating for their son's problem. They made sure that he knew that he had a problem but that his parents loved him and supported him.

Bladder size is a family heritage. Most children find it very helpful when their father or uncle tells them that they used to wet the bed. When the child learns that it is not the worst thing in the world and there are ways to solve the problem, their future looks a lot sunnier and a lot less lonely.

Many families try to restrict liquids for some time before bed. This has limited help due to the fact that the human body is mostly water. There is plenty of liquid for your child to urinate with later. I do get concerned when children are limited liquids at dinner. Your child needs plenty of clean water for healthy growth.

WE NEED TO ENLARGE YOUR CHILD'S URINE STORAGE CAPACITY.

Your child needs to have a urine bladder storage capacity of at least 12 ounces to be able to sleep dry throughout the night. Buy a 16 ounce measuring cup. Make sure you get one with 1 ounce lines clearly marked.

Think of the bladder as a water balloon

To keep the water in the balloon you have to hold the opening very tightly.

kidney

ureter

bladder, full

bladder, empty

urinary sphincter   urethra

FIGURE 1

The first thing to do is to teach your child about how his body works. You explain that he has two kidneys and that his kidneys filter waste from his blood. The kidneys mix the waste with water and float the waste in the water to the storage tank called the urinary bladder. Use graphics such as Figure 1. Kids find it fascinating to learn about their guts. Explain that the bladder is like a balloon that gets bigger as more urine gets stored inside. Teach your child that the bladder can grow if it is slowly stretched. And, once it is stretched, it will stay big.

Explain that if his bladder was bigger, he would be able to store all the urine his kidneys could make while he slept. Once that happens, he will not have to let the urine out at night before he wakes up.

Explain that he can make his bladder bigger by slowly stretching it a little bit every day. Most kids find that it is pretty easy and in about a month their bladder is much bigger.

The way to stretch his bladder is to make it hold more urine for a little bit. This is pretty simple. Tell your child that when he feels the need to urinate he should go into the bathroom and get ready. Just as he gets ready to urinate he should stop and hold as long as he can. At first he may only be able to hold for 5 to 10 seconds. However, after a few days he will notice that he can hold it longer and longer, maybe even a minute or two.

Then, when he does urinate, he should do so into the measuring cup. This is so we can keep track of how much urine he can hold. Give your child the responsibility of pouring the urine into the toilet and rinsing out the measuring cup so it is ready for the next time. When he is away from home (i.e., school, friend's house, etc.) he should just practice the holding part and not worry about the measuring.

A chart is kept in the bathroom to keep track of the process. For older kids we tend to keep a calendar and simply log the amount. For younger kids we draw up a chart in the shape of a measuring cup. A copy of the chart I give out at my office is printed here for your convenience. Make copies if you wish.

Make this a team effort. Make it fun. As your child learns about his internal signal, he can hold his urine without being right at the toilet. At first it is best to practice holding right in the bathroom. Daytime accidents are embarrassing and defeat the goal of this activity.

I generally recommend against attaching an external reward to this activity. Your child is getting a lot of reward by conquering a real life problem. I have seen lots of bribery techniques help kids <u>wet</u> the bed for years. (See Chapter 1: BRIBERY DOES NOT WORK)

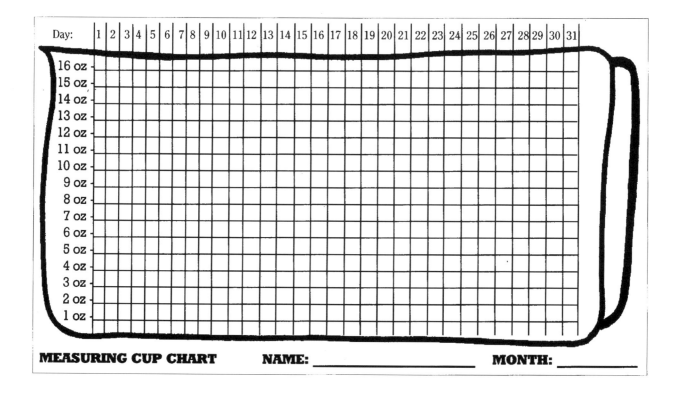

WE NEED TO STRENGTHEN YOUR CHILD'S URINARY BLADDER SPHINCTER

At the bottom of the urinary bladder there is a tube that takes the urine out of the body. This tube is kept closed by a ring of muscles called a *sphincter*. Often this muscle needs to be strengthened.

There are two relatively easy ways to strengthen this sphincter. Many moms may recall this exercise from their own pregnancy preparation.

The first exercise is to start and stop urine flow while voiding. Teach your child to urinate a little then stop the flow and count to 10. Then repeat the process until empty. In only a few weeks the sphincter tends to show great improvement. This can be done in association with the measuring cup as described in number 2.

The second exercise is the Kegel exercise developed by Dr. A. M. Kegel in the 1950s. This exercise can be done anywhere for a total of 20 minutes. The muscles that control the bladder are the pubococcygeal muscles. The exercise consists of tightening the anal sphincter. Simulate preventing a bowel movement. Then relax. Tighten the anal muscle, then relax, and breathe deeply. Repeat 20 -30 times in an exercise set. Do this exercise set 3 or 4 times every day.

By improving the quantity of urine your child can store and the muscle tone of the bladder, your child will find dry nights in his future. Be patient, it takes most children 2-3 months to stretch and tone completely.

WE NEED TO TEACH YOUR CHILD TO NOTICE THE "WAKE-UP AND GO TO THE BATHROOM SIGNAL" EVEN IN A DEEP SLEEP.

When your child is able to store 12 ounces of liquid at a time but he is still having wet nights, I recommend you continue the techniques above and add a fourth method — a bell and pad conditioning device.

Some children sleep so soundly that they do not notice the internal signal telling them to go to the bathroom. A relatively inexpensive device can be purchased from most pharmacies that will help your child learn to notice his internal signal.

The battery powered device is very safe and comes in two forms. One is a special moisture sensitive pad that is placed under your child. The second is a small moisture sensor that is attached to your child's underwear. When the moisture sensor detects liquid an alarm is set off. (Some even turn on a light.) The alarm disturbs your child's sleep enough for him to notice the internal signal ... "Get up and take me to the bathroom!"

Research shows us that in a few months about 70 percent of children benefit from this apparatus. Of this 70 percent group, some 30 percent relapse and need to use the apparatus again.

It has been my experience that parents try the "bell and pad" method too early, looking for a quick fix for their child's bed-wetting. I have found that the "bell and pad" are useful for only a few. Children who enlarge their bladder and strengthen their muscle tone tend not to need it.

FURTHER READING:

A Parents Guide to Bed Wetting Control: A Step-by-Step Method, by Nathan Azrin and V.A. Besalel, Simon and Schuster, 1979

Childhood Encopresis and Enuresis: Cause and Theory, by C.E. Schaefer, Van Nostrand Reinhold, 1979

LYING

For the sake of discussion, I am going to break lying down into three distinct sections:

a. Fabrication
b. Childhood lying
c. Teen lying

In each section we will investigate why kids lie.

FABRICATION

> My five year old is a little fibber. He will create a whole story versus tell the truth. Even when there is nothing to be gained by it. I'm so worried that he will turn out to be an immoral person.

Fabrication is the sign of a young child's emotional and verbal development. Many parents become extremely concerned about the fantasy life their child talks about. Rest assured that fabrication in early childhood is normal and should be encouraged. If your child says to you, "There is an elephant under my bed." Participate in the fabrication. Allow your child to develop his imagination. It is a good idea to ask your child, "Tell me more of the story."

If your child tries to use a fabrication as an excuse, calmly ask what part of the problem is he involved with. Focus on solving the problem, not on how your child wants to avoid his role in the problem.

If your child grows a wonderful imagination it will lead to many new and exciting things for us all. If you think about it, societal change comes from adults asking themselves, "How can I do this differently?"

If fabrication is getting out of hand, tell the story of *The Boy Who Cried Wolf*. Over a few weeks of discussion, young children learn to preface their words with, "I have a story," or "I know a tall tale", or "I want to tell you a shaggy dog story." It is important for parents to remember that

©1997 CoptichInc.com

WHEN STEVEN KING OFFERS TO TELL A BEDTIME STORY.

separating fact from fiction is a learning process for children. Most children master this skill by age seven or eight. Also, if your child is really good at telling tall tales, encourage her to write them down. If a person does strange stuff it is a big problem, but if a person writes about fanciful strange stuff, we call them an author. I wonder what types of fanciful stories Steven King told his parents?

CHILDHOOD LYING

I have tried everything to get my son to stop lying. No matter how hard I punish him he doesn't stop. What can I do? I don't want him to grow up to be a criminal.

As parents we need to deal with the reason children lie much more than the fact that they lie. Many parents are horrified when I make such a statement. One woman at a PTA meeting was indignant,

PTA mother: So, you're saying it is OK that my children lie?

Dr. Phil: No, ma'am. Do you think that I am fat?

PTA mother: No, not really, you are little overweight ...

Dr. Phil: But, ma'am I weigh 300 pounds!

PTA mother: OK, but you wear it well.

Dr. Phil: 300 pounds. Do you know how fat that is? I haven't seen my feet since 1942.

PTA mother: You're not that fat; You have a weight problem I guess.

Dr. Phil: Honestly I don't, I have a food problem. I eat too much. I am fat because I eat too much food.

PTA mother: OK, I guess you're fat, but that's OK.

Dr. Phil: I only bring it up because in our society we do not go out of our way to hurt people's feelings. It is considered rude to call a fat person fat. But, it is the truth. I have noticed that people will protect my feelings rather than tell me the truth. Personally, I like that, but isn't it a form of lying?

Truth is always strange.

Byron

It is twice as hard to crush a half truth than a full lie.

Austin O'Mallery

The point here is that we all lie, children and adults. But, as parents we are so upset when our children lie that we lose track of the big picture. Lying is very difficult for children to understand. There are many types of lies. We have white lies, polite lies, and bold face lies. It is important for parents to help children understand their reason to lie. Only then will the need to lie substantially decrease.

TYPES OF LIES TO HELP CHILDREN COMPREHEND

a. Lies to get you out of trouble (fearful of punishment or rejection, feeling threatened or cornered):

Often children lie to get out of trouble or to avoid getting into more trouble. From the standpoint of the child, lying for this reason is logical. From the point of view of the parent/child relationship this leads to mistrust. It is important that parents focus on the long term nature of their relationship with their child. A parent needs to emphasize to their child that their relationship has to be based on trust and without this trust they will have to constantly second guess each other. I have pointed this out to my children by saying (more than once over the years): "If you are going to lie about such and such, I am concerned. If you are going to lie about something as small as such and such, then when you say, 'Good night daddy, I love you' to me tonight, how will I know something as big as that is the truth?" I leave this as an open ended thought. Over the next few weeks we talk about it many times when life is calmer and feelings are not raw. (This is also a common theme when we talk about, "What is a friend?")

b. Lies to save face (fearful of disappointing others or feeling dumb):

Often children lie to keep from being judged harshly by others. This is often an issue of self esteem. As the child's self esteem grows, this type of lie will greatly diminish. A parent needs to be concerned when their child needs to make themselves look better because they are feeling unsure of how wonderful they actually are.

c. Lies of omission (what mom and dad don't know, won't hurt them):

Many parents have a hard time with this one. Many feel it is OK if they omit part of the facts. But, it is hideous if their child lies to them by omitting part

> Dishonesty, cowardice and duplicity are never impulsive.
> George A. Knight

of the facts.

Many parents *teach* lies of omission to catch their children in lies. For example, if the school calls and tells you that your fifteen year old skipped fifth period, some parents will ask, "So son, how was school today?" This is a verbal ambush. We are setting up our child to lie by using a lie of omission. It is much healthier for the parent/child relationship to state what you know. (See TEACHING HONESTY in Chapter 2) "The school called and stated that you skipped fifth period, what's up?" Honesty is learned. Anything that is learned can be taught. A wonderful teaching method is modeling (see Chapter 4).

Children omit information usually to protect themselves from punishment and to protect their parents' feelings. If your child feels judged by you she will not expose her pain to you.

TEEN LYING

I often tell the following story to parents of teens to illustrate why teens lie:

Bobby is sixteen years old and a proud new license owner. The third time Bobby gets to take the family car out for the evening he returns home with alcohol on his breath. Mom and dad are furious and very concerned about Bobby drinking and driving. Bobby is very remorseful and embarrassed. He is surprised that he broke such an important rule.

Bobby talks this problem over with his parents on a few different occasions. He volunteers to join the school's anti drug group. He seems to enjoy the group and brings home information about the societal problem of driving under the influence of alcohol and drugs.

When Bobby asks if he can use the car to take his girlfriend to the junior prom, his parents are concerned. The family talks openly about this concern and mom and dad give their <u>conditional</u> agreement. Mom and dad are adamant about no drinking at the prom. Curfew is extended until 2 AM due to the nature of the evening. As Bobby leaves for the evening, mom and dad talk about how mature he is and how proud they are of him. Mom and dad enjoy a quiet evening. At 11:00 dad, a Highway Patrol Officer has to go to bed. He has to get up at 4:30 to go to work.

Logic is the technique by which we add conviction to truth.
Jean De La Bruyer

At 2 AM no Bobby. At 2:15 mom starts to get worried. At 2:30 mom calls the girlfriend's home to learn that she has been home since 12:30. At 2:45 mom wakes up dad. Dad assures mom that Bobby is fine. Mom thinks she hears a car out front.

To mom's surprise, Bobby parked the car half in the driveway and half in her rose garden. He opens the car door and falls out. He staggers up to the front door. Mom opens the door and states with a scream, "My god, you've been drinking!" Bobby, obviously intoxicated, falls through the front door, landing on his knees. He carefully picks himself up and tries to straighten his neck tie. Mom again screams with horror, "You've been drinking!"

Bobby breathes his brewery breath all over her and announces as he wobbles, "No I haven't. Who says I've been drinking!"

At this point mom goes ballistic. She races to her bedroom to confront dad, "Bobby is drunk and he says he isn't! How stupid does he think I am. I'm not going to allow a stinking drunk to drive my car!!!"

At this point Bobby goes into the bathroom and kneels at the porcelain altar. His body rejects the poison in his stomach. As he pours himself into his bed, he thinks to himself. "Why is she yelling so loud ... God my head hurts"

Now, I ask you. What is the number one reason teenagers lie to their parents? Why do they look into your face and talk to you like you're stupid? Why did Bobby lie?

Teens lie to distract. If they make their problem your problem, you'll get caught up in it as your problem, and their life goes on.

Teens lie to distract. So, when you are discussing something with your teen and your blood pressure starts to boil, think, "Bingo, he is distracting me, I'm right, great! What the heck were we talking about?" Then stay focused on the issue, not on the teen lie. One mom summed it up nicely, "Dr. Phil, once I feel flustered and confused I know I'm right. I don't let him distract me. I've got his number. I just know I'm right and stick with the Must Rules!" It was music to my ears.

DEALING WITH LIES

I advocate that lying should be seen as an indication that there is probably a more serious problem. It is our goal, as parents, to help our child uncover the real problem and deal with it. To this end I

> When you have to make a choice and don't make it, that in itself is a choice.
>
> William James

hope that parents write Must Rules that focus on the problem much more than the lie. At any one time we can deal with the lie, but if we do not deal with the cause for the lie, our children will not be able to avoid the root problem and the lying is most likely to continue. One major problem that occurs is that when parents only focus on the lie, the child learns to lie better, so as not to get caught. This is a disaster for the child in the long run. I wish for your children to be skilled at dealing with their problems, not skilled in covering up their problems with lies.

Many families find the following Must Rule works well for them:

Must Rule: No lying

Consequence: (Young child) Time Out followed with support with the real problem.

(Older child) Sent to room to calm down followed up with discussion about the following question. "What is the lie distracting us from dealing with?"

Some parents and teenagers find that having the youth write an answer to this question while in their "calm down" area is very helpful. Many teens find it difficult to find the correct words when talking to adults. Writing down their thoughts helps them to master the skill of thinking through a conflict.

SIBLING RIVALRY

I live with the Bickersons. My three children argue about everything. It has gone on for years. I have talked to friends who tell me "it's normal, all kids bicker." Is it true? Do all kids bicker? My kids drive me nuts. And, even worse, I worry that when they grow up they will not like each other.

People that live under the same roof tend to bicker, sorry it's a species specific behavior. When it comes to our children we call it sibling rivalry. Sibling rivalry is the "normal" arguing, bickering, tattling, teasing and moderate hostility siblings express towards each other. Usually, it is a developmental stage children experience as they practice growing up. When your children are two - three years of age they tend to push, hit, bite and scream their displeasure. When they are five - seven sibling feuds become name calling, tattling, and silly teasing. By age eight your children become skilled at hateful teasing, angry hostility, and spiteful competition. On the surface this sounds horrifying, but it need not be. If this acting out behavior is dealt with correctly by parents and teachers it is merely a mild annoyance.

Many parents want to know *why* their children seem to have the need to bicker all the time. The simple answer is competition. Children need lots of things from the very powerful people they call mom and dad. Anything that distracts mom and dad from taking care of them is a potential conflict for your children. The test of all relationships is conflict. To this end, if mom is taking sister to skating, mom is not taking care of me. It is only a small skip in thought for brother to growl, "You're always taking Sally places, you don't do stuff for me." When mom mistakenly gets caught up in the argument: "Bobby, I do lots for you," she feeds the emotional fire. In this situation it is necessary to read between the words and help Bobby experience and understand his feelings. The same situation:

Bobby:	You're always taking Sally places, you don't do stuff for me.
Mom:	You're not happy that I'm taking Sally to skating?
Bobby:	No. I don't care about dumb skating! (Note the skillful dig at Sally's beloved skating.) I just want to... ah... you know.
Mom:	I'm not sure, what do you want me to do?

We must learn to live together as brothers or perish together as fools.

Martin Luther King, Jr.

Sin has many tools, but a lie is the handle that fits them all.

Oliver Wendell Holmes

Bobby:	I want you to do stuff with me.
Mom:	Me too. I want to do stuff with you. Do you want to ride with me to skating?, We can visit on the way.

This active listening on the part of mom will, over time, teach Bobby to keep perspective and to plan his needs. Most people need about thirty years of practice before this is a skill they have mastered. (I see your questioning look. We all know forty-five year olds that are selfish toad lickers, but most people tend to master this skill by thirty.)

For most families I work with I advocate the following Must Rule:

For parents of younger children:

Must Rule: Be nice to self and others

Consequence: Short Time Out to get your feelings in check. Followed by a discussion.

For parents of teenagers:

Must Rule: Be nice to self and others

Consequence: Teen is excused from the room until they feel that they can discuss their concerns in an appropriate manner. Followed by a discussion.

For me, *be nice to self and others* is the proverbial "Golden Rule." (One should behave toward others as one would have others behave toward oneself.) I expect people I am around to treat others kindly. I expect it out of myself as well as my family and friends. I point out to my children that this is one of the major factors in how I pick friends.

WHAT CAN A PARENT DO TO LIMIT SIBLING RIVALRY?

MUST RULE

Implement a Must Rule that allows your child a moment to think through the conflict. Avoid harsh punishment as this leads to acts of revenge. Allow your child a safe place to work out choices. Ask, "How can you do it differently?"

My salad days, when I was green with judgment.
Shakespeare

The only way to have a friend is to be one.
Ralph Waldo Emerson

RESPECT THE INDIVIDUAL

Keep in mind that your children are individuals. Don't try to make everything equal. Strive to make your children's lives personal. For example, if you return from a trip with a gift for each child, make the gift personal to your relationship with each individual child. Fret little about the dollar amount, focus on the person you are giving to.

RESPECT PRIVACY

If at all possible, give each child their own private place. Then, let them do with their private space as much as you can. Allow their private place to be their creative place. Respect your child's individuality as it is shown in their private space.

If children live in a cramped situation, it should be expected that they will get on each other's nerves.

SHARE YOURSELF AS AN INDIVIDUAL WITH AN INDIVIDUAL

Plan time with each of your children. Do things with each member of the family. It is wonderful to take the kids to the park, but make some time to take just one child at a time to the park. Let your children invite you to do something with them as an individual. If one child likes chess, play chess. If the other likes checkers, play checkers. It is counterproductive to force the chess player to play checkers just so he can spend time with you.

THE PARENTAL DOUBLE CHECK

Check to make sure you are treating each child fairly as well as treating them as individuals. Over the years I have heard horror stories that just break my heart. Without belaboring the point, if you're bringing a gift for one child, bring for all. It is better to bring just yourself than fuel sibling rivalry by slighting the other child. This is especially a problem in blended and step-families.

TEACH PROPERTY RIGHTS EARLY

It is important that parents teach children that their property is theirs and that other people's property is not theirs. Children need to be taught early to ask for permission before touching another's property. This teaching is done in word and action. I advocate that parents ask for permission before they touch their child's belongings. This is an amazing teaching tool, as well as polite. If I say to my

There is no such thing as justice, either in the courtroom or out.
Clarence Darrow

The nature of all men is so formed that they see and discriminate in the affairs of others, much better than in their own.
Terence

son, "Ethy, can Josh and I use your giant tub of Legos?" He usually gives his permission with a powerful lift to his self esteem. Once he did pull rank with a smile, "You can dad, but put them away when you're done. I don't want to get them Ching Chinged." (See The Ching Ching Box, elsewhere in this chapter.)

At a round table there is no dispute about place.
Italian proverb

DO NOT FORCE SHARING

Your child's property is theirs. Teach the virtue of sharing, but do not force it upon your child.

For example. If your child has just gotten a new, must-have-toy, let him enjoy the newness. Many parents question me on this. But, would you like to share your brand new, over priced car with the neighbor, just because he wants his turn really badly?

SOILING

> My son is eight years old. He has messes in his pants almost every day. We have tried everything to get him to notice that he needs to go to the bathroom. But he just doesn't seem to notice that he has to go to the bathroom. A few times recently, he has messed in his pants at school. His teacher is very concerned that she may be pressuring him too much in class. His father and I were divorced three years ago, about the time when we think this problem started. We were kind of hoping that our son would just grow out of it.

Quick Reference Guide

encopresis: The repeated passage of fecal matter, by children older than four, in inappropriate places.

"Messing" in one's clothing is often called soiling. The clinical term is encopresis. The elimination disorder, encopresis is the repeated passage of fecal matter, by children older than four, in inappropriate places. Usually this "accident" is involuntary, but sometimes it is purposeful. Soiling is not as prevalent a problem as enuresis. Studies show that about two percent of eight year old boys and one percent of eight year old girls have regular problems with soiling. Soiling is very rare by adulthood.

Soiling is usually misunderstood by parents and school personnel. Many adults see soiling as anger related and controlling. Most families are embarrassed by the problem and thus reluctant to seek help. Many families become punitive with the soiling child; this tends to worsen the problem.

It is rare that "poor" toilet training is the cause of soiling. It is very rare that children spitefully soil. (Although I have worked with children in in-patient facilities who did learn to control their parents by soiling into their own hand and throwing the fecal matter at them.) I stress that this is rare, and it has been my experience that parents readily ask for professional help in this type of situation.

In the vast majority of soiling situations the problem is the side effect of severe constipation due to feces retention. Ally, a little girl of seven, was very upset about a new baby entering the home. She refused to use the bathroom even though she had been toilet trained for over three years. She begged and pleaded with her parents to let her use a diaper. At first no one noticed that she was not toileting herself. About two weeks after her little brother came home from the hospital Ally had an accident when she was walking home from school. Over the next few months she soiled almost every afternoon. Ally's mother talked with the family doctor who assured her that Ally "...was just adjusting to the new baby in the house." When I met Ally she was the center of the family. Everyone was worried about her. Even Ally. She thought that she was sick and her "guts were going to fall out."

The above situation is typical of how soiling can become a

major problem. Research has shown us that most encopritic children have no medical condition that is causing the problem. But, interestingly enough, one of their parents were prone to constipation when they were a child. The cycle begins this way. For whatever reason a child begins to resist defecating. It may be because they are upset about the attention a new baby is getting or they just feel out of control in some part of their life. The child feels control within themselves by not going to the toilet. This retention leads to constipation. Constipation leads to discomfort when defecating. This leads to further retention. In a matter of a few days to a week the child is impacted. She loses the urge to defecate. The child keeps eating, but no waste gets out. As the retention continues, the bowel stretches. As the lower bowel becomes more and more distended (swollen from internal pressure) the child's anus remains partially open. A little seepage occurs even though a true bowel movement is restricted by the retained blockage.

It is common for the psychological factors that attributed to the initial retention to be solved and the soiling to continue. Ally, had been soiling for over three months, long after she got used to the new baby.

BEHAVIORAL INTERVENTIONS

Parents have had great success in stopping soiling by using behavioral interventions. There are three parts to this process. Your child may need all three or just one or two.

1. Your child needs to feel safe within the family.
2. We need to regulate food intake.
3. We need to get your child toileting on a routine.

YOUR CHILD NEEDS TO FEEL SAFE WITHIN THE FAMILY.

I cannot over emphasize the fact that your child needs to share his problems with others within the family. I advocate that your child hear that "we" have a soiling problem. Parents need to advocate for their child. I am sure he feels deep shame due to the soiling. This shame tends to be exhibited as an "I don't care attitude" for older children and adolescents.

I advocate that parents focus on how their child is dealing with the problem, versus the problem itself. Depending on the emotional maturity of the child he should be dealing with the soiled clothing and take responsibility for keeping clean. The goal is for this to become a Minor Rule in the future. At this point the process of taking care of himself should be a Must Rule. One family found the following Must

Rule very helpful (This child tended to soil between 4-6 PM):

Must Rule: If you soil yourself, you will take responsibility to clean yourself, rinse out your soiled clothing and place them by the washing machine.

Consequence: If you are soiled for more than three minutes, for every minute it takes you to get into the shower you choose to lose ten minutes of TV.

Please note that the consequence was not directed at the soiling. It was directed at the child taking care of himself appropriately.

WE NEED TO REGULATE FOOD INTAKE.

The human body has a tube (the digestive system) running through it. This tube starts at the mouth and ends at the anus. We need to deal with the impacted colon so that your child can digest and evacuate waste properly.

Once the colon is distended (swollen by internal pressure) your child will not notice the natural alarm that indicates the need to defecate. As long as the child is impacted this alarm will not trigger correctly.

So, first things first. Your child needs to pass the impacted waste. Obtain from you local drugstore two Fleet enemas. Follow the directions on the packaging carefully. Most children are able to pass the retained blockage with one enema. Sometimes two enemas are needed. This is not a punishing situation. Explain to your child about the process described above and how important it is that his bowel function correctly. Most children are looking forward to solving the problem, so they are cooperative. Sometimes parents need to elicit the help of the child's medical doctor to administer the enema. (Most doctors turn this medical procedure over to their nursing staff.)

Once the blockage has been passed it will take a few weeks for the colon to reestablish normal muscle tension. During this time, and into the future, what goes into the mouth is most important. Simply put, your child should eat a well balanced diet of food that does not get soft in water. The intestines need roughage (fiber) to squeeze against as it forces food from the stomach to the anus. This process is called peristalsis, a wave like muscular contraction that moves digesting matter through the digestive system. Aim for fresh and cooked vegetables, fresh and dried fruits, and pastas. Avoid sweets, pastries, and low fiber "fluffo" breads.

In the beginning most parents find that a few prunes a day really helps their child keep the digestive tract running smoothly. (If

Quick Reference Guide

peristalsis: A wave-like muscular contraction that moves digesting matter through the digestive system.

things are running too smoothly, cut back on the fruit.)

This tends to solve about half of the problem. The problem of your child being constipated. We also have to reteach your child to recognize the "call to" defecate.

WE NEED TO GET YOUR CHILD TOILETING ON A ROUTINE.

This is often harder than it sounds. We need to reteach toilet training. Not the whole process, just the, "Oh yeah, I need to poop" knowledge. This is done by setting a routine. Simply put, your child needs to perch his derriere on a toilet three times a day until he is noticing his need to use the toilet. This works best by having your child sit on the toilet for ten minutes after every meal. And, please note, the meals need to be at regular times. Say breakfast at 8 AM, lunch at noon, and dinner at 6 PM This routine is very important in changing the cycle of soiling. In a week or two it will become apparent that at a certain time (sometimes twice) your child needs to defecate. At that point, the potty perching schedule can change to reflect your child's new self control. Most families find it helpful to keep a chart.

If there is an incident of soiling, then the schedule is reevaluated. One family I worked with found that 8, noon and 6 didn't work. For their child wake-up and just before bed worked perfectly.

If your child is in discomfort it may be best to consult with your family doctor. Your doctor can evaluate if a stool softener medication would be in order. A registered dietician can be very helpful in developing a healthy diet for your child as well as your whole family. Soiling is a treatable problem. Please reach out to local professional resources. With the correct diet, routine toileting, and a supportive environment, most children tend to retrain their lower bowel in a few months.

FURTHER READING:

Childhood Encopresis and Enuresis: Cause and Theory by C.E. Schaefer, Van Nostrand Reinhold, 1979

Healthy Snacks For Kids by Penny Warner, Bristol Publishing, 1996

STEALING

Over the years I have found that children steal for four major reasons. Three reasons will be discussed here, while the fourth will be covered under its broader category.

The four major reasons why children steal:

1. Because they really want the item they steal.
2. Because they wish to teach someone something.
3. Because they enjoy the process of stealing.
4. They steal to cover the cost of the drugs that they want. (This will be covered under: WHAT DO I NEED TO KNOW ABOUT DRUGS, later in this chapter.)

BECAUSE THEY REALLY WANT THE ITEM THEY STEAL

> My son is nine years old. He has been caught stealing three times in the last month. My husband and I suspect that he has also stolen money from our bedroom as well as from his older sister's purse. We have spanked him and grounded him, but he does not seem to care.

The vast majority of children (under age fourteen) steal for the most basic of needs. They want something—so they take it. It is not unusual that there is no more thought than just that. *I want it, so I take it.*

If you ask around (I have) everyone seems to have the "I got caught stealing and my mother did ..." story. The most common story is,

> I got caught and I had to go and confess. I was so embarrassed. I could feel my heart pounding. But my mom was so mad at me. She marched me right back to the store and made me confess to the store manager. I never stole anything again.

For most children, being marched back to the store to talk to the manager is a wonderful life lesson. I definitely advocate doing just that, but it is no longer 1940 America so we need to call the store and make sure that the manager is willing to play his part well (most are). I have had parents tell horror stories of managers that flipped out on them and chased them out of the store. And then there was the story of the manager who tried to befriend the child who was crying by saying, "It's OK little girl. It's only a candy bar so don't worry about it." It is best to call the manager and ask them to take a few minutes to explain how when people steal from his

Be good and you will be lonely.

Mark Twain

store it hurts him personally and also raises the cost for everyone who shops at the store.

Most parents over react to their child stealing by being punitive and forgetting to teach. Many children steal because it is their only way to get what they want and they do not see anything wrong with getting their needs met. If a parent becomes extremely embarrassed they tend toward character attacks and spanking. Some parents exaggerate the situation and call their child *thief* or tell them that they are going to *go to jail*. It is important that parents use this problem as a teaching tool. It is important that parents <u>discuss</u> the following with their child:

a. People who have things stolen from them have feelings.
b. Trust in the family is very important.
c. Others trust you by not locking up their belongings. This trust in you does not give you permission to steal from them.
d. If you have a want, how could you get this need met?

It is important for parents to focus on the process of fixing the problem. It is important that children make restitution whenever possible. Children need to be responsible for their behaviors.

BECAUSE THEY WISH TO TEACH SOMEONE SOMETHING

> It has gotten so bad that I have had to put a lock on my bedroom door. My daughter is a little thief. If it isn't bolted down she will steal it. I hate living like this, but we have to. I had to put a chain with a lock on the refrigerator.

Often stealing within the family is a form of acting out in a-round-about-way to teach someone a lesson. It is important to figure out what the underlying problems are. Often this is easy, such as when little brother keeps stealing big brother's Legos. When you ask him "Why?" he shouts back, "You like Bobby better, he gets all the cool stuff!" If it is this straight forward then you want to help little brother deal with his real feelings. Little brother needs to learn how to get his needs met, while respecting other people's property. (See Chapter 2.)

Sometimes it is not clear exactly what your child is trying to say. It will take time and effort to sort out what the child is trying to teach. But, this is very important, not only for the present situation, but also for the child in the long run. Your child needs to know that his feelings are appropriate, but his behavior (stealing) is not.

I worked with a forty-five year old man who had lived for forty years getting back at people who he thought had wronged him. He told story after story of making things right, in his mind, by getting people back. He had slashed tires, peed on potted plants, and spat on others' food. The interesting thing was that he hated himself for it. He sought therapy because he wanted to learn how to tell people his feelings. When I asked him about his earliest memory of righting wrongs *his way* he said,

> When I was five, I stole my brother's pocket knife. I got a beating and sent to bed without dinner. I remember, as if it was yesterday, that I stayed up for hours planning my revenge. To this day, I can't talk with my brother without hating him.

This man learned to take revenge instead of learning how to communicate his feelings and get his emotional needs met in an appropriate manner.

BECAUSE THEY ENJOY THE PROCESS OF STEALING

As we discussed in Chapter 1, behaviors are learned. The secondary gain (thrill) of stealing is very rewarding. I have worked with many teenagers, as well as adults, who steal simply for the excitement. It usually starts with small stuff then becomes very large.

This learned behavior is very hard to unlearn. Most teens and adults need to experience a severe punisher to change their behavior. Because of this it is important that parents do not overly protect their children when they get caught. If your child learns that you will protect him from the police, the stealing will most probably increase after the initial fear of being caught subsides. For most teens this takes about two weeks.

If your child is coming home with items that are not theirs, <u>you</u> must deal with it. I worked with a parent who was surprised when the police searched her home. They found thousands of dollars of stolen property in the form of a stereo, TV, VCR, leather jacket, and jewelry. When I asked the mom where she thought the stuff came from, she said, "He said his friends gave it to him." It is very hard for teens to make money, even when employed, so it is important that parents stay aware of their child's property.

I AM OFTEN ASKED WHAT TO DO IF A TEEN COMES HOME WITH POSSIBLE STOLEN PROPERTY

I advocate that in most cases stealing within the house is a family problem and stealing outside of the house is a community problem. To this extent, I advise parents to deal with small crimes within the house. I advise parents to make their children accountable to the community outside of the home. This can take the form of taking your child back to the store (young child) to calling the police and reporting a crime (teenager).

Parents often ask me if they should turn their own teen in for, let's say, stealing a car. And I emphatically say, **"Yes!"** It is very simple. I want your child to know, for a fact, that there are powers much greater than their parents. And I want your child to learn this fact well before they are adults, at which point society is not very forgiving.

In closing, if a parent covers up a crime for a child, the child learns that they are not responsible and their parent will cover for them. In my experience this leads to larger crimes and much greater danger. One young adult told me:

> When I was strip searched on my sixteenth birthday— after getting arrested for drunk driving and joy riding ... I knew that I had to change. In jail I was treated like a nonperson. I was only there three hours, but I grew up ten years.
>
> (The young man is now a third year college student studying Business Finance. His parents had called the police when he arrived home intoxicated in an unknown car.)

The following are Must Rules used by families with great success:

Family with three teens with minor run-ins with the law:

Must Rule: No Stealing!

Consequence: Inside the house: One week grounding.

Outside the house: Explain your behavior to the police.

Family with seven and eight year old girls:

Must Rule: You must have specific permission to use another's property <u>before</u> you <u>touch</u> it.

Consequence: Fifteen minutes of sitting on your bed.

Family of fifteen year old with a history of stealing from neighborhood homes:

Must Rule: Terrance is not allowed to steal. Terrance is not allowed to borrow anything from anyone outside of the family. Terrance can borrow from mom and dad only with prior permission.

Consequence: Room restriction for one week; report to probation officer for review. Possible probation violation and legal charges if deemed necessary by probation department.

TEACHING RESPONSIBILITY

There are three major sore points with parents in regards to responsibility. These are:

a. My children procrastinate.
b. My children won't pick up after themselves.
c. My children are late with homework, chores, or curfew.

The above are major irritants that, in most cases, are a sign of normal or abnormal maturity. This may sound contradictory at first read, but it is not. Some parents have unrealistic ideas of what they can expect from a child at any particular age. This can be a real problem. If the parents' expectations are unrealistic it will fuel great conflicts within the home.

One father was adamant that when he was a child he had to do his homework as soon as he got home or he would get a beating. Between the first and second session I asked him to call his mother and ask if her memory was the same. He started out the second session by explaining,

> I called my mother and she said that I fought doing my homework until high school. She told me a few stories of how hard I was to live with because of my dislike of homework. I just remember being stuck at the kitchen table.

For most fathers, memories of their behavior and their athletic ability improve as they become older memories. For most mothers, memories of their behavior and their ability to deal with boys improve as they become older memories. I am always amazed at how many star little league ball players I meet in their thirties and forties.

Unless you're around many children it is hard to know what is "average" skill level for them. Most of the time, parents I work with learn that their child's responsibility level is relatively average. This is in no way an excuse for messy or late homework assignments. But it is simply a reminder that responsibility is a learned behavior.

Parents should use the techniques discussed in the first four chapters of this book to teach responsibility. In addition, in this section we will look at some tricks of the trade that will help prod your future adults along.

MY CHILDREN PROCRASTINATE

Many parents complain that their children do not use time wisely. They call it dawdling, laziness, or procrastination. Most families feel frustration during the transition times of the day— morn-

It is easier to pull down than to build up.
Latin proverb

ings, meals, homework, and bedtime. It is at these times of the day parents need the cooperation of their children to accomplish the task at hand. Many parents consult me with the same problem, "I can't get my child to ..." Their frustration leads to nagging, arguing, and punishment— which produced no real change in their child's behavior.

Time management is a learned behavior. Most children do not understand the concept of time until about age ten. A four year old is starting to understand the concept of annual, such as their birthday, Christmas, or summer. By age five, children are starting to understand days, months, and a year. These are very generalized concepts until around age eight. Between eight and ten children start to grasp the accumulation of a minute and what it feels like to wait five minutes. They are starting to develop their *internal* clock. At the same time their internal clock is influenced by their moods and expectations. Until age eight, parents need to help children compartmentalize their time. "You have six minutes to pick up your toys, I'll set the timer," is very helpful to a six year old. "I'll help you pick up the toys, I wonder how long it will take?" clues four year olds into the ticking of the clock.

People who try to command respect are wasting their time. Respect can't be commanded, it has to be earned.

The concept of understanding the passage of time is a developmental milestone. Which means, it cannot be taught until your child is mentally developed enough to accept the new information. At the same time, time comprehension is not simply turned on in your child's brain. It takes external stimulation to trigger the nerves to develop. What this means for us parents is that we have to spend a lot of time talking about time with our children. Calm and supportive supervision of time management is an important parental task. All things being equal, be patient. (It is interesting to note that the lack of employee time management skills is a leading concern of corporate business management.)

Parents need to be careful that time does not become a battle ground between themselves and their child. The following are some parenting land mines to avoid:

THE POWER STRUGGLE

As we have discussed before, life is a process of cause and effect. Often the parent that pushes her child finds her child moving at a snail's pace in freezing January. The harder you push, the more your child resists. In parent/child power struggles everyone loses. Power struggles should be avoided by the parent. A power struggle is a spiral of emotion that pulls the parent and the child into the black hole of emotional conflict. The process is quite simple. The child feels pushed into doing something that they do not wish to do. They resent being told what to do, so they slow down. This is their behavioral way of saying, "You can't control me." This slow down gets them nagged at which feels like attention and is rewarding to the child. In the end everyone is angry with each other and you're still late. (See Chapter 1: HOW CHILDREN LEARN)

I advocate that parents write Must Rules based on behaviors to be accomplished by a particular time. The older the child gets, the less support the child will need to accomplish the behavioral task. For example, do not focus on getting out of the house, focus on your child putting on his seat belt by a particular time.

> Must Rule: You will have your seat belt on by 7:42 so we can start the car and drive safely to school.

> Consequence: For every minute late, five minutes of early bed.

Parents need to resist telling their school age children and teenagers how to get to the car by 7:42. This is your child's responsibility. Respect their ability to learn and grow. (See Chapter 2: ADVOCATING VERSUS JUDGING YOUR CHILD)

CHILDREN MISUSE TIME TO AVOID STRESS

Many children act lazy or procrastinate to avoid personal stress. They find it is easier to try to miss the perceived stress than it is to deal with it head on. A child that hates school just can't seem to get started on school mornings. But they are bright eyed and bushy tailed on the weekends. Some kids that hate school just can't figure out how to sit down and start their homework. Homework will be discussed later in this section.

Some children fall into daydreaming to avoid stress throughout their day. The daydreamer avoids conflict by enjoying fanciful misdirection. My experience with daydreamers is that as you help them raise their self esteem the time they spend daydreaming will be used to get things done. (See Chapter 2: HOW TO BUILD YOUR CHILD'S SELF ESTEEM)

I do not see it as often, but some children become perfectionists to deal with their interpersonal stress. The perfectionistic child is able to look busy but accomplish very little. She may take twenty-two minutes to put her socks on, while being able to honestly say, "Mom, I'm putting my shoes and socks on." The perfectionistic child is trying to avoid conflict by accomplishing perfection but finds constant conflict because of time management. It is important to deal with the underlying fear in order to help the child proceed at a reasonable level of proficiency. (See Chapter 2: HOW TO BUILD YOUR CHILD'S SELF ESTEEM)

MY CHILDREN DON'T PICK UP AFTER THEMSELVES

Please allow me to semi brag for a moment. I do not know what you spent on this book, but most parents tell me that the following problem solution is worth millions in parental stress reduction.

We have all stepped on those parent land mines called Legos. As much as I love the creativity Legos encourage in children, and I do highly recommend them as one of the best educational toys for children, I surely hate stepping on them. One night I stepped on one and its "sharp" little self impaled my heel. I walked crooked for two days. People asked, "Are you OK?" and I would grunt in pain, "No, my children are trying to maim me!"

Picking up after their children is probably the main reason why parents have lower back pain. I have no scientific proof, but I think Chiropractors give children a commission for every parent who walks into their office stooped over in agony.

Picking up after oneself is a learned behavior. As a learning tool I advocate the use of the Ching Ching Box. The Ching Ching Box has its own partially accurate story:

> Many years ago, back in B.C. (Before Children), when Dr. Phil could see his toes, he would walk around the office picking up toys that were left around. Back then the goal was to keep the office picked up. Those were the good old days, when Dr. Phil only bent over four or five times each day, and never on weekends. Many years went by with no lower back pain.
>
> We entered A.D. (After Diapers) when little ones roamed around the house spilling things and saying "No!" As the little ones went from diaper to demolition, Daddy Phil started to think about the good old days, when it was safe to walk around the house barefoot.
>
> One day, Daddy Phil was walking through the living-room picking up lots of colorful toys when he felt his eyes start to spin inside his head. As he stood erect, his eyes kept spinning and then came to a sudden noisy stop, "Ching Ching!" "I have an idea," he exclaimed to the large purple dinosaur he was holding. "I should get paid for being the maid!"
>
> "If I'm enslaved to pick up after my kids, they should have to earn their toys back!" The dinosaur voiced no dissent. An idea was hatched— The Ching Ching Box.

The Ching Ching Box procedure is quite simple. Anything unattended can and may be picked up by a parent and placed in the Ching Ching Box. Once it is imprisoned in the Ching Ching Box the owner must negotiate with the parent or teacher for its return. It is only fair. We caring parents protected our children's stuff for them, now they have to earn it back.

Things are earned back at the level of the owner. A five year old may have to do two jumping jacks to earn back a sneaker. While a ten year old may have to do a load of laundry or sweep the kitchen floor. The process is a negotiation. Both parent and child need to agree on the "repurchase price." Big ticket items are baseball gloves, homework assignments, or favorite articles of clothing.

The Ching Ching Box is a teaching tool. My goal isn't to fill it up. My aim is to focus my children on taking responsibility for their belongings. On a regular basis one of us will say to the other, "Are you planning to Ching Ching before dinner?" "Oh yes," the other one plays along, "I'm really looking forward to getting the stuff over by the ..." This leads to a scurry of little feet and victorious faces grinning, "You didn't get my ..."

In the Copitch house we use a box that held ten reams of copy paper. It was "decorated" by *the boys* many moons ago. When it starts to get full, we pull it out and hold a Ching Ching auction. Whoever owns the item gets to discuss how to get it returned to them. Any item that is not worth earning back is auctioned off to another family member, usually at a very reasonable price. Mind you, we are not talking about money. Children earn their stuff back through chores. Our family is highly involved in Martial Arts so we do *sell* back items *paid* for with push-ups, sit-ups, or jumping jacks. Similar to the "punishments" given out by coaches in sports. Everything is negotiable. An ability that will greatly assist your children down the road in the adult business world.

If a child gets upset because his brother left out his property, I advocate for the situation. "It is sad that your brother is not taking responsibility for his behavior, but the property is yours, how would you like to earn it back?" Often one of my children will earn back another's belongings because they caused the item to end up in the Ching Ching Box. But I never get involved in that negotiation. It is important that our children learn to pick their friends by judging the other's level of responsibility. This is a wonderful practice for our children to learn about borrowing and personal responsibility to another.

I am regularly asked by one of my boys, "Dad, are you planning to Ching Ching ?" to which I advocate, "Not right now, but in a little while, how come you're asking?"

Many parents find that one child accuses another of using their belongings without permission, then getting it Ching Chinged. It is tempting for parents to play police officer and try to solve the problem. I advise that you do not. Negotiate the item as discussed above and table the issue of stealing until an appropriate time. (Usually the next meal or house meeting.)

It is important that the Ching Ching Box be seen by the parents as a learning tool not a form of delayed punishment. Keep it light

One family I worked with believed that clutter was their number one family conflict. To make sure that they were ready to Ching Ching they obtained a refrigerator box from an appliance store, decorated it, and set out to, as dad put it with clenched fist

Education is a social process ... Education is growth.... Education is, not a preparation for life; education is life itself.
John Dewey

hearted and humorous. Oh, just so you know, some families allow Ching Chings by one parent of the other parent's stuff. I hear the repayment negotiations get quite interesting.

Finally, only parents can Ching Ching! Only parents can take an item out of the Ching Ching Box. A child who removes an item from the box is stealing!

MY CHILDREN ARE LATE WITH HOMEWORK, CHORES, OR CURFEW.

This is simply an issue of your children doing what they want to do versus what they *must* do. Let me make this point bluntly,

Why doesn't your teen poop in the living room?
Why doesn't your eight year old potty on the couch?
Why doesn't your eleven year old make *dodo* at the dining room table during Sunday dinner?

The answer is: they have internalized the Must Rule about toileting that you taught them during the potty training phase of their younger life. I point this out because, unless your children "believe" that they must do their homework, they will do what they want to do. Unless your child believes that they must be home by curfew, they will do what they want to do. Unless your child believes that they must do their chore at a particular level, they will do what they want to do.

Central to most task completion issues is that the child does not believe her adults.

Make your books your companions.
The Talmud

You need to honestly question yourself. Is homework a *Maybe* (a preference) in your family or a Must Rule? (See Chapter 4: MUST, MAYBE, AND MINOR RULES) If you are teaching your children that homework is a preference, then your child will play before she does her work. If your child believes that cleaning her room is a parental preference (Maybe Rule), then riding her bike is more likely to be her choice.

The following are actual Must Rules that families have found usable: (See Chapter 4: HOW DO YOU WRITE A MUST RULE)

Homework:

You can lead a boy to college, but you cannot make him think.
Elbert Hubbard

Must Rule: Homework must be done as soon as you come home. Nothing else is allowed until homework is done. (Go to the bathroom first, then go to your homework area.)

Consequence: For every minute you procrastinate you earn four minutes of room restrictions.

Must Rule: Homework must be completed and placed on the front hall table by 6 PM. Mom or Dad will check all homework during dinner. Homework corrections (after dinner) will be done before any TV.

Consequence: If homework is not on table by 6 PM, you have earned room restrictions that evening.

Must Rule: Mom will be available to help with homework from 7-8 PM Monday through Friday, and Saturday morning from 9 AM to noon.

Consequence: School is your job. I am here to help, but I am not willing to nag. Any midterm or final grade below a "C" earns house restrictions until it is raised to a "B."

Chores:

Single father with three children ranging in age from eight to sixteen.

Must Rule: Chore list is posted on Sunday morning. You must do your chore as listed on the chore list.

Consequence: If your chore is not done correctly, as defined by the chore list, you are grounded for the rest of the day and earn an extra chore.

Note: The chore list had specific expectations, clearly spelled out, for each household chore.

A blended family with 4 teenagers:

Must Rule: There are four family chores that must be done every day. Morning Dishes, Upstairs Bathroom, Living-Room Pick-Up, and Dinner Dishes. It is the responsibility for our four children to work out a procedure to get the chores done, as needed, throughout the day.

Consequence: If any chore is undone, your beloved parents go on strike until the chores are done. (On strike means that (step) mom or (step) dad will not help any of their teenagers to do anything, i.e., lend car, take phone messages, cook.)

Single mother with young children:

Must Rule: Bobby must set the table for breakfast.

Sally must set the table for lunch.

Mary must help mommy set the table for dinner.

Consequence: If table is not set on time, responsible person loses his or her dinner dessert.

Revenge is sweet, sweeter than life itself— so say fools.

Juvenal

Curfew:

Must Rule: You must be home at or before 9 PM.

Consequence: If you are late, you have chosen to be grounded for one week.

Must Rule: Before you get to leave, you must write the agreed upon curfew on the refrigerator white board.

Consequence: For every minute you are late, you are grounded for one day.

There are no excuses for being late, even alien abduction is not a good reason.

Must Rule: Randy's curfew is exactly 11 PM.

Sue's curfew is exactly 10 PM.

Robert is too young for a curfew.

Consequence: If you are late, even by a second, you lose your license for three days. Three curfew infractions in any thirty day period, you are grounded for one month.

Each of the above rules are from different families. All of the families were having problems getting their children to follow the family rules. When the rules moved from the Maybe Rule column to the Must Rules column the children started to let their parents parent. Please note that each family wrote the rule specifically for their family and situation. (See, HOW DO YOU WRITE A MUST RULE in Chapter 4) Must Rules with clearly defined consequences are essential for teaching your child responsibility and, in the long run, relieving your personal frustrations.

"You have chosen" puts the responsibility where it needs to be, with the

UNCOOPERATIVE BEHAVIOR IN SCHOOL (8 YEAR OLD)

The following information was documented during the initial treatment session with a mother concerned about her son's poor school performance.

Happiness is more often remembered than experienced.

> My son, Tony, is eight years old. To tell you the truth, he has always been a handful. He is very active and often rude. He is now in second grade. Kindergarten and first grade were a mess. I kept hearing from the teachers that my son was "hyperactive" and that he needed medication. I put him on medication and he is still a handful. The principal and the teacher have worked it out that if my son gets his name on the board three times he is sent home. At least once a week I am called to come pick him up from school. I take him home and put him on room restrictions. The principal told me that if I keep him in his room he will choose to act better in class so he doesn't have to go to his room.
>
> I am very concerned that my son is learning very little in school. I dread the phone ringing. The school secretary told me that my son was troubled and I should seek help. The school isn't helping ... they just send him home.

The story above is very common. Parents and the school in conflict and worry about a youngster. This isn't the forum for me to discuss this problem from the institutional level. But, suffice to say, I believe that the school is there to help your child learn. Sometimes, before a child can learn, we have to help her get control over herself.

For some children medication can go a long way in helping them to control themselves. But, for most children a behavior modification program is all that is needed. Most of the children I see do not need medication. In fact, many of the children I work with need to be weaned off the medication program they are on so that they can start to practice their new found interpersonal skills.

Please note, I am not anti-medication. Some children really need it. But, I do advocate caution. Over the years I have seen many more children on medication who didn't need it, than children not getting the medication that they did need. I am always surprised when a parent tells me that "Johnny can't do such and such because he is hyper." Some parents use the fact that their child is on medication as a sign, "I'm still a good parent, my son is diagnosed with ADHD!" Personally, it is much more interesting to me to see what a child *can do* versus what they can't do.

Also, medication does not solve the acting out behavior for most children. It simply allows the child to notice his interactions with the world. It allows his cognition to work better for him. I am concerned when medication is prescribed for attention deficit and hyperactive disorders without behavioral management follow-up and evaluation.

Let's get down to the task at hand. Little Tony is having problems staying in school. We all know that it is best for Tony to stay in class, but his behavior is so disruptive that he is often asked to leave.

The first thing we must do is find out how often Tony is kicked out of class. This is our **baseline study**. This is the starting point. It lets us see where we are and if what we are doing is helping the situation.

We checked the school records (most schools keep very good records) and found that over the last month (20 school days) Tony was sent home 11 times. He was also sent to the office, then returned to class, 26 times. So our baseline number is 37. Thirty-seven times in 20 days that Tony was removed from his class. This has to be a big problem for the classroom teacher. The teacher is there to teach and almost twice a day she needs to stop her class to deal with Tony to the point where he is sent out of the room. This level of distraction is very hard on the whole class.

Once we have the baseline, the starting point, we need to develop a treatment program to decrease this baseline number. This tends to be a bone of contention for most teachers and parents. They want the number to become zero as soon as possible. Unfortunately, this seldom happens. It took a long time (usually weeks) for the negative behavior to escalate to its present level. As we discussed in Chapter 1: SHAPING, you can't get a dolphin to jump out of the ocean by yelling "Jump" over a boat's P.A. system.

The way we solve this problem is also by using successive approximation, shaping. The nice thing is that we tend to see positive change from day one.

A BEHAVIOR MODIFICATION TEAM FOR TONY

The adults involved with Tony's education met at the school. The participants were:

Teacher: Mrs. Cramer
Classroom aide: Mrs. Cohan
Principal: Mrs. Bloom
School psychologist: Mr. Delman
Mom: Mrs. Diaz
Tony's therapist: Dr. Phil (I asked for this meeting and also asked for permission, from the principal, to facilitate it.)

At first there was a little tension in the room. The school personnel were frustrated about the escalation of Tony's behavior. Mom was down right upset. She really wanted to blame the school for wasting her child's first 2 1/2 years of education. I changed the tone by explaining:

> I am happy to see everyone here. I appreciate that you are all taking your time to help Tony. I am sure there are many demands on your after school time and I think it is wonderful that you have chosen to stay after school to help Tony.
>
> I am concerned that the problem of Tony's outbursts will get worse. I have been invited here by Mrs. Bloom and Mrs. Diaz to help organize a treatment program for Tony.
>
> My goal is to take the burden of controlling Tony's behavior off of your shoulders and to place this burden back where it belongs ... on Tony. Tony needs to control himself. Tony has to let you all teach him. Tony has to let his mother parent him.
>
> To get Tony back on track I am going to need your help. But, only a little bit of help, in the way of a minute here and a minute there. From what I have been told, Tony demands huge chunks of time, distracting the whole class.

It is important to note that teachers choose teaching as a profession because they wish to teach. I can only imagine the personal discomfort and frustrations Tony's behavior must be imposing on the school staff.

In all my years, I have never had a teaching team refuse to help children like Tony. What usually happens is that the team learns how to help Tony. Then they copy Tony's treatment plan to help Sally, Randy, and George. I have had numerous schools invite me in to teach all their teachers at the same time how to defuse the classroom blowups and re-spark learning in a child that is seriously acting out.

Tony's teaching team wanted to help. We set up a positive / negative token economy to shape Tony's behaviors. Our goal was to help Tony deal with his outburst before he exploded and to help him win his teacher's attention and his mother's attention by staying on target throughout his school day. A token economy, by definition, is a behavior modification system that uses a token as a conditioned reinforcer. In a token economy behavior is shaped towards becoming more socially acceptable. (See Chapter 1: THE POWER OF THE TOKEN ECONOMY)

Most token economies are what I call "positive token economies." This means that the child only earns tokens. Personally I prefer a Positive/Negative Token Economy. In this more sophisticated system, the child can earn (reward) as well as lose tokens (punishment). (Please note that this is much more work for the adults.) This behavior modification system is a lot of work for the teacher because the child's academic and personal needs must always be factored into the equation. A Positive/Negative Token Economy tends to be a warm learning environment that encourages personal responsibility.

A SMILEY CHART FOR TONY

We used a Smiley Chart to keep track of the positive and negative token economy. Checkers, paper "money" and stickers are often used, but I have found that for young acting out children, a stationary chart seems to last throughout the day or week. It keeps the problem of "I lost my ..." or "He stole my token," from occurring.

Smiley	Point value	Name
	+2	A full smiley
	+1	A half smiley
	0	A flat smiley
	-1	A half yucky face
	-2	A full yucky face

Once I found a nine year old girl with hundreds of my "PC's" covering two pieces of paper. When I pointed out, "I remember doing that when I was a teenager. I practiced my initials for days until I liked what I wrote.

She looked surprised. "It's not that hard, it took me only about an hour."

Tony, like most children, seemed to do quite well when the teacher or the aide was supporting him 100% of the time. But, as you know, Tony has to support himself most of the time and allow teachers and aides to help him on an as need basis.

We wanted to give Tony constant, but reasonable reinforcement. Constant meaning, Tony could win his teacher's attention for positive behaviors. Reasonable meaning Mrs. Cramer could support Tony in just a few moments of actual one-on-one time. (She had 26 other children who also need her attention.)

The Smiley Chart which follows was used. Each symbol has its own name. The "nose" initials have two purposes. First it informs the parent who filled out that time period. Second, it keeps the children from filling in their own Smiley Chart.

On the following pages you will find a single day Smiley Chart. Tony got a new Smiley Chart taped to his desk every school morning. The Smiley Chart is broken down into segments.

From the teaching team discussion the following segments were devised: Morning Calendar/Reading, Recess, Lunch, Math, Recess, Group (Science, Language Arts, Study Skills by skill level)

The teaching team's goal was to give Tony information about

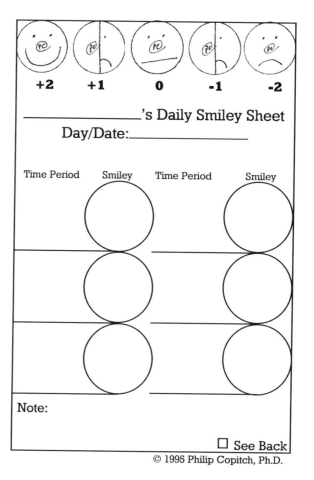

© 1995 Philip Copitch, Ph.D.

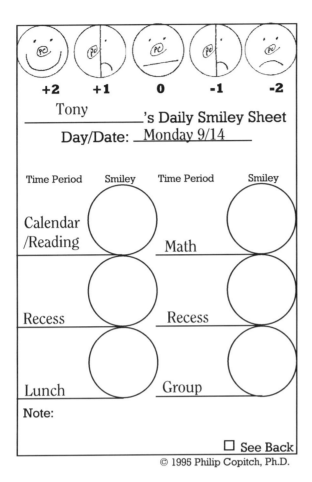

his behavior many times throughout his day. The feedback points of the day were based on Tony's individual needs. Some areas were only 20 minutes while others were as long as 90 minutes. The team thought that the transition time from just before recess until just after recess was very difficult for Tony, so extra attention was placed on that 20 minute time period. For the same reason the team was comfortable with Group time being one segment, even though the time was 1 and 1/2 hours. Tony seemed to do quite well in a small group of three or four others and the aide.

At the appointed moment Mrs. Cramer would draw the appropriate Smiley on Tony's chart. This ritual only took a moment, but it was very formalized. With Tony sitting at his desk Mrs. Cramer would say, "Let's see how you have done this period." Then she would draw in the appropriate Smiley. Whatever the "score," Mrs. Cramer would take a moment to talk about choices and how happy she was that Tony was in her class. Her time commitment was usually less than a minute. For Tony it was the invaluable feedback that he so desperately needed to help him monitor his own behavior.

WHAT THE SMILES "EARNED" TONY

It was possible for Tony to earn a total of 12 points. (2 per time period) When the teaching team filled out, from memory, the smiley sheet for the last three days, it was estimated that Tony would have earned 4 points on one day and less than 3 points on each of the other two days. I suggested that we start the shaping at 5 points. (You start the rope under the waterline to teach a dolphin to jump. With Tony I advocated starting at 5 because with just a little positive reinforcement he was able to get to 4 points.)

At the end of each day, Tony's mother came to school to pick him up. The new Must Rule was:

> **If** Tony earns 5 or more Smiley points **Then** he gets to play for 15 minutes with mom after school at the playground. This is to be one-on-one time.

Mom was the reward. Tony got to *win* mom. And, mom was happy to be won. It was the teaching team's responsibility to "talk this up" (centered around mom and Tony's relationship) throughout the day.

> Wow, you earned 1 smiley point, that's great ... you're getting really close to taking your mom to the park.

> That's rough, a half a yucky face ... Well, I guess you'll have to turn that around.

Children quickly learn (in one or two days) that if you get a -2 it takes a +2 to get back to zero. With this information, their outbursts tend to be of a shorter duration. If a child has a very bad period the teacher can remind him, when he gets his Smiley Chart filled out, that this period is now history and the next time period is a brand new slate. This compartmentalization with suggestive feedback helps the child to look at his choices. This is the beginning of making better choices. When the child realizes he has the choice to act positively he starts to understand how he impacts his world. He learns that he is an individual who can control himself. This is an important notion. For a lot of children it *feels* safer to be out of control than in control of their behaviors. When out of control they are just reacting. For them it is easier to react than it is to understand their environment.

If Tony had a truly bad day his mother was to focus on her hope that he would do better tomorrow. " I'm really looking forward to playing on the swing with you tomorrow." The goal was for mom to talk about how she lost her fun if Tony didn't get to take her to

Sylvia was an intelligent child of seven. The school was very concerned that when Sylvia did not get her way she would scream. She would scream at a high pitch hurting the ears of others in the room.

I suggested that when Sylvia controlled the room with her screaming the teacher should request that she scream louder. Then louder. Then louder.

The teacher had to repeat the scene three times in one day. Once Sylvia could not control with her high pitch, she stopped screaming.

A few days later when Sylvia heard a "no" from her teacher. She rolled her eyes back and muttered as she returned to her seat, "I know, scream

the park.

If Tony had a wonderful day, the goal was for Mrs. Diaz to outwardly enjoy going to the park, and throughout the rest of the day she was to tell people that her son took her to the park because he was doing so well in school. Mrs. Diaz noted, "When I told people that Tony took me to the park, Tony would stand tall and smile ear to ear. It was great ... he was getting talked about instead of getting yelled at."

In individual therapy Tony and I talked a lot about how to make choices. We explored the situation by asking Tony, "What could you do differently?" and followed up with If/Then statements. (See Chapter 3: ADVOCATING FOR GOOD CHOICES) Mrs. Cramer and Mrs. Bloom started asking the same supportive type questions during the second week of the behavior modification program.

The following shows Tony's progress over the first two weeks (10 school days).

Day	Score	Outcome
1	7	Went to park. Great evening at home.
2	4	Did not earn trip to park. Destroyed own room in anger.
3	6	Went to park. Great evening at home.
4	8	Went to park. Normal evening at home.
5	8	Went to park. Normal evening at home.
6	9	Went to park. Normal evening at home.
7	5	Went to park. Great evening at home.
8	9	Went to park. Normal evening at home.
9	11	Went to park. Normal evening at home.
10	10	Went to park. Normal evening at home.

The classroom teacher reported that "a different kid" came to school starting the third day. On the afternoon of the tenth day I met with the teacher and the mother to reevaluate the behavior modification program. We made one minor change. Tony had to earn 9 points to win mom. This change was explained to Tony.

The following shows Tony's progress over the next two weeks (10 school days.)

Day	Score	Outcome
11	11	Went to park. Normal evening at home.
12	11	Went to park. Normal evening at home.
13	11	Mom couldn't go to park due to a dental appointment. Tony got to pick menu for family dinner from three choices.
14	4	Tony was sent home.
15	7	Tony spent 2 hours in office.
16	11	Went to park. Great evening at home.

17	12	Went to park. Normal evening at home.
18	12	Went to park. Normal evening at home.
19	11	Went to park. Normal evening at home.
20	11	Went to park. Normal evening at home.

As you can see, when mom broke the rule (**If** Tony earns nine or more Smileys **Then** he gets to play for 15 minutes with mom after school at the playground. This is to be one-on-one time.), Tony's security fell apart.

On day twenty I met again with the teacher and mom. At this meeting we decided to make the "rope" a little higher. Up to this point Tony had been judged on what the teacher expected out of Tony. (Tony the problem child.) Starting day twenty-one I asked the teacher to judge Tony based on what she expected out of the average child in her class. This mind set change was not told to Tony. It had always been our goal to help Tony fit into an average second grade class by using successive approximation. That had not changed. It was now time for Tony to elicit more appropriate behavior to earn his reward (mom).

On day twenty-three I met with Tony and his mother. At that time I told Tony that the teacher, mom, and I were very proud that he was letting his teacher teach him. Now he had earned a chance to win more than just the park. The Must Rule was changed to:

> **If** Tony earns 10 or more Smiley points **Then** he gets to play with mom 2 minutes for each smiley he earned. This is to be one-on-one time. Tony can pick:
> -Play at park
> -Go on a bike ride
> -Have story time at home

The following shows Tony's progress over the next two weeks (9 school days. Teacher training, one day, no school.)

Day	Score	Outcome
21	10	Went to park. Normal evening at home.
22	11	Went to park. Normal evening at home.
23	10	Went to park. Normal evening at home.
24	11	Bike ride. Great evening at home.
25	11	Bike ride. Great evening at home.
26	12	Story. (Rainy day) Normal evening at home.
27	12	Bike ride. Normal evening at home.
28	12	Bike ride. Normal evening at home.
29	11	Bike ride. Normal evening at home.

This was a vast improvement in the course of about five weeks.

And, please note that the teacher also increased her expectations over the time period. At first Mrs. Cramer was happy to get Tony not to push other kids and to semi stay in his seat. By the third week she expected him to be doing his work and raising his hand if he needed her assistance. By the fifth week she told the principal (who told me), "Tony isn't a problem, but Ashley and Marla need a Smiley Chart."

It is also interesting that during week six of Tony's treatment, Tony was invited to his first birthday party at the Mecca of birthdays, Chuck E. Cheese Pizza. I point this out because it is significant. Tony was starting to make friends. He wasn't seen by the other students as the "bad boy," as he told me. Now Tony was seen as one of the kids in class.

Five months after the smiley sheet had started, mom and the teacher went to a weekly progress report. As mom put it, "Tony really wants to play with his friends after school, not his mom. But we still plan on bike riding every Saturday afternoon."

During the summer we took Tony off all his medication. Third grade is going well. His mother is now complaining about "...all the parties kids get invited to these days." As Tony internalized his new skills, the behavior modification system became obsolete.

A note about rewards. I very seldom use anything other than parental one-on-one time as the reward for appropriate school behavior. I find that it is by far the best for helping a child to develop appropriate social skills. (See Chapters 1-4)

On the following pages you will find daily and weekly smiley charts. They are here for you to make copies of and use. I advise you to lend this book to your child's teacher (or gift them a copy) and to work with the team to help your child. Most teachers and principals have had some training in behavior modification and they will be of great help to your family. If the behaviors are severe please consult with your doctor about a referral to a family therapist that specializes in behavior problems in childhood.

The following forms are available as a free PDF download
from www.CopitchInc.com

	+2	+1	0	-1	-2

_____'s Daily Smiley Sheet

Day/Date: _____

Time Period	Smiley	Time Period	Smiley
	◯		◯
	◯		◯
	◯		◯

Note:

☐ See Back

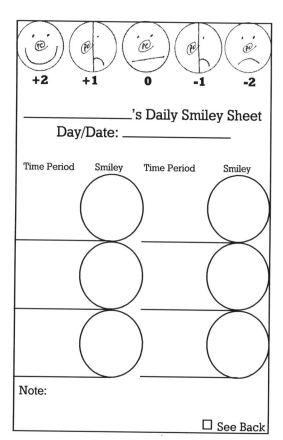

	+2	+1	0	-1	-2

_____'s Daily Smiley Sheet

Day/Date: _____

Time Period	Smiley	Time Period	Smiley
	◯		◯
	◯		◯
	◯		◯

Note:

☐ See Back

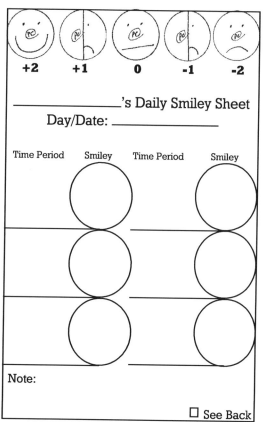
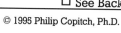

	+2	+1	0	-1	-2

_____'s Daily Smiley Sheet

Day/Date: _____

Time Period	Smiley	Time Period	Smiley
	◯		◯
	◯		◯
	◯		◯

Note:

☐ See Back

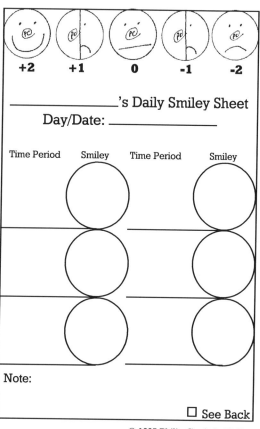

	+2	+1	0	-1	-2

_____'s Daily Smiley Sheet

Day/Date: _____

Time Period	Smiley	Time Period	Smiley
	◯		◯
	◯		◯
	◯		◯

Note:

☐ See Back

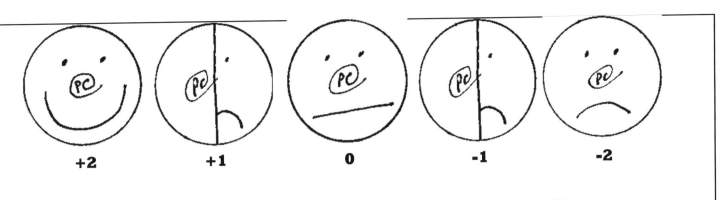

+2   +1   0   -1   -2

_____'s Weekly Smiley Sheet

Week Of_____

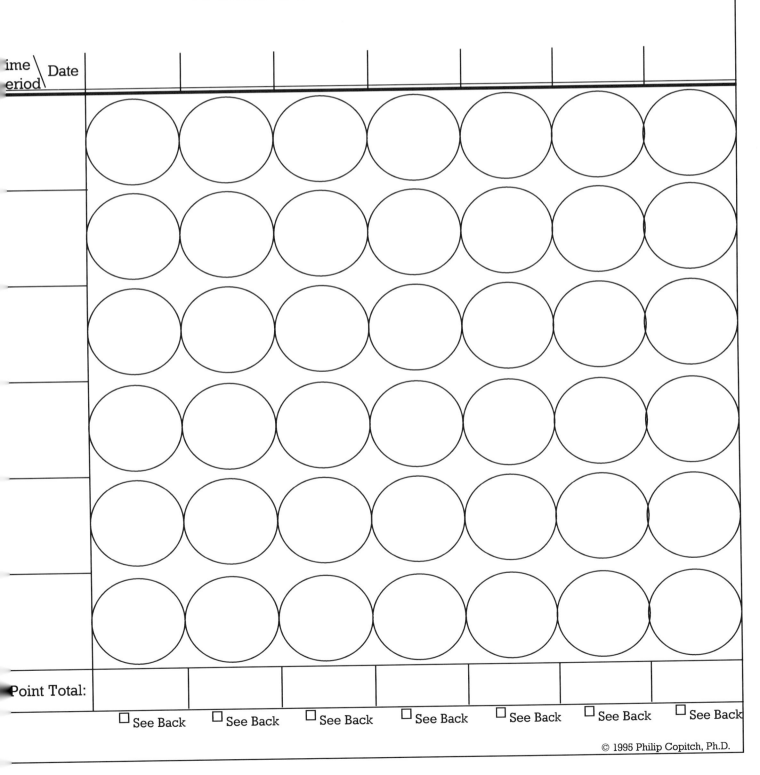

Time Period \ Date							
Point Total:							

☐ See Back   ☐ See Back   ☐ See Back   ☐ See Back   ☐ See Back   ☐ See Back   ☐ See Back

UNCOOPERATIVE BEHAVIOR: SCHOOL MORNINGS, (TEENAGER)

My son is sixteen years old. He is intelligent and good. But I have a problem. I can't get him out of bed on school mornings. I have tried everything. I have begged. I have screamed. I have taken away his belongings to punish him. Nothing seems to work. He just says he is tired and that school is "boring."

At first glance there are two problems that catch my attention. First, why is getting up mom's problem? It sounds like mom is able to get up. Getting out of bed should be the child's responsibility. Second, whenever I come across the problem of teens unable to get up there is always a concern about drugs and/or clinical depression. (Please see, WHAT DO I NEED TO KNOW ABOUT DRUGS elsewhere in this Chapter.)

Chuck was sixteen years old. He was having trouble getting out of bed in the mornings. His mother and father were at odds with him about "the normal teenage stuff:" his hair, his clothes, his friends, and his school tardiness. Chuck lived ten minutes away from school and he was almost always late. It was such a problem that the school placed Chuck on academic probation because he was failing first period. He was doing "C" and "B" work in his other classes.

Chuck's mother, Mrs. Koclowski explained:

Chuck is a great kid. We have been blessed with him. Until this year he has not been a problem. Both of our kids are great. Chuck's older brother is a freshman in college this year. I have tried everything to get Chuck out of bed, He just lays there. My mother told me to pour cold water on him if he refuses to get up, but it felt wrong and Chuck was so angry with me, he just swore at me and laid in the wet sheets. We have taken away his belongings and grounded him. He has nothing left to take away. Every morning it is a big fight to get him out of bed. I hate the mornings.

The problem here is the ownership of the problem. It is not the parents' responsibility to get their teen out of bed. It is the parents' job to instill responsibility into their children. As we discussed in Chapter 4, *All things being equal, teens do what they want to do.*

Who is responsible to get to school on time? In this case it is

Chuck. At the present time, the unwritten Must Rule is, "Mom gets upset and Chuck sleeps through it." This is not a well written rule.

When the question was asked, "What is the reward Chuck is earning for sleeping in?" Mom, dad, and Chuck came up with:

1. Chuck hates first period English. He was getting a "D," even when he went to class.

2. Chuck was winning mom in the morning by making her act crazy.

3. Chuck was tired and could not get up, so the sleep was a reward.

When I asked Chuck about his future, he stated, "I'm going to college then getting a really good paying job."

When I asked what Chuck did at night instead of sleeping, Chuck said, "I just kick and listen to music. I don't get into any trouble."

The new family rules (discussed by all, but written by mom and dad) were as follows.

Must Rule: Chuck will attend every class.

Consequence: Set by school.

Must Rule: Chuck will maintain a "B" average.

Consequence: Loss of driving privilege until grades are raised to a "B" average.

Must Rule: No music in house after 10 PM on school nights; midnight on non-school nights.

Consequence: Loss of stereo for 24 hours.

Must Rule: Mom and dad cannot complain about any music group.

Consequence: For every negative statement, Chuck receives a quarter to go towards buying music.

At the end of the second session, Mrs. Koclowski lingered

Thy fate is the common fate of all;
Into each life some rain must fall,—
        Longfellow

as the family left the room. She whispered, "We've done all this ... I don't think it is going to work." "That may be so," I smiled, "but you have to follow the Must Rules."

Starting the next day, Chuck got himself up and out on time. He earned three dollars towards music and the family conflicts diffused. By the one month mark, Chuck had bought two used CD's (about $11) and his parents were happy to see their old Chuck back. Chuck had earned and completed two "Saturday Schools" for being tardy.

What happened? Where did the big fight go? The big fight centered around Chuck proving to his parents that he could make his own choices. To prove his point he stayed up most of the night and listened to music. That caused him to be too tired, but his mother took the blame for that (by working so hard to get him up) so Chuck never had to.

Only a few things really changed in Chuck's world. The major change was that he got to listen to music while he was doing his homework. This was never allowed in the past. This had bothered Chuck because he saw this as an insult to his ability to make good choices. Another change was that Chuck's parents stopped verbally attacking Chuck's music. This was a big deal, because Chuck took the attacks as a personal attack on his character. (See Chapter 2: HOW TO BUILD YOUR CHILD'S SELF ESTEEM.)

By putting Chuck back in control of his responsibilities, Chuck did a reasonable job. It was interesting that one of the used CD's that Chuck bought was a *Best of Pat Boone* that he gave to his parents as a present. In the card was the statement, "Not my kind of music!" Glued onto the card was a quarter.

UNCOOPERATIVE BEHAVIOR IN SCHOOL (TEENAGER)

Martin is sixteen years old. He is uncooperative and defiant in school. He verbally states that he does not wish to stay in school. He wants to "start his life." Martin's parents have been divorced for over five years. His mother is a waitress and his father is a long haul truck driver. Martin openly states that he hates school and wants to be a long haul trucker like his father. Martin's mother is dead set against the whole idea. "I don't want no son of mine," she exclaimed, "Wasting his life driving a truck." She wants her son to go to college and "To make something out of himself."

The day I met Martin he had just been sent home from the continuation high school because he was smoking on campus. He was asked to leave his neighborhood high school the year before due to daily disruptive behavior.

As I do with all cases of teens exhibiting disruptive behavior, I had Martin tested for drugs. To the surprise of his mother, he was clean.

When I met with this family, it was obvious that Martin was stuck in the middle of his parents' angry divorce. It seemed that Martin had picked his father's side because his father's life looked more exciting. His father traveled all over the country and seemed to have an easy life. Lots to see, cash in his pocket, and little pressure.

Over the course of three weeks I got mom to reluctantly agree to let Martin ride with his father for the whole summer. Martin would get to live the life of the trucker. To see, first hand, if it was for him. This was not an easy situation for mom to agree to. She was sure that trucking was the reason for her divorce and she didn't like the idea of her "baby" living on the road. She also knew that living with Martin was getting impossible and she had to do something.

Two months into the three months of summer trucking, Martin unexpectedly returned home on the bus. It took him three more days to tell his mother what was going on.

It was stupid. All I did all day was sit in a truck. When we did get to some town, the load wasn't ready and someone would yell at dad. It wasn't dad's fault, but if you're a trucker the people in the office treat you like dirt. I just couldn't handle sitting any longer, so dad gave me bus fare home.

While Martin was away, mom and I worked on a contingency

Youth is a wonderful thing; what a crime to waste it on children.
George Bernard Shaw

plan, just in case Martin returned home. The new Must Rules devised by mom and presented to Martin were as follows (Martin was much easier to talk to now that he was "choosing" to live with his mother):

Must Rule: Martin must go to all his classes.

Consequence: School consequences and 1 chore for every class missed.

Must Rule: Mom will not bad mouth dad.

Consequence: Mom has to make a dessert.

Must Rule: Martin will not smoke in the house or at school. He can smoke on back porch and walking to and from school.

Consequence: Martin does own laundry for one week. (Mom seemed to like to do Martin's laundry, but refused to do mine when I offered to drop it off.)

Two years later I got a call from Martin. He was graduating from high school and joining the Army. When I asked him what his future plans were he proudly said, "I want to be a fire fighter."

Note: The teen has the power over the parent when it comes to their actions. We can advocate for them but they must do their own choice making. When mom started advocating for Martin, he learned that the fantasy life he thought trucking was, wasn't for him. With information (education), most people make better choices, most of the time.

Mrs. Rallof was very upset the first time I met her. She told me,

Jack (sixteen years of age) is a good boy. He is very smart and has lots of potential. He can do anything he puts his mind to. The problem is that he just doesn't care about acting good. I had a meeting with his dean and was told that Jack was on his last chance. One more referral slip to the dean and Jack will be suspended for five days. When I tried to talk with him he just said, "They can't do that to me, I'm not that big of a problem.

Over the next week I met with the Rallof family three times. Jack's drug test was negative and mom was correct, Jack was very smart. He presented himself as arrogant and I could see how a teacher would find his attitude hard to live with. Overall, the Rallof family was functioning quite well. The only real problem was Jack's attitude about being in school. Mr. and Mrs. Rallof only wrote one Must Rule. (Even though I asked for more. The parents were as hard to teach as their son!)

Must Rule: Jack's job is to get through his class day without being in conflict with his teachers.

Consequence: Mom will follow Jack around school to make sure he is following the rule.

Mrs. Rallof contacted the dean and requested permission to supervise Jack throughout his day rather than suspending him. The dean agreed. It only took until lunch the next day for Jack to test the dean's and his mother's resolve. Mrs. Rallof followed the rule. She shadowed Jack around for one full day. She sat at the back of Jack's classes and walked a few yards behind him in the hallways. She supervised his behavior because he was unable to do it himself.

Jack's behavior improved dramatically. For the next two years Jack earned not one referral slip to the dean's office. Once Jack believed that his parents expected appropriate behavior in school he stopped testing the size of the behavioral envelope and acted appropriately in class.

The best memory is that which forgets nothing but injuries. Write kindness in marble and write injuries in the dust.
Persian proverb

"Momma, where do storks come from?"

WHAT DO I NEED TO KNOW ABOUT STREET DRUGS?

OVERVIEW OF THE PROBLEM

I need to start off with a serious warning. If your family presently has a member with a drug or alcohol problem, this section will be of limited assistance. A drug problem needs the support of people outside of your family. I advocate that families seek the professional support of a competent family therapist or drug treatment facility.

The secrecy that surrounds most families who have a member with a drug problem tends to inadvertently support the drug abuser. Please seek help outside of your family. At the end of this section you will find national contact information.

The goal of this section is to provide interested parents with the basic facts concerning drugs that surround their children. It is a fact that our society is inundated by drugs. I cannot think of any section of our community that drugs has not infected. Our country has declared a war on drugs. Most people agree that it has been an expensive failure. I once asked a high ranking police officer if he thought his department was making a dent in the drug trade, to which he replied, "You can tell by the price that drugs are everywhere. Drugs are sold by supply and demand economics and, unfortunately, drugs are relatively cheap."

So, what is a parent to do? How do you keep your children away from drugs? Chapter Two explains how you assist your child to develop a high self esteem. This will be your best hedge against the destructive nature of drugs. Also, information is power. As a parent you need information and your children need information about the dangers and realities of drugs.

Your children are listening from the very beginning. You need to be careful that you are giving a clear message about drugs. What are your attitudes about the socially acceptable drugs, caffeine, alcohol, and tobacco? Do you encourage your children to take their daily vitamin pill as a quick fix to a well balanced meal?

When your children are adolescents they will, by nature, be "invincible." This is a dangerous time for them. Invincible beings do not see the dangers of drugs.

I advocate that parents share their feelings on a daily basis with their children. If I hear a news report about how some actor harmed himself with drugs, I question out loud, "I wonder how such a talented person allowed drugs into his life?" When a character on TV is acting drunk I bring up, "Boy, he is a good actor, if he was really drunk he couldn't remember his lines." When my child tells me that he heard that there are lots of homeless people I discuss that in my experience many homeless people have a drug or alcohol

The time has come to stop the sale of slavery to the young.
Lyndon Baines John-

problem. When a college student told me, in front of my nine year old, that he went to an all night kegger party, I asked him how he felt the next day. He said "Oh, I was sick as a dog!"

"It was a party that you got sick as a dog at, don't your friends care about you? I wouldn't want any of my friends to get sick as a dog at my party." The point is, parents need to condone and expect mature and safe choices and help people in their life to expect the same for themselves.

GATEWAY DRUGS

Parents need to watch out for, and guard against, the gateway to drugs. It is commonly stated that marijuana is the gateway to the hard drugs. And, that people who smoke pot are more likely to move onto harder drugs. The physiological evidence for this is limited. In addition, on the surface I find it to be a limited parenting tool to tell a child that they cannot use the "soft drugs" because they *may* lead to the hard drugs.

I want parents to watch for gateway behavior as a signal that there is potential trouble. If your child wants to wear a tee shirt that is adorned with a giant marijuana leaf, I am concerned about the behavioral presentation. Who is your child wearing the shirt for? It could be a simple act of thumbing his nose at authority. Or, it could be a way to get accepted into the drug scene. It is a fact that the drug subculture of your community has very strict social regulations. Your child will have to follow these regulations to fit in. The gateway to the drug scene is your child's behavioral choices. Parents need to keep their eyes and ears open.

Over the years I have consulted with hundreds of parents who have said something like, "I just can't believe it, not my baby!" Then as the parents begin to learn what the drug scene looks like I hear, "I had no idea. When he did that I thought it was no big thing." Please watch and listen to your children. If you hear your child talking about "pot," "Ludes," or "Demmies" you need to understand his world.

It is common for teens to pay for their drug habit by stealing. Most teens steal from the family before they start to steal from the community at large. Stealing within the home must be dealt with immediately, it is often an early sign of a larger problem.

Parents need to be clear with their children about the Must Rules concerning drugs. This will be discussed in the next subsection.

In our overview we will learn the basic information that every parent needs to have to appropriately protect their family. The federal Drug Enforcement Agency (DEA) has devised the following drug classification listing. This information will be referenced as we discuss the different types of drugs your child may encounter.

Any clinician in this day and age who overlooks and fails to check for drug and alcohol abuse as a primary component of negative teenage behavior is either irresponsible or incompetent.
Tough Love Solutions
Phyllis York
Davis York
Ted Wachtel

Water taken in moderation, cannot hurt anybody.

Mark Twain

DRUG ENFORCEMENT AGENCY (DEA)
CLASSIFICATIONS
(This will be indicated in the charts to follow)

I: Illicit drugs with no medical use; high potential for abuse.

II: Prescription drugs with high potential for abuse and physical dependence.

III: Drugs with less abuse potential than schedule II; have moderate to low physical dependence, but may have high psychological dependence.

IV: Prolonged use of these drugs may lead to limited physical or psychological dependence; lower abuse potential than schedule III.

I have broken down the drugs available on the streets into sections based on how they will affect your child. These sections are:

a. Drugs that depress the central nervous system
b. Drugs that stimulate the central nervous system
c. Drugs that cause hallucination
d. Drugs that relieve pain

DRUGS THAT DEPRESS THE CENTRAL NERVOUS SYSTEM

<u>Behavior changes associated with depressant drug usage:</u>

· Drowsiness (low level of drug)
· Coma (higher level of drug)
· Lack of coordination
· Speech impairment (slurred speech, stuttering)
· General mental confusion
· Muscle tremors (usually localized)
· Decreased muscle tone
· Feelings of paranoia
· Emotional outbursts (anger or elation not appropriate for setting)
· Dramatic change in sleep pattern with ongoing usage

<u>When the drug problem is exposed:</u>

· The user often talks about guilty feelings concerning drug

We believe that the normal struggle of adolescence is distorted and made pathological by the abuse of drugs.
Tough Love Solutions
Phyllis York
Davis York
Ted Wachtel

usage

·   The user is regretful for things that they have done

·   Other family members want to believe and can be used by the user, because they care *too* much

The most common central nervous system depressant is alcohol. However, all depressants will make the user seem drunk. As the name implies, this classification of drug depresses the body's normal nervous system abilities. There is a danger of physical harm and even death from overdosing with depressants. Most families learn to live in fear of the angry outbursts depressant users are prone to. It is not unusual for me to work with families that have numerous holes in their walls from angry outbursts that endanger all members of the family.

DEPRESSANTS / SEDATIVES / HYPNOTICS

BARBITURATES

Type of Drug	Name	Street Name	Time detectable in Urine	DEA
Phenobarbital	Luminal	Downers, Goofballs	Short-Acting	IV
Secobarbital	Seconal	Barbs, Reds	1 Day	III
Pentobarbital	Nembutal	Nembies	Long-Acting	III
Butabarbital	Butisol	Bute, Stoppers	2-3 Weeks	III
Amobarbital	Amytal	Yellow Jackets		III
Aprobarbital	Alurate	Barbs, Downers		III

BENZODIAZEPINES

Type of Drug	Name	Street Name	Time detectable in Urine	DEA
Chlordiazepoxide	Librium	Downs, Nerve Pills, Tranks	Therapeutic	IV
Clonazepam	Clonopin	Downs, Nerve Pills, Tranks	dose: 3 Days	IV
Diazepam	Valium	Downs, Nerve Pills, Tranks		IV
Flurazepam	Dalmane	Downs, Nerve Pills, Tranks	Chronic use	IV
Lorazepam	Ativan	Downs, Nerve Pills, Tranks	over period of	IV
Oxazepam	Serax	Downs, Nerve Pills, Tranks	months or	IV
Alprazolam	Xanax	Downs, Nerve Pills, Tranks	years: 4-6 wks.	IV
Chlorazepate	Tranxene	Downs, Nerve Pills, Tranks		

METHAQUALONE

Type of Drug	Name	Street Name	Time detectable in Urine	DEA
Methaqualone	Quaalude	Ludes	14 Days	IV

For every question, there is an answer that is simple, unequivocal, and usually wrong.
Robert Kuttner

TRICYCLIC ANTIDEPRESSANTS

Type of Drug	Name	Street Name	Time detectable in Urine	DEA
Amitriptyline	Elavil	None	No Data	
Nortriptyline	Aventyl			
lmipraniine	Tofranil			
Desipramine	Norpramin			
Doxepin	Sinequan			

ALCOHOL

Type of Drug	Name	Street Name	
Ethanol	N/A	Booze	After absorption ($\sim$ 1 hr.) blood alcohol decreases $\sim$ 0.02 gm%/hour.

INHALANTS

Technically inhalants are a depressant. Children as young as six up to around sixteen are the most common users. The most common inhalants are "airplane" glue, gasoline, harsh smelling cleaners, and harsh smelling solvents. The initial intent of the sniffer is to get a quick high. This early high tends to be experienced as dizziness and memory loss (feelings of drunkenness). Due to tolerance, children quickly graduate to long durations of sniffing using plastic bags, cloth, or small jars to concentrate the odor. Regular users exhibit slurred speech, memory loss, constant drowsiness, dulling of affect, and weight loss.

Sniffing of glues and gasoline can cause permanent brain damage.

DRUGS THAT STIMULATE THE CENTRAL NERVOUS SYSTEM

Behavior changes associated with stimulant drug usage:

· Irritability, mood change
· Rapid speech
· Agitation
· Problems with concentration
· Cold symptoms (Due to nasal irritation, cocaine)
· Sleep cycle problems
 (User may not sleep for days, then sleep for days.)
· Dilated pupils (User may hide behind sunglasses.)
· Itchy skin, may develop open sores

This classification of drug stimulates the body's nervous system. When the drug is initially ingested the user may seem drunk.

As the drug is broken down by the body, the user tends to seem depressed and suffering from the flu.

Most teens use stimulants because of the euphoric feeling they give for several hours. The body has a high tolerance for stimulants and the user tends to need more of the drug to obtain the same feeling of euphoria. It is common for users to first feed their habit by selling their belongings. When they run out of money many teens turn to burglary and prostitution. (Users will even steal from their family to get their drug needs met.)

It is important to note that stimulants tax the user's body. Stimulants cause heartbeat irregularities, increased blood pressure, blood clots and muscle spasms. Stimulant usage can cause sudden death due to heart attack. Many teens scoff at this fact believing that they are young and that they have a strong heart. A review of the medical literature shows that even healthy individuals who are young and athletic have died from moderate doses of stimulants.

STIMULANTS

Type of Drug	Name	Street Name	Time detectable in Urine	DEA
Amphetamine	Benzedrine, Obetrol 10/20	Speed, Crank	24-72 Hours	II
Methamphetamine	Desoxyn	Upper, Snot, Clue, Meth	24-72 Hours	II
Cocaine	None	Coke, Rock, Crack, Snow, Blow, Toot Nose candy	24-96 Hours	II

DRUGS THAT CAUSE HALLUCINATION

Behavior changes associated with hallucinogenic drug usage:
(Excluding cannabis which will be discussed separately.)

· Profound changes in mood
· Unpredictable behavior (overly pleasant or frightened)
· Seeing things that are not there
· Hearing things that are not there
· Smelling things that are not there
· Dilated pupils
· Profuse sweating
· May have flu-like symptoms

The person under the influence of an hallucinogen tends to show psychotic-like behaviors. The user may have a "good" or a "bad" *trip.* The user suffering a bad trip may exhibit drug induced psychotic behaviors: severe panic, disorientation and overwhelming fear. A bad trip constitutes a medical emergency. A user having a good trip experiences unrealistic flows of thought and sensation.

HALLUCINOGENS: EXCEPT MARIJUANA

Type of Drug	Name	Street Name	Time detectable in Urine	DEA
Lysergic acid diethylamide				
	None	LSD, Acid	1.5-5 Days	I
Phencyclidine	None	PCP, Angel Dust	14-30 Days	II
		K-J (marijuana soaked with PCP)		
Methyenedioxyamphetamine				
	None	MDA, Love Drug	No Data	I
Methylenedioxymethamphetamine				
	None	MDMA, Adam, Ecstasy	No Data	I

HALLUCINOGENS: MARIJUANA

Behavior changes associated with marijuana usage:

· Extreme calmness
· Loss of drive
· Loss of age appropriate judgment
· Emotional disturbance
· Loss of time
· Loss of orientation
· Hunger
· Delirium (rare)

Teens in most communities in the United States have relatively easy access to marijuana and hashish. Marijuana and hashish are harvested from the same plant, *Cannabis sativa*. Marijuana is the dried leaves and flower, while hashish is the concentrated resin of the plant that grows relatively easily throughout the world. The active ingredient, delta-9-tetrahydrocannabinol (THC) gives the user the feeling of relaxed euphoria. The effects of THC are relatively benign for most individuals. However, research shows that individuals with emotional disorders tend to find that marijuana increases their psychotic or neurotic disorder.

I wrote above that THC is relatively benign, but it is by no means a good idea for teens or most adults to indulge. I find it is important to explain this clearly to teens. Many adults try to scare kids into abstaining. What I have experienced is that teens do well with information. The biggest problem with marijuana comes when kids avoid conflicts by getting high. When teens deal with problems in their life by getting high, they rob themselves of the practice of learning how to deal with problems. Pot takes the creativity and future orientation away from regular users. I regularly see twenty-five year olds that have used pot daily since age fifteen. Of interest is that these individuals are quite often emotionally retarded in their interpersonal abilities. By age forty, I find that regular pot users are emotionally functioning at about the age of twenty-five. I am not saying that they are youthful, I am saying that they are immature. They have spent thousands of hours procuring and using their drug of choice, and have limited their emotional growth by avoiding lessons on how one can deal with conflicts.

Chronic marijuana users tend to develop a tolerance, causing them to increase their dosage to obtain their desired euphoria.

HALLUCINOGENS: MARIJUANA

Type of Drug	Name	Street Name	Time detectable in Urine	DEA
Cannabinoids	"Medical marijuana"	Grass, Pot, Smoke K-J (marijuana soaked with PCP) Hash, Sh-t, Thai, Thai Stick, Weed, Dope	*	I

*CANNABINOIDS - DETECTION TIME	
Light smoker or acute dosage	1-3 days
Moderate Use (4 times/week)	3-5 days
Heavy Smoker (daily)	10 days
Heavy, Chronic Use (5+ joints/day)	10-21+ days
Oral Ingestion	1-5 days

DRUGS THAT RELIEVE PHYSICAL PAIN

Behavior changes associated with pain killer drug usage:

· Depressed state, fear of failure
· Prone to agitation and aggression
· Prone to carelessness
· Feelings of hopelessness
· Impulsive behaviors
· Low level of frustration
· Demand for immediate gratification

Most prescribed pain killers are opiate based or a synthetic chemical that mimics morphine. The word opium comes from the Greek word for juice. It is produced from the milky juice of the immature seed sacks of the poppy plant. From this heroin and morphine are produced. In the laboratory we synthesize (man made) morphine-like chemicals that are routinely used around the world to relieved pain, suppress coughs, and as anesthetics.

ANALGISICS (Semi-Synthetic)

Type of Drug	Name	Street Name	Time detectable in Urine	DEA
Codeine	Empirin, Tylenol w\ Codeine	Schoolboy	24-72 Hours	III
Morphine	Raxanol	M," Morph	24-72 Hours	II
Diacetylmorphine		Heroin, Horse, Smack, "H," Speedball (w/Cocaine)	24-72 Hours	I
Hydrcodone	Hycodan, Vicodin	None	24-72 Hours	-
Hydromorphone	Dilaudid	Juice, Dillies	24-72 Hours	-
Oxycodone	Percodan	Percs	24-72 Hours	-

ANALGISICS (Synthetic)

Type of Drug	Name	Street Name	Time detectable in Urine	DEA
Meperidine	Demerol	Demmies, Pain Killer	No Data	II
Methadone	Dolophine	Dollies, Meth	72 Hours	II
Pentazocine	Talwin	T's	No Data	III
Propoxypene	Darvon	Pain Killer	6-48 Hours	IV

MUST RULES CONCERNING DRUGS

The following are Must Rules written by families. All the families reported that their Must Rule solved problems within their family.

Family with four teens, no history of drugs:

> Must Rule: No drugs! Period. Unless given to you by your parents as prescribed by your doctor.

> Consequence: One month grounding. No unsupervised time for six months.

Home school family with teen with a drug history:

> Must Rule: You are not allowed to use or even hold illegal drugs.

> Consequence: You will not be allowed out of my sight for one month. You will be drug tested, randomly for one year.

<u>Foster home with residents with a history of juvenile law problems:</u>

Must Rule: OUR HOME IS A DRUG FREE ZONE.

No drugs are allowed within 1000 yards of our property. All residents have signed a drug free lifestyle pledge. Medication can only be give out by the house parents.

Consequence: Any violation of our drug free environment will be prosecuted to the highest degree of the law. House parents are mandated by law to report all criminal activity to the police and your probation officer.

<u>Family with six children ranging in age from 6 to 20:</u>

Must Rule: You are not allowed to use or be around drugs or alcohol. You will not get into a car without permission. You will call for a ride, no matter what the hour, without your parents judging you.

Consequence: Loss of license for six months plus house restrictions for one month.

DRUG AND ALCOHOL ABUSE CONTACT INFORMATION

Most counties have a Drug and Alcohol Abuse Program. It will be listed in your local phone book.

Most of this list was developed by the National PTA and/or the Partnership for a Drug-Free America.

American Council for Drug Education
164 West 74th Street
New York, NY 10023
1-800-488-3784
www.acde.org

California Department of
Alcohol and Drug Abuse Programs
1-800-879-2772

Creative Partnerships for Prevention
www.CPPrev.org

Department of Education: Safe & Drug Free Schools Program
600 Independence Avenue, SW, #604
Washington, DC 20202-6123
1-800-624-0100 (publications)
202-260-3954 (office)
www.ed.gov/offices/OESE/SDFS

Department of Health and Human Services: Keeping Youth Drug-Free
200 Independence Avenue, S.W.
Washington, DC 20201
202-619-0257
www.health.org/pubs/drugfree/keep-menu.htm

Food and Drug Administration: Children and Tobacco
(HFE-88)
Rockville, MD 20857
1-888-FDA-4KIDS
www.fda.gov/opacom/campaigns/tobacco.html

Join Together
441 Stuart Street, 7th Floor
Boston, MA 02116
617-437-1500
www.jointogether.org

The National Center on Addiction and Substance Abuse at Columbia

University (CASA)
152 West 57th Street, 12th Floor
New York, NY 10019-3310
212-841-5200
Fax: 212-956-8020
www.casacolumbia.org

The National Center for
Tobacco-Free Kids
1-800-284-KIDS
www.tobaccofreekids.org

National Clearinghouse for Alcohol and Drug Information (NCADI)
P.O. Box 2345
Rockville, MD 20847-2345
1-800-729-6686
1-800-487-4889 TDD
www.health.org/index.htm

National Council on Alcoholism and Drug Dependence, Inc.
12 West 21st Street, 7th Floor
New York, NY 10017
212-206-6770
1-800-NCA-CALL
www.ncadd.org

National Families in Action
2296 Henderson Mill Road, Suite 300
Atlanta, GA 30345-2739
770-934-6364
Fax: 770-934-7137
www.emory.edu/NFIA

National Inhalant Prevention
Coalition
1201 W. Sixth Street, Suite C-200
Austin, TX 78703
1-800-269-4237 or 512-480-8953
Fax: 512-477-3932 or
E-mail: nipc @io.com
www.inhalants.com/

National Institute on Drug Abuse (NIDA)
National Institutes of Health
5600 Fishers Lane, Room 10A-39
Rockville, MD 20857
1-800-662-HELP
Fax: 301-443-6245
www.nida.nih.gov

Parents' Resource Institute for Drug
Education, Inc. (PRIDE)
50 Hurt Plaza, Suite 210
Atlanta, GA 30303
404-577-4500
1-800-677-7433
www.prideusa.org

Partnership for a Drug-Free America
405 Lexington Avenue, 16th floor
New York, NY 10174
www.drugfreeamerica.org

The Willow Tree Teen Institute
P.O. Box 265
Green Village, NJ 07935
973-301-9104
E-mail: willowsue@worldnet.att.net

Alcohol and Drug Treatment

Al-Anon/Alateen Family Group Headquarters, Inc. (For families and friends of alcoholics)
1600 Corporate Landing Parkway
Virginia Beach, VA 23454-5617
For Free Literature Packet:
1-800-356-9996 USA
1-800-714-7498 Canada
For Meeting Information:
1-800-344-2666 (USA)
1-800-443-4525 (Canada)
www.al-anon-alateen.org/

Alcoholics Anonymous World Services
P.O. Box 459
Grand Central Station
New York, NY 10163
212-870-3400
www.alcoholics-anonymous.org

Narcotics Anonymous
P.O. Box 9999
Van Nuys, CA 91409
818-780-3951
www.wsoinc.com

Nar-Anon Family Groups
P.O. Box 2562
Palos Verdes Penninsula, CA 90274
213-547-5800

National Drug Information,
Treatment and Referral Hotline:
1-800-662-HELP (662-4357).

The National Association for
Children of Alcoholics
11426 Rockville Pike, Suite 100
Rockville, MD 2085
1-888-554-COAS
www.health.org/nacoa

MORE DRUG ABUSE INFORMATION PROGRAMS

African American Family Services
2616 Nicollet Avenue
Minneapolis, MN 55408
612-871-7878

Al-Anon Family
Group Headquarters, Inc.
1600 Corporate Landing Parkway
Virginia Beach VA 23454-5617
757-563-1600 (USA)
613-722-1830(Canada)

Alcoholics Anonymous World Services
475 Riverside Drive
New York, NY 10115
212-870-3400

American Council for Drug Education
164 West 74th St.
New York, NY 10023
800-488-DRUG

American Health Foundation

320 East 43rd St.
New York, NY 10017
212-687-2339

Boys and Girls Clubs of America
1230 West Peachtree St., NW
Atlanta, GA 30309
404-815-5700

Camp Fire, Inc.
4601 Madison Ave
Kansas City, MO 64112
816-756-1950

CDC National AIDS Clearinghouse
P.O. Box 6003
Rockville, MD 20849-6003
800-458-5231

Center for Substance
Abuse Prevention (CSAP)
Substance Abuse and Mental Health
Services Administration

5600 Fishers Lane, Room 800
Rockville, MD 20857
301-443-0373
800-729-6686
(National Clearing House)

Center for Science in the Public Interest
1875 Connecticut Ave, NW, Ste. 300
Washington, DC 20009-5728
202-332-9110

Center for Substance
Abuse Treatment (CSAT)
5600 Fishers Lane, Room 618
Rockville, MD 20857
(301) 443-5052

Clearinghouse on Family
Violence Information
P.O. Box 1182
Washington, DC 20013
800-394-3366
Community Anti-Drug
Coalitions of America (CADCA)

901 North Pitt Street, Ste 300
Alexandria, VA 22314
703-706-0560
800-54-CADCA

Drug Strategies
2445 M. Street NW
Suite 480
Washington DC 20037
202-663-6090

Families Anonymous
P.O. Box 3475
Culver City, CA 90231
800-736-9805

Girls Incorporated
30 East 33rd Street, 7th Fl.
New York, NY 10016
317-634-7546 (National)
800-374-4475

Hazelden Foundation
Box 11
Center City, MN 55012
800-328-9000

Join Together
441 Stuart Street, 6th Fl.
Boston, MA 02116
617-437-1500

"Just Say No" International
1777 North California Blvd., Ste. 210
Walnut Creek, CA 94596
510-939-6666
800-258-2766

Mothers Against Drunk Driving
511 East John Carpenter Freeway, Ste.
700
Irvington, TX 75062
214-744-6233
800-GET-MADD

Nar-Anon Family Groups
P.O. Box 2562
Palos Verdes Peninsula, CA 90274
213-547-5800

Narcotics Anonymous
11426 Rockville Pike, Ste. 100
Rockville, MD 20852
301-468-0985
National Association for Native American Children of Alcoholics
611 12th Avenue South, Ste. 200

Rockville, MD 20852
301-468-0985

National Association for
Children of Alcoholics
11426 Rockville Pike, Suite 100
Seattle, WA 98144
206-324-9360
800-322-5601

National Black Child
Development Institute
463 Rhode Island Avenue NW
Washington, DC 20005
202-387-1281
800-556-2234

National Center for
Tobacco-Free Kids
1707 L St. NW, Ste. 800
Washington, DC 20036
202-296-5469
800-284-KIDS

National Clearinghouse for
Alcohol and Drug Information
P.O. Box 2345
Rockville, MD 20847-2345
800-SAY-NOTO

National Coalition of Hispanic Health
and Human Services Organizations
1501 16th, NW
Washington, DC 20005
202-387-5000

National Council on Alcoholism
and Drug Dependence, Inc.
12 West 21st, 7th Fl.
New York, NY 10017
212-206-6770
800-NCA-CALL

National Crime Prevention Council
1700 K Street, NW, 2nd Fl.
Washington, DC 20006
202-466-6272
800-627-2911 (information requests)

National Families in Action
2296 Henderson
Mill Rd, Ste 300
Atlanta, GA 30345
770-934-6364
National Family Partnership
9220 S.W. Barbur Blvd. #119-284
Portland, OR 97219

Phone:(503) 768-9659
Fax: (503) 244-5506

National Head Start Association
201 North Union Street, Ste. 320
Alexandria, VA 22314
703-739-0875

National Inhalant
Prevention Coalition
1201 W. Sixth St., Ste. C-200
Austin, TX 78703
800-269-4237

National Institute on
Drug Abuse (NIDA)
5600 Fishers Lane, Room 10A03
Rockville, MD 20857
301-443-4577

National Urban League:
Substance Abuse Program
500 East 62nd Street
New York, NY 10021
212-310-9000

Office of Minority Health Resource
Center
P.O. Box 37337
Washington, DC 20013-7337
800-444-6472

Office of National Drug Control Policy
(ONDCP)
P.O. Box 6000
Rockville, MD 20849-6000
800-666-3332

Parents' Resource Institute for
Drug Education (PRIDE)
50 Hurt Plaza, Ste. 210
Atlanta, GA 30303
404-577-4500
800-853-7867

Safe & Drug-Free Schools Program
U.S. Department of Education
1250 Maryland Ave. SW
Washington DC 20024
800-624-0100

Students Against Driving Drunk
200 Pleasant Street
Marlboro, MA 01752
508-481-3568
Toughlove
P.O. Box 1069

Doylestown, PA 18901
215-348-7090
800-333-1069

National Domestic Violence Hotline
800-799-7233

Treatment Facility Referrals and Helpline
800-HELP-111

**Quick
Reference
Guide**

2 SUPER SITES

Recommended Web Information sites for parents with an interest in learning more about drug treatment and prevention.

The National PTA and GTE Corporation have created: Common Sense: Strategies for Raising Alcohol and Drug-Free Children. www. pta.org/commonsense

###

Partnership for a Drug-Free America www. drugfreeamerica.org

###

Both of these sites are extremely well written, informative and authoritative. A must surf for every parent.

FURTHER READING ABOUT DRUG ABUSE PREVENTION:

Preparing for the Drug-Free Years: A Family Activity Book, by J. David Hawkins, et al., 1988. Developmental Research and Programs, Box 85746, Seattle, WA 98145. $10.95.

Team Up for Drug Prevention with America's Young Athletes. Drug Enforcement Administration, Demand Reduction Section, 1405 I St., N.W., Washington, DC 20537. Free.

Ten Steps to Help Your Child Say "No": A Parent's Guide. 1986. National Clearinghouse for Alcohol and Drug Information, P.O. Box 2345, Rockville, MD 20852. Free.

The Fact Is...Hispanic Parents Can Help Their Children Avoid Alcohol and Other Drug Problems. 1989. National Clearinghouse for Alcohol and Drug Information, P.O. Box 2345, Rockville, MD 20852. Free.

The Fact Is...You Can Prevent Alcohol and Other Drug Problems Among Elementary School Children. 1988. National Clearinghouse for Alcohol and Drug Information, P.O. Box 2345, Rockville, MD 20852. Free.

The Fact Is...You Can Prevent Alcohol and Other Drug Use Among Secondary School Students, 1989. National Clearinghouse for Alcohol and Drug Information, P.O. Box 2345, Rockville, MD 20852. Free.

Young Children and Drugs: What Parents Can Do, 1987. The Wisconsin Clearing House, 1954 E. Washington Ave., Madison, WI 53704. $6.00 per 100 brochures.

What Works: Schools without Drugs, U.S. Department of Education, 1986, revised in 1989. National Clearinghouse for Alcohol and Drug Information, P.O. Box 2345, Rockville, MD 20852. Free.

A Parent's Guide To Prevention: Growing Up Drug Free, U.S. Department of Education. National Clearinghouse for Alcohol and Drug Information, P.O. Box 2345, Rockville, MD 20852 or call 800-624-0100

What Every Parent Can Do About Teenage Alcohol and Drug Abuse: Hope and Help from Parents Who Have Been There, Parents and Adolescents Recovering Together Successfully (P.A.R.T.S) 12815 Stebick Court, San Diego, CA 92130-2418 or call (888) 420-7278 $9.95

Buzzed: The Straight Facts About The Most Used And Abused Drugs From Alcohol To Ecstasy, by Cynthia Kuhn, Phd., et al, 1998, W.W. Norton and Company. $14.95.

WHINING

> My son is twelve. He is an uncomfortable child to be around. He whines constantly. He wears me down until I give in to his demands.

> My daughter is very bright. She whines and whines until she gets her way. What can I do to teach her that when I say "no" I mean it. She just doesn't believe me!

Fear not a jest. If one throws salt at thee thou wilt receive no harm unless thou hast sore places.

Latin proverb

As I said earlier, if you, the parent, say something twice you are nagging. The same is true about children. If they say it twice, or more likely twenty-seven times, they are committing the kid version of nagging, whining.

Whining is a learned behavior and anything that can be learned can be unlearned and replaced with a more mature and useful behavior. (See Chapter 1: HOW CHILDREN LEARN)

For about the first four years of life a child needs to be demanding of her parents. As her communication skills develop she learns to speak her needs, versus cry, as a form of alert that she has a need. After age four, a child who does not communicate her needs, at an age appropriate level, is acting immaturely. This should be a concern for the child's parents.

I have seen teens that still <u>expected</u> their parents to cut their meat and make their bed. These teens exhibit clingy behaviors. It is interesting that most parents with overdependent children do not seem to notice the immature behavior.

Children from age four to eight tend to complain with the "Why can't? or Why does?" "Why can't I stay up and watch the show?" "Why can't Bobby come over?" "Why does Mary get tooooooo ..." This is normal manipulation for their age. It becomes whining when the child refuses to accept your answer and keeps asking the same question.

WHY DO KIDS WHINE? WHY DO KIDS WHINE? WHY DO KIDS WHINE? WHY DO KIDS WHINE? WHY DO KIDS WHINE? (Sorry I couldn't resist. "Starting")

Kids whine because it works. They tend to get their way. And the more it works, the more they whine. Bluntly, you have taught your child to whine at you. Mr. and Mrs. Johnson came to my office because of a concern with their nine year old daughter, Nan. Mrs. Johnson explained:

> Nan is a brilliant girl, her teachers have always said how smart she is. The problem, very simply is ...

whatever I say she argues with and whatever Dick (Mr. Johnson) says she just does. No fuss. She is happy to listen to her dad.

Dr. Phil: Dad, any idea why your daughter listens to you?

Mr. Johnson: Not really, I guess it's because I mean it when I tell her to do something. I just won't get into an argument with her. She is too smart. She could sell a sin to the Pope. I just won't argue with her.

I think Mr. Johnson was correct. Nan had her mother's number. She knew that if she gently pushed, her mother would come around to see things her way. Mom saw it as whining, Nan saw it as winning. (See DR. PHIL'S RULE OF 10:1, 100:1, 1000:1 in Chapter 1.)

WAYS PARENTS ARE MANIPULATED BY THEIR CHILD'S IMMATURE BEHAVIORS

PLAYING THE BABY

Some children learn that if they act charming or naive some adults will like them. For the adult this child's behavior makes them feel wiser, mature, and needed. Some parents are fearful about their child growing up, thus they reinforce childish behaviors that prove to them that they are still needed.

CHILDISH POWER TRIPS

Some children learn that by whining they can get attention from their parents. The reverse of this is when a child feels overpowered by his parents so he acts useless as a way of punishing (feeling power over) his parents.

NARCISSISTIC BEHAVIORS

The self-centered child sees his parents as tools to control so he can get his own needs met. This is more common in teenagers. The self -centered teen sees anything that a parent wants to do for them as a weakness on the part of the parent. They feel that it is their parent's fault that they are weak, so exploiting them is only fair. The parent tends to feel overwhelmed with the self centered belief system of their child. (It is usually best to seek professional assistance for you and your child to deal with this type of emotional disorder.)

PARENT HAS PROBLEM SETTING LIMITS

One of life's little ironies is the fact that when you finally master a tough job you make it look easy

One of the most important responsibilities of a parent is limit setting. Some parents are so concerned that their children like them that they become extremely inconsistent with their limit setting "to keep the children happy." I had a mother exclaim, "What do you mean that I am not supposed to be my child's best friend!" I explained, "You're supposed to be your children's mother. Part of being their mother is being their *friend*, but you do your children a true disservice if your goal is to make your children happy all the time.

This mother was uncomfortable with my belief that she could not be or should not be her children's *friend* first and parent second. In friendship it is not necessary to set <u>parental</u> limits on the other's behavior. In fact, if that is occurring between friends, wouldn't it be an unhealthy relationship? I do not wish to get caught up into the semantics of the word "friend," but parenting is much more than friendship. (See Chapter 4: FAMILY RULES, THE ART OF DISCIPLINE) It is important that a parent feel comfortable with the fact that their children will not always be happy with them.

"So does this mean that our kids have to listen to us now?"

IN CLOSING

A few years ago my wife, Geri, suggested that we take the family to a favorite camping area of her youth. She painted a beautiful picture of secluded campgrounds dotting a reflective lake in the Adirondack mountains of up state New York. She told of how we could rent canoes and paddle to the silent woods. She spoke of her hope that, if we were lucky, we could get the campground on the small island in the middle of the picture postcard lake.

Over the next few weeks we made plans to fly to the east coast and meet up with other family members to camp at Forked Lake. Our summer vacation plans came together.

As we drove to Forked Lake from Grandmother's house, the skies were gray and threatening. The weather had been cold and rainy for many days. We talked openly about how we were going to have to make the best of our camping trip, no matter the weather. When we got to the state campground entrance the cloud cover opened and patches of bright blue snuck through. The first thing we did was check on the availability of the island campsite. The Ranger was blunt, "It's been raining for near two weeks, take your pick." We rented the island campsite and were afloat in the canoes in record time.

The lake was choppy and the wind cold. The sun threatened to burst into full light, but for now it was just hope. The boys and I started off in our canoe. The first ten minutes were exciting as I steered the bow of the canoe towards the island. In short order, the canoe trip to the small island became work. The boys quickly

If at first you don't succeed, you'll get a lot of advice.

More of better is not always the best way to succeed. Sometimes it's simply a matter of doing what needs to be done.

The more you say the less people remember.

lost their enthusiasm for the sea. Josh was in serious need of a nap. The wind was cold and damp. The camping equipment laden the boat.

The mountain storm had washed a lot of debris into the lake. Steering around the floating branches and entertaining the boys became cumbersome. After twenty minutes of paddling we met up with a cross flow of water. The wind was bitterly moist and cold. The boys were complaining. To my surprise, the island seemed very far away.

Between the wind and drizzle, cross current, and debris the canoe trip took over an hour. A very long hour. Setting up camp was a chore and getting everyone warm was work. But, it all worked out. We spent a magical sunny week on "our" private island.

A few months later I was talking with a couple about their two week summer vacation. It was horrible. Many things went wrong. It tried their relationship to the breaking point. By the end of the fourth day, they returned home, completely upset with each other and filed for divorce. On the advice of their friends they sought marriage counseling.

I told them the story of Forked Lake. Then continued:

> I have thought about that canoe trip often. After the weather turned nice, we canoed the same route many times. It was a leisurely twenty minute trip.
>
> I found myself thinking about how the first canoe trip was so hard. As it happened I felt frustrated. I constantly had to redirect my canoe. Something seemed to constantly pull me away from my target.
>
> I think of my marriage and my family in a similar way. I know where I want to be say, in fifty years. But, something is constantly pulling or pushing me away from that goal. On the rainy canoe trip my goal was the island. When something misdirected me, I had to navigate around it. I found a way to deal with it, as best I could, then pointed my canoe back at my target.
>
> It seems to me, that in life we are constantly blown off course, and have to deal with the problem and then get ourselves back on target.

So, in closing I hope that you hear that the process of raising your children counts. The end result is your target island, your goal, your dream. But, the day to day process of getting to your island is the hard built foundation that is your family.

Allow yourself the peace of mind to know that you will be blown off course. And the serenity that comes from knowing that you will deal with the problem and redirect yourself toward your island. The process counts.

Thank you for taking your time to read my book. I hope you have found it helpful for you and your family.

Thank you for encouraging my behavior,

We have all drunk from wells we did not dig and have been warmed by fires we did not build.

Show me a man who makes no mistakes and I will show you a man who doesn't do things.
Teddy Roosevelt

We realize that what we are accomplishing is a drop in a vast ocean. But if this drop were not in the ocean, it would be missed.
Mother Teresa

Index

Symbols

3M list
  Typical 112

A

Advocate 66
Advocated Child 67
Advocating 75, 91
Alcohol 212
Alcohol problem 208
All things being equal, people do 113, 117
Analgisics (Semi-Synthetic) 216
Analgisics (Synthetic) 216
Antidepressants, Tricyclic 212
Arbitrary consequence 138

B

Barbiturates 211
Baseline study 191
Bed-wetters, Continuous 157
Bed-wetters, Discontinuous 157
Bed-wetting 156
  Medical conditions 157
Behavior modification 191
Benzodiazepines 211
Bribery 38
Briggs, Dorothy 57
Building trust 59

C

Character 62
Childhood lying 165
Ching Ching Box 185
Chores 187
Classical conditioning 13, 22
Conditioned response 14
Conditioned stimuli 14
Consequence, arbitrary 138
Consequences 137
Consequences, Logical 137
Consequential thinking 154
Continuous bed-wetters 157

Continuous schedules of reinforcement 31
Controlling Chaos 149
Copitch Cash 32, 40
Curfew 187

D

Daily Smiley Sheet 194
Dawdling 182
Depressants 211
Desensitization 19
Development of a Must Rule 141
Discipline 84
Discontinuous bed-wetters 157
Dr. Phil's Rule of 10:1 34
Drug and alcohol abuse contact information 218
Drug Enforcement Agency (DEA) Classifications 210
Drug problem 208
Drugs 208
Drugs that cause hallucination 213
Drugs that depress the central nervous system 210
Drugs that relieve physical pain 215
Drugs that stimulate the central nervous system 212

E

Encopresis 174
Enuresis 156
Envelope of freedom 107
Expectation 75

F

Fabrication 164
Family night 56
Fixed-ratio schedule of reinforcement 33
Freedom 105

G

Gateway drugs 209
Generalization 18
Ginott, Haim 65
Goal of Time Out 87

H

Hallucinogens 214

Hierarchy of fear 20
High self esteem 44, 47, 56
Home not just a house 105
Homework
  Assignment 51–52
  Revisited 73
   187
Honesty 60
How would you teach a dolphin to jump over
    a rope 36
Hypnotics 211

I

"I do it for the kids" 101
I don't care 95
"I want to talk code" 98
If/Then statement 93, 117, 127
Immature behavior 223
Infant 46
Inhalants 212
Interpersonal conflict 153

J

Judged child 67
Judging 62, 65, 75

L

Labeling is disabling 65
Law of Effect 25
Laziness 182
Limitations 106
Limits 65
Logical consequences 137
Love 57
Low self esteem 48
Lying 164
  Childhood 165
  Teen 167

M

Marijuana 214
Maslow, Abraham 52
Maybe Rules 110
Maybe Rules cause constant conflict 113
Media hype 44
Medium self esteem 48
Methaqualone 211

Minor Rules 110, 147
Modeling 37
Must Rule 110, 127, 129, 141
Must Rules build a family 123

N

National PTA 221
Negative sounding list 50
  Revisited 64
Nurturing 55

O

One Maybe Rule = Child's Behavior + Parent's Mood 121
One Rule = Child's Behavior + Parent's Behavior 117
Operant conditioning 25
Ownership of the problem 202

P

Parent 102
Parenting 102
  Time 58
Partial schedules of reinforcement 33
Partnership for a Drug-Free America 221
Pavlov, Ivan 13
PeopleToons 10, 24, 42, 55, 61, 82, 100, 1
    48, 155, 164, 207, 219, 224
Personal makeup 46
Positive consequence list 126
Positive consequences 125
Positive List 72
Positive sounding list 50, 72
  Revisited 71
Positive/Negative Token Economy 193
Power struggle 183
Praise 68, 69
Procrastination 182
Punishment 28, 84
Punishment versus discipline 102

R

Reinforcement, negative 26
Reinforcement, positive 26, 196
Respect 73
Responsibility, Teaching 182
Rivalry, Sibling 170

Rules
    Maybe 110
    Minor 110
    Must 110
Rules, Unclear 122

S

Schedules of reinforcement and extinction 33
Secondary gain 95, 180
Sedatives 211
Self esteem 45, 46, 47, 49
    And behavior 52
    Build 44
    Continuum of 47
    High 47
    Influence 49
    Low 48
    Medium 48
Self work 87
Shaping 36
Shure, Myrna 151
Sibling rivalry 170
Size of the envelope 106
Smiley Chart 193, 194
Smiley, Weekly Sheet 201
Smith, Jeffrey 57
Soiling 174
Stealing 178
Stimulants 213
Stolen property 180
Stop gap measure 83
Street drugs 208
Struggle, power 183
Successive approximation 37

T

Teaching honesty 60
Teaching respect 73
Teaching responsibility 182
Teen lying 167
Temperament 46
The Little Prince 149
Thorndike, E.L. 25
Three M's 111
Time Out 83, 86, 98
Token economy 40, 192

Token, Positive/Negative Economy 41
Tricyclic Antidepressants 212
Trust 59
Types of lies 166

U

Unconditioned response 13
Unconditioned stimulus 13

W

Weekly Smiley Sheet 201
"What could you do differently?" 93, 197
What do you want for your child? 43, 136
What is a rule? 117
Whining 222
Word combinations 151
Write A Must Rule 128

BOOKS BY DR. PHILIP COPITCH:

See: Amazon.com, Kindle, iPad, or Smashwords.com
For more information please see: CopitchInc.com

FOR THE KIDS:

(To motivate reading and have a little fun.)

- Jokes I Can Read To You: Plus cartoons!
- Jokes, Cartoons, And Funny Stories I Can Read To You

FOR THE ADULTS:

- Basic Parenting 101 The Manual Your Child Should Have Been Born With
- Chutzpah Marketing: Simple Low Cost Secrets to Building Your Business Fortune
- Anatomy For Martial Artists
- Chutzpah Marketing for Mental Health Professionals: The missing manual from your graduate school education
- Phone Scripts For Mental Health Professionals That Fill Your Schedule
- How To Make Money From Your Website or Blog: From basics to money in five hours
- Change: How to bring real change to your life: The psychology and secrets of highly effective people
- Life's Laws For New Adults: Mastering Your Social I.Q

DR. PHIL'S ADULT JOKE BOOK:

Jokes I Told My Therapist Plus Cartoons, tall tales, and funny true stories

WANT A MUG?

Many of Dr. Copitch's cartoons are available at www.zazzle.com/copitch*

You can get them in full color on lots of stuff such as a shirt, mug, or apron.

Made in the USA
San Bernardino, CA
22 September 2018